The Rise and Fall
of the Future

ALSO BY GORDON ARNOLD

*The Afterlife of America's War in Vietnam:
Changing Visions in Politics
and on Screen* (McFarland, 2006)

The Rise and Fall of the Future

America's Changing Vision of Tomorrow, 1939–1986

GORDON ARNOLD

McFarland & Company, Inc., Publishers
Jefferson, North Carolina

LIBRARY OF CONGRESS CATALOGUING-IN-PUBLICATION DATA

Names: Arnold, Gordon, 1954– author.
Title: The rise and fall of the future : America's changing vision of tomorrow, 1939-1986 / Gordon Arnold.
Other titles: America's changing vision of tomorrow, 1939-1986
Description: Jefferson, North Carolina : McFarland & Company, Inc., Publishers, 2020 | Includes bibliographical references and index.
Identifiers: LCCN 2020027927 | ISBN 9781476677446 (paperback : acid free paper) ∞
ISBN 9781476641010 (ebook)
Subjects: LCSH: Social prediction—United States—History—20th century. | Technological forecasting—United States—History—20th century. | Exhibitions—United States—United States—History—20th century. | Popular culture—United States—History—20th century.
Classification: LCC HN57 .A695 2020 | DDC 303.4973—dc23
LC record available at https://lccn.loc.gov/2020027927

BRITISH LIBRARY CATALOGUING DATA ARE AVAILABLE

ISBN (print) 978-1-4766-7744-6
ISBN (ebook) 978-1-4766-4101-0

© 2020 Gordon Arnold. All rights reserved

No part of this book may be reproduced or transmitted in any form or by any means, electronic or mechanical, including photocopying or recording, or by any information storage and retrieval system, without permission in writing from the publisher.

On the cover: cutaway view of Bernal Sphere, artwork: Rick Guidice (NASA Ames Research Center)

Printed in the United States of America

McFarland & Company, Inc., Publishers
  Box 611, Jefferson, North Carolina 28640
  www.mcfarlandpub.com

Acknowledgments

This book has a long history. It was originally conceived a decade ago in a slightly different way, but in a way, its genesis can be traced back to summer nights in 1962 and 1963 when I would look into the night sky from my family home in rural America, pondering the stars and hoping to catch a glimpse of a satellite crossing the sky high above.

As the book took shape off and on over the last ten years, I benefited from conversations with and observations from many people. There are too many to name, but a few stand out—my friends and work colleagues Stacy Thomas-Vickory, Ethan Berry, Erin Dionne, Martha Buskirk, Megan Brown O'Connell, and others at Montserrat College of Art and also my former student Meghan Hawkes.

I am, of course, thankful for the help and support of Kimberlee Arnold, who had many good suggestions while I was writing, as well Gregory Arnold and Jeffrey Arnold, who provided inspiration and technical assistance.

A book such as this requires many bits of information, some of which are quite obscure. For services in tracking down and making available many items, I gratefully acknowledge the helpful assistance of several fine libraries, especially the Boston Public Library, Worcester Public Library, Westborough Public Library, Northborough Free Library, Shrewsbury Public Library, and the McAuliffe Branch of the Framingham Public Library. Without their help, completing the book would have been a much greater task.

Table of Contents

Acknowledgments v
Preface 1
Introduction 6

1. The World of Tomorrow 15
2. From War to Renewal 36
3. A Consumer's Future 58
4. A New Frontier 81
5. Peak Future 105
6. The Specter of Doubt 126
7. Fading Tomorrows 147

Epilogue 168
Chapter Notes 185
Selected Bibliography 195
Index 199

Preface

On October 12, 1961, a young man named Harold M. Graham gave what was probably the performance of his life. At Fort Bragg in North Carolina, a group of observers that included President John F. Kennedy waited to see the young man do something remarkable. It was obvious that something important was about to happen. The audience was ready for the event to begin.

Graham was well prepared. Wearing a strange-looking 150-pound suit, he stood in "an amphibious vehicle in the middle of a lake,"[1] as a newspaper account described it, waiting for the signal to begin. Finally, Graham gave the small crowd what they came to see. He ignited the thrusters that were mounted to the back of his specialized suit and quickly ascended 20 feet into the air. Then, as the engines roared, he "flew horizontally some 200 feet before landing abruptly in front of the startled president."[2]

Graham's brief demonstration of the Bell Rocket Belt fit neatly into the expectations of an era when almost any fantastic innovation seemed to be possible. Yet, like many things that were once expected, jet packs, as such devices are often called, never became everyday devices. There were too many issues associated with them—the very short range being a key one—to become practical for routine use. Yet, jet packs were tantalizing devices at a time when Americans still believed in the dream of a near-utopian future world. They were powerful symbols of the glorious world of tomorrow that seemed to be just around the corner.

From a broader perspective, many Americans in the middle decades of the 20th century presumed that a combination of innovation and American know-how would soon usher in a bright and shining future—a world that would be filled with technological miracles and free from worry and stress. This mid-century American futurism, which in many respects was carefully crafted, proved to be a compelling vision. It was a specific kind of optimism born of Americans' abiding faith in technology, consumerism, and their nation. It did not last very long, but for several decades, it was a

A powerful symbol of mid-century futurism, jet packs captured the imagination of many Americans in the 1960s. The most successful and widely known of such devices was the Bell Rocket Belt. A working prototype of the device was presented to the public at numerous events in that era, including this demonstration at Wright-Patterson Air Force Base in Ohio, 1965 (iStock.com/NNehring).

powerful force in the nation's popular and political culture. The breathtaking rise and fall of this techno-consumerist futurism in the United States of the 20th century is the subject of this book.

In some ways, the optimistic and, at times, utopian vision of tomorrow's world is a perplexing artifact of an often-turbulent century. That such a positive view of the future would develop and thrive during times that were often characterized by doubt and crisis was by no means a given. Yet, from the last days of the Great Depression until the middle of the 1960s, many Americans were captivated by this optimistic spirit, even when times were dark. They eagerly anticipated a time when their lives would be better than ever before. Miraculous innovations would make it all possible, they thought. America's mightiest institutions would soon deliver a consumer's paradise—a sleek and shiny future that would wash away the hardships and trials of recent memory. A life of comfort and security seemed just around the corner.

For a time, the future seemed without limits. America's optimistic spirit unleashed a plethora of fantastic concepts, images, and speculations about an extraordinary life ahead—a world filled with wonder. There would be flying cars, undersea cities, household robots, space travel, and a vast array of astonishing technologies that would transform everyday life.

Americans imagined lives without worry and monotony. Instead, adventure, comfort, and security were on the horizon. In the years following World War II, this portrayal of the future was especially alluring. Despite Cold War fears of that era, Americans remained mostly positive, believing that the country would overcome its problems en route to an astonishing tomorrow.

But then, the unimaginable happened. America's dreams of a glorious future began to fade. It did not happen overnight or within a single year. But eventually, a series of conflicts and discontents rattled American confidence about what was to come. Within a few short years, the future, which only months earlier seemed safe, no longer seemed secure.

As Americans began to lose hope about the future, they began to look ahead with dread. Their vision of a near-utopia mostly evaporated. It was replaced by an image of the future that was dark and bleak. Indeed, by the 1970s, the optimistic world of tomorrow was only a memory. It disappeared before delivering on its promises—or many of them, at least—leaving Americans with feelings of loss for what might have been. At the same time, the representation of the future in popular culture grew ever more dystopian. Indeed, as the year 1984 drew closer, the frightening world that novelist George Orwell had described many years earlier in his most well-known book, *Nineteen Eighty-Four*, seemed, to many people, less like fiction and more like the direction in which the world was heading. The euphoric, promising picture that mid-century futurism had described, meanwhile, seemed hopelessly naïve and the product of wishful thinking.

This book traces the unexpected rise and dramatic fall of mid-century futurism, examining both how it took hold in the public sphere and how it subsequently lost its allure. The book is decidedly not an exercise in nostalgia for a world that never materialized, nor is it a critique of specific predictions that did or did not come true. Rather, the following chapters examine the social construction and destruction of an idea—techno-consumerist futurism—that was a significant part of the American mindset during pivotal years in U.S. history.

This type of futurism inspired many people, but it was also a way of thinking that had significant blind spots. Indeed, for all its public appeal, it possessed what appears to be a fatal flaw. While the proponents of the techno-consumerist future were somewhat successful in imagining the role that science and technology would have in reshaping American life in many respects, they largely ignored and misjudged the social and political changes that would also exert enormous influence over what future life would be. With its heavy emphasis on technology and consumerism, mid-century futurism tended to emphasize tomorrow's world as "a matter of things," as some writers conclude. To this way of thinking, the social aspects of life would remain mostly the same as revolutionary technologies and zealous consumerism propelled society toward an idyllic tomorrow. That presumption proved to be very far from the mark, as events in the 1960s made clear.

Yet, techno-consumerist visions of tomorrow ruled the day for a time. In part, it was probably an antidote to perceived existential threats and to the sometimes-downbeat times that Americans endured. The optimism of mid-century futurism looked beyond immediate gloom and dangers. It was a promise, of sorts, that in the end, everything would be all right. That is likely the reason that it continued to have appeal even when people seemingly had little reason for optimism.

Mid-century futurism was always more than that, however. In bad times, its positive attitude about tomorrow's world likely acted as a distraction. It provided a respite for ordinary people who had limited influence over dangerous world events. It was a buffer against the uncertainties of the here and now.

More than that, the success of techno-consumerist futurism as a cultural phenomenon was undoubtedly aided by aggressive marketing efforts that promoted it. Importantly, however, those efforts were not coordinated or overarching. It could not have been so since this brand of futurism was not the result of a single vision, nor of a single source or time. Instead, mid-century futurism was built bit by bit with many pieces and contributing voices. Its relative coherence as a movement resulted not from an explicitly articulated philosophy or vision, but rather from common threads running through a variety of sources.

If there was no single vision and no manifesto, how did the vision of a techno-consumerist future spread across the nation? To some degree, the answer to this question is relatively simple: Mid-century futurism was packaged for and sold to the American consumer, its primary target audience. The public encountered futuristic visions in many places. Pictures of the world of tomorrow arrived in the form of advertisements, expositions, trade shows, newspapers, magazines, movies, and public declarations from experts, politicians, and writers. The "future," therefore, appeared in news reports, advertising campaigns, and entertainment of all sorts. Indeed, these wide-ranging sources provide much of the source materials that inform this book.

These varied sources sometimes differ in the details of the tomorrow that they present. Yet, from these disparate voices, some commonalities are evident. And from these many individual articulations of future, a picture emerges that is larger than the sum of the parts—a picture woven together by pervasive consumerism and deep faith in technology.

It is important to note that this vision was not just anyone's vision. It was a distinctly American one. Indeed, implicit in mid-century futurism was the notion that the world ahead mostly would belong to, and be a reflection of, the United States. An American way of looking at things was usually taken for granted as if there could hardly be any other viable options. True to the tenets of American exceptionalism, most people in the United States presumed that America was the natural leader of the world and that the future would be crafted in its image. Other perspectives, if they were voiced at all, gained little traction in the public sphere.

Another of the many intriguing characteristics within techno-consumerist futurist thinking is that it mythologized a world that had yet to come, and indeed, a world that, in some respects, was never going to come. Although wishing for the presumed glories of the past—for the "golden age"—is a familiar phenomenon, applying this near-nostalgic perspective to thinking about the future is less obvious. Nevertheless, in the middle decades of the 20th century, Americans sometimes became attached to the future that they imagined to the extent that it sometimes took on mythic dimensions. This feeling was not so much about the desire for a specific invention or futuristic gadget or any set of such things. Instead, it was a longing for a certain kind of life overall—a life that would be considerably better than any life people already knew.

The future, in this respect, was not so much about the gadgets, inventions, and innovations that people imagined. Instead, it was about what these things represented. The material world that mid-century futurism envisioned, therefore, was powerful because of what it symbolized. It spoke to Americans on a deep level—in a way that was bound up in their sense of their identity.

This book is *a* history of mid-century futurism, but it does not pretend to be *the* history of that topic. There are, of course, other approaches and other ways to interpret America's visions about the world ahead during the middle of the 20th century. Yet, the roles of technology, consumerism, and Americanism in shaping the public's attitudes about the world-yet-to-come remain intrinsically interesting and have something to tell us about the United States in one of the most tumultuous periods of its history.

Introduction

Mid-century futurism thrived during a critical period in America's history. With its brightly colored visions of a world of leisure and wonders, it was fueled mainly by a uniquely American faith in consumerism and technological innovation. This techno-consumerist way of looking ahead fit congruently with mainstream American ideology, which tended (and tends) to place the United States as the natural leader of the world in nearly all things. Whether this is true or not is an interesting question, but in thinking about its place in mid-century futurist thinking, what matters is that it was almost universally taken to be obviously true by most Americans. They knew that a future was coming, and they expected the United States to take the lead in meeting it, using the power of consumer production and consumption and the nation's continuing scientific and technological prowess as its engines.

Unsurprisingly, this strand of futurist thinking was not entirely new in all its dimensions. Rather, it built upon already-existing ideas. Americans had been encountering highly imaginative visions of tomorrow for many years. So, although it may sometimes seem that techno-consumerist futurism as it crystallized in the late 1930s was an abrupt break from the past, this was hardly the case. Taking a long view, it is apparent that it was less of a revolutionary change in thinking than a result of several decades of evolution.

A few brief observations about the road leading up to mid-century futurism can help set the stage for the examination of this movement that is the focus of the following chapters. Consider, for example, some key developments.

A more or less "modern" way of thinking about the future was already taking shape in the 19th century. Sparked by dramatic scientific and technological developments, many people at that time began to explicitly speculate about the world ahead in new ways that reflected these shifts in humankind's understanding of how the physical and social worlds work.

Some of these new visions were grounded in reality, and others were extremely fanciful. But regardless, they almost always placed human ingenuity and a strong sense of progress at their center.

French writer Jules Verne is perhaps the best-known fiction writer to explore these themes. Much of his imaginative work is built upon the idea of scientific progress, though he took many liberties to fill in unknowns and move his stories forward. His books, *From Earth to the Moon* (1865), *Twenty-Thousand Leagues Under the Sea* (1870), and others, reached a broad, international audience and brought a mostly new kind of futurism to the foreground. Readers were enthralled with his stories of travel into space and deep beneath the sea. Somehow, he projected a faith in the idea that, of course, such things might one day be possible—a faith that humans would continue to unlock nature's secrets.

Verne did not invent science fiction, but he helped popularize it. And by the early 20th century, many writers were working in the genre. Indeed, in the early years of the 20th century, science-fiction stories and the ideas behind them became familiar to many people as such stories became widely available in books, newspapers, and magazines.

Another author whose work pushed ideas about a future that would be transformed by science and technology was the English writer H.G. Wells. Today, he is best known for his science-fiction classics, such as *The Time Machine* (1895) and *The War of the Worlds* (1897). In his day, however, Wells was also famous in his capacity as a public intellectual. Indeed, beyond science fiction stories, Wells wrote history, social commentary, and on a variety of nonfiction topics. One such work was *Anticipations*, a remarkable treatise that was published in 1901. (The full title of the work is notable for its length—*Anticipations of the Reaction of Mechanical and Scientific Progress upon Human Life and Thought*.)

Although little known today, *Anticipations* became a bestseller and proved to be influential in its time. In it, Wells cataloged many technological advances and looked forward to what kinds of further innovations might appear in the new century. It was predictive and imaginative and in some ways it was a harbinger of the thinking that would gain considerable traction in the years ahead.

Wells continued to develop this theme in *The Discovery of the Future*, a work that was first published in 1902. By then, he was thinking even more deeply about how humankind envisioned what was ahead and how people might do so more effectively. Wells observed, for example, that humans tend to look at the future in one of two ways. Most commonly, he thought people imagine that the future will be like the past, so they model their ideas about what is yet to come on what has already happened. Less often, in his view, some people look at the future as a

Astonishing visions of human flight captured readers' imaginations by the early years of the 20th century. In this fanciful drawing that appeared on the cover of *All Story* magazine in October 1908, artist Harry Grant Dart shows a woman piloting a futuristic aircraft as a male passenger sits beside her (Library of Congress).

clean slate that is not necessarily tightly tethered to past experiences. According to Wells, the first of these perspectives, by continually looking back, is limiting and too often leads to the replication of old ways of doing things and the perpetuation of old problems. The future, in other words, becomes an endlessly repeating bad habit. However, the less common way of thinking about tomorrow, which Wells supported, presents many more positive possibilities because it unchains the future from the burdens of the past, and, in Wells' view, opens the future as an arena for new ideas and innovations.

Although Wells argued for the second approach, he was aware that most people are reluctant to deviate from tradition. In trying to explain the pull of the past, he concluded that this was partly because of the widespread belief that the future is wholly unknowable—that it is mostly a series of surprises waiting to happen, with the implication that there is nothing to be done about it. "It is our ignorance of the future and our persuasion that that ignorance is absolutely incurable," he writes, "that alone gives the past its enormous pre-dominance in our thoughts."[1]

Wells was realistic enough to know that, in some sense, that perception was correct. He acknowledged that there would always be things about the future that no one would be able to predict. However, Wells had faith in reason and in the progress that humankind had made in analyzing and understanding the world. With some qualifications, therefore, he argued that giving up on knowing the future and presuming it is entirely unpredictable is a mistake. "I am venturing to suggest to you," he wrote, "that along certain lines and with certain qualifications and limitations a working knowledge of things in the future is a possible and practicable thing."[2] To this, he added, "I believe that the time is drawing near when it will be possible to suggest a systematic exploration of the future."[3]

Beneath Wells' belief that tomorrow's world is in some ways discoverable in advance was his abiding faith in rational analysis and the methods of science. As he said, "Everything seems pointing to the belief that we are entering upon a progress that will go on, with an ever-widening and ever more confident stride.... We have struck our camp forever and we are out upon the roads. We are in the beginning of the greatest change that humanity has ever undergone."[4]

Wells was not the only person who was thinking about such things, but he was among the most vocal advocates for conceiving the future in a new, analytical way. He would continue making predictions and speaking about the future in works of fiction and nonfiction for many years.

Other developments in the print-media world also proved to be important in promoting wide-ranging visions of the future world. In the early decades of the 20th century, for example, newspapers published many stories (though of varying journalistic quality) about new inventions and scientific breakthroughs that seemed to be on the horizon. Popular magazines, such as *Frank Reade Weekly Magazine*, featured sensational stories, complete with illustrations of fanciful inventions, of adventures that had futuristic implications.

Popular magazines with scientific and technological themes brought many speculations to public attention in the 1910s and 1920s. An intriguing proposal for a "floating railroad" was discussed in the December 1923 issue of *Science and Invention* (collection of the author).

Print publications dominated the mass media of the era, and by the 1910s and 1920s, a plethora of magazines similarly popularized speculative futuristic innovations. Their titles may seem mundane, but the so-called "hobby" magazines, such as *Electrical Experimenter, Science and Invention, Popular Science,* and *Popular Mechanics,* regularly focused on a fantastic array of futuristic technologies and lifestyles. The bright, colorful images and enthusiastically written articles in their pages brought speculative predictions to public attention.

By the 1920s, cheaply produced, mass-market pulp magazines, which published exciting stories on a wide range of subjects, were all the rage. The science fiction genre came to hold a prominent place in these publications. Probably the most famous of the early science-fiction pulps was *Amazing Stories*, which debuted in 1926, but it did not take long for many other science-fiction pulps to join it on America's newsstands. Indeed, by the 1930s, a large selection of science-fiction pulps—*Science Wonder Stories, Astounding Stories*, and others—regularly enthralled readers with futuristic adventures. Within their pages, writers such as Edgar Rice Burroughs used the science-fiction genre to tell stories of thrilling adventures on distant worlds. There was little actual science in them, but the far-off settings—Mars, Venus, the Moon, and other worlds—captured the imagination, evoking a sense of wonder in the process.

In 1936, a new pulp magazine titled *Flash Gordon Strange Adventure Magazine* was introduced. It featured the swashbuckling rocketeer Flash Gordon character, who was already the subject of a popular syndicated newspaper comic strip. At the time, a rival comic strip, *Buck Rogers*, was also a fan favorite. Both characters later appeared in serialized movies, further extending their fame. With their appearances in multiple entertainment media, Flash Gordon and Buck Rogers drew much attention to adventure-oriented futurism in American popular culture of the 1930s.

Many portrayals of the future appeared in exciting fictional adventures or in starry-eyed plans for improving the real world. However, it would be a mistake to presume all future-oriented thinking was filled with adventure and a generally positive outlook. There was always a darker side in thinking about tomorrow's world, and it sometimes surfaced in different ways. Some of the most remembered versions of a bleak future appeared in Europe, where artists and writers sometimes peered into the world of tomorrow through a dark lens.

Interestingly, the very word *Futurism* (or *Futurismo*, in Italian) had distinctly aggressive associations in the art world of Europe. Since the second decade of the 20th century, the term was often associated with an Italian art movement of that name that advocated a violent break with the past. Its advocates wanted to destroy vestiges of everything that had come before.

The Futurist art movement was well-reported in the United States. Many accounts implied its adherents possessed a strange, antagonistic point of view. A story in a 1911 edition of the famous New York newspaper *Evening World*, for instance, reported that Futurism was a "new cult in art" that declared "everything in the past [was] all wrong."⁵ Indeed, the Futurists believed that destroying vestiges of the past was a necessary step if they were to build a bold, new future. The movement seems to have been somewhat a precursor to fascism, however, and it was hardly the type of optimism that appealed to most Americans at the time.

Meanwhile, in the European film world, some movies, especially after World War I, portrayed the future in very ominous ways. The most well-known example is probably Fritz Lang's epic *Metropolis* (1927). Made in Germany near the end of the silent-film era and before the rise of Nazi ideology, the film is distinctive, in part, for its depiction of the future in decidedly dystopian terms. Most people portrayed in the film are condemned to lives of hard labor and little freedom. Meanwhile, the privileged few live luxuriously in skyscrapers, remote from the enslaved population. The film's visual design emphasizes the stark contrasts between the wealthy few and the enslaved masses, the latter of which are shown existing in dreary, oppressive environments that seem like concrete prisons. This future, it would seem, is nothing that most people would want to see come true.

Several years later, the 1936 British sound film *Things to Come* presented the future in a similarly downbeat manner. Based on material from H.G. Wells, who was involved in its production, it is a cautionary look ahead that features many bleak scenarios. Indeed, the world of tomorrow, as depicted in this movie, is one of war, fear, and conflict.

The world depicted in the films *Metropolis* and *Things to Come* both possess some similarities in theme and tone to a widely known book from that era, *Brave New World* (1932) by the English writer Aldous Huxley. Like those films, *Brave New World* represents the generally pessimistic worldview that sometimes found expression in Europe and even, at times, in the United States.

These are only a few cursory examples, of course, but they serve to demonstrate that a high-profile and quite ominous picture of the future was widely known in Europe. While it is true that something similar to that view was also present in American culture at times, it was far less prominent in the United States as it was in Europe. Perhaps this is not surprising. For the most part, social and political conditions in Europe, where these works originated, differed markedly from those in the United States.

Throughout the 1920s (and beyond), Europe was still recovering from the death, destruction, and psychological blow of World War I. The United States, meanwhile, faced a far less somber situation, at least in the 1920s. In the decade known as the "Roaring Twenties," Americans remained mostly optimistic. And even in the years after 1929, when the Great De-

Introduction 13

pression brought a more pessimistic mood, Americans, overall, never fully succumbed to a dystopian view of the future. Through it all, some glimmer of optimism continued to run through U.S. social and political culture. Although it would be a mistake to extrapolate too much from it, the extraordinary popularity of the song-filled Disney cartoon *Three Little Pigs*, a vibrant full-color short that appeared in 1933, was one of the more unusual symbols of America's resistance to the gloom of economic crisis, for example. Indeed, as unlikely as it may now seem, Disney's cartoon was widely interpreted as a parable about America's ability to withstand and overcome the adversity of the Great Depression.

Another source of futuristic thinking in the early decades of the century could be found in the world of architecture. In thinking about and planning for how people would live in years to come, architects sometimes explored designs that imagined urban landscapes that differed from the traditions the 20th century had inherited. The French artist-architect Le Corbusier, for example, examined ways of reorganizing basic architectural premises to bring about new opportunities for urban living. By the 1920s, he brought geometric forms and other design elements from his Cubist painting style into his architectural plans, creating what is still often regarded as a futuristic look in the process.

In some ways, the great age of skyscraper construction in cities such as New York also evoked a sense of tomorrow. These new architectural marvels hinted that life on the horizon, which presumably would be lived in modern and reconstructed cities, might differ dramatically from the past. In some ways, such visions already seemed to be coming true. By the 1930s, many forward-looking physical buildings dotted American cityscapes, creating new skylines that were unlike anything that had come before.

Perhaps more importantly, in addition to plans for real-world construction, many architects also drew up designs for structures and urban environments that would never be built, and, in some cases, were never meant to be built. The significance of that work was not so much the designs themselves, but rather the willingness to revisit and rethink the presumptions of the past. In many ways, architects were among the first to embrace the idea that the world ahead did not necessarily need to resemble the world people already knew. This represented a meaningful change in thinking—the kind of change in mindset that H.G. Wells had advocated some years earlier.

There already existed an ongoing series of public spectacles in which these kinds of ideas could find expression before a wide audience. Indeed, formalized international expositions—elaborate events such as world's fairs—represented one arena in which many of these strands of future-oriented culture found fruitful expression. World's fairs became opulent displays that attracted global audiences.

These expositions highlighted futuristic ideas and concepts. By the end of the 19th century, for example, London's spectacular Crystal Palace Electric Exposition in 1882, Paris' 1889 Exposition Universelle (which introduced the Eiffel Tower), and Chicago's World Columbian Exposition in 1893 were among the world's fairs that captivated visitors' imaginations with spectacular exhibits and architecture. To some extent, these events looked at previous achievements and possessed the triumphalist tone that was common in the era of Colonialism. In other ways, however, they touted scientific and technological developments that were only starting to reshape the world.

These expositions remained popular in the early 20th century. In 1933, during the Great Depression, a commanding new world's fair opened in Chicago. Dubbed the "Century of Progress Exposition," it offered visitors dazzling exhibits and architecture. The event suggested a future that would be quite different from the past. Even its motto, "Science finds, Industry applies, Man adapts," was telling. Although it emphasized past achievements, the 1933 Chicago World's Fair, like its motto, was a bold assertion that the world was undergoing a profound transformation. The overall implication was that businesses—especially American businesses—would bring modern science and technology into the home. It was a theme that would be refined and amplified in the years ahead.

These remarks obviously only touch lightly upon a few of elements in the background to the view of tomorrow's world that held sway in U.S. culture in the middle decades of the 20th century. Yet, even this abbreviated account established that futurism, as a general phenomenon, was well established in the United States by the early 1930s. However, the continuing economic plight of the Great Depression limited the ability of one key player—the American consumer—to fully participate in the optimistic future that was taking shape. Indeed, consumers were still shackled by the economic distress that cast a shadow over the Chicago World's Fair. Soon, however, that picture would change, setting the stage for rapid evolution in the way Americans would think about the world to come.

1

The World of Tomorrow

Thirteen-year-old George had waited a long time, but now the big day had come. On the morning of April 30, 1939, he left his home in the Kew Gardens section of Queens, New York, and made his way to nearby Flushing Meadows. There, he joined a crowd of people—eventually numbering almost 200,000—who had come to experience the grand opening of the 1939 New York World's Fair.

Just beyond the gates, visitors encountered a fantastic world with many fascinating exhibits and pavilions to see and explore. As George headed down the pathway to the Fair's center, a gleaming-white, three-sided pylon towering 700 feet into the sky stood before him. It was attached to another strange object—a massive white orb, some 200 feet across. "So, this is the World of Tomorrow!" he exclaimed.[1]

George had the right idea. When organizers had started planning the Fair some months earlier, evoking the future was just what they had in mind. They had approached the whole project hoping to influence visitors to think about the coming world positively. That outcome would be a considerable feat considering the nation had not fully recovered from the Great Depression.

Nevertheless, they were confident and aiming high. What they imagined was a bright and bountiful future that would surpass anything at expositions that had come before and sweep away doubts about the future. Officially, organizers announced the theme as "Building the World of Tomorrow with the Tools of Today," but people soon boiled that idea down to its essence—the "World of Tomorrow."

It was a bold statement, but in some ways, devising the theme was the easy part. By contrast, making the Fair a reality was a more challenging undertaking. Organizers selected a former ash dump in the Flushing Meadows section of Queens to serve as the fairgrounds. To prepare the site for construction, 30,000 workers cleared the property and hauled away seven million cubic yards of fill. Then they sculpted the land in preparation for construction, creating two artificial lakes in the process.[2]

Construction crews then began building infrastructure, pavilions, and walkways. At an estimated cost of $155 million,[3] they created an impressive collection of exhibit halls, auditoriums, restaurants, houses, offices, and entertainment spaces. After months of hard work, the former ash dump was no more. In its place, there now stood a miniature city filled with architectural wonders, laid out along pristine boulevards. It all led up to the Fair's opening day when, at last, the public finally got to see the Fair and its vision of the World of Tomorrow.

The 1939 New York World's Fair was the most comprehensive presentation of the future ever to be presented to the American public. Its many pavilions and displays gave specific form to ideas that might otherwise have seemed too abstract or too fantastic to look real. It created the picture of a life that would be comfortable and appealing in the years to come. Light years from the discouraging mood that characterized the Depres-

With its theme of "The World of Tomorrow," the 1939 New York World's Fair provided the American public with a comprehensive look into the future as it was envisioned by many of the nation's leading corporations. The futuristic Trylon and Perisphere, which symbolized a coming world of wonders and innovation, were strategically placed at the center of the fairgrounds (National Archives).

sion, the future as the Fair presented it would bring the long-anticipated "good life" to American families.

To some extent, the Fair's depiction of the future was not entirely new, of course. Hints about the future appeared in other expositions hosted by the United States in that decade, including the 1933 "Century of Progress" World's Fair in Chicago and the 1939 Golden Gate International Exposition in San Francisco. The New York World's Fair, however, was not a celebration of American "progress," as had been the case with previous expositions. It was an emphatic statement about times yet to come.

Still, many of the ideas it presented were refinements of concepts that had percolated in U.S. culture for several decades. They could be found in newspaper reports, magazine articles, pulp novels, comic strips, radio, and movies. The Fair provided a context in which many of these ideas could be brought together and shown to the public in a controlled environment. For the modest price of admission, people could see and experience an expansive vision of the future in a single visit.

Visions of the future had long appeared in popular culture, but this was different. It was not a picture of a coming world in the mold of Buck Rogers or Flash Gordon, whose fanciful futuristic adventures were well-known. Instead, the 1939 World's Fair aimed to do more than provide visitors with an entertaining distraction or unrealistic predictions. Fair organizers framed the future more practically, even though in some ways it looked new and unfamiliar. They wanted the World of Tomorrow that the Fair offered to appeal to average people and everyday lives. Their target audience, then, was composed of those who could imagine how marvelous their lives would be with the addition of the scientific and technological wonders that the exposition showcased. Fair organizers, in other words, wanted to present compelling scenarios that would attract the interest of the American consumer.

Overall, the Fair's exhibits and attractions skillfully communicated this futuristic theme, and they did so with a sense of flair and high drama. Sophisticated designs aimed to inspire awe and wonder, and the sights and sounds of the future were engineered to achieve maximum effect. In one sense, much of the Fair resembled a stage or movie set.

Although some parts of the Fair were far less devoted to portraying the future than others, the sections explicitly focusing on the World of Tomorrow theme created environments that aimed to be as immersive as practical in that era. By setting the "stage" in this way, exhibitors were able to tell their stories about the future against a backdrop that reinforced their general message.

This theatrical presentation was particularly evident in evening hours when state-of-the-art lighting transformed the Fair to marvelous effect.

Organizers had realized that the type of illumination incorporated into the design would make a difference in the quality of the visitors' experience. With that in mind, they hired electrical engineer Bassett Jones, who had designed the Empire State Building's complex elevator system, as a lighting consultant for the Fair as a whole.[4]

The results were impressive. The president of the Illuminating Engineering Society was so admiring that he said the lighting at the World's Fair had "advanced by at least a decade the science of illuminating engineering."[5]

Many of the stunning illumination effects were the work of Richard C. Engelken. A highly imaginative lighting engineer, he was responsible for designing creative lighting for the Radio City Music Hall, the Hayden Planetarium, the Museum of Natural History, and many other prominent venues along the East Coast. At the Fair, his work could be seen in the "brilliant, variety-colored illumination" that dramatically lit the Lagoon of Nations as well as the lighting for the Trylon and Perisphere.[6]

In an article published in 1940, Engelken explained the approach that he used to achieve these effects:

> A zoning and color scheme adopted prior to construction insured architectural unity, and harmony of plan, design, and treatment throughout the whole area.... Starting with white at the Theme Center, color treatments of red, blue or gold radiate outward with progressively more saturated hues. The illumination was fitted to this scheme as to maintain the basic pattern by night as well as by day, but with new and added interest and charm after sunset.[7]

The carefully designed illumination surely did reinforce the futuristic aura of the grounds and the stunning architectural elements. Lights in a dazzling array of colors gave the Fair the atmosphere of a "fairyland," according to one account, which continued: "Thousands thrilled to the light-and-shadow designs, the beams of color piercing the skies." [8] If this was the World of Tomorrow, then it promised to be a world of wonder and enchantment.

All these considerations added up to a particular way of looking at the future. It was a way that very much reflected the perspectives of American society's most powerful institutions and especially the business community. The general message of the 1939 Fair seemed to be that when the world of tomorrow arrived, America's mightiest businesses would deliver it to the public. This orientation was hardly a surprise. According to Robert W. Rydell, a historian of international expositions, the "idea of selling the future through world's fairs seized the imaginations of corporate executives."[9] Indeed, corporate leaders poured millions of dollars into their pursuit of the idea.

1. The World of Tomorrow

The giant white pylon and orb that George had encountered on opening day symbolized the bright future that Fair organizers had in mind. The gleaming, other-worldly exteriors of these structures suggested something striking and new. There was little about their appearance that connected these structures to the past. That, of course, is the effect that fair planners wanted to achieve.

Officially named the Trylon and Perisphere, the towering pylon and massive orb were strangely compelling structures. They unambiguously announced the Fair's bold, futuristic theme. When first encountering them, visitors knew they were not looking at anything representing the world as it already was.

A contemporary newspaper article ventured to explain what the structures meant, saying that the Trylon represented humankind's "aspiration," while the Perisphere symbolized "the world around us."[10] Of course, people probably interpreted the buildings in many ways. The structures may have functioned as unintentional Rorschach tests, prompting a variety of associative interpretations. Whatever the specific intentions, however, the buildings made an enormous impression on the public. According to Richard Wurts, they "were regarded as the most imposing symbol for any fair since the Eiffel Tower of 1889"[11] at the time.

The Trylon and Perisphere stood at the Fair's center, both literally and metaphorically. Since they were intended to emphasize the World of Tomorrow theme, many details were taken into account to achieve that purpose. For example, to help set them off visually from surrounding buildings, they were covered with special white paint. It was formulated to be brighter than the paint used on nearby structures.[12] Visitors may not have directly noticed this subtlety, but the choice of color helped the buildings stand out in a way that surrounding structures did not.

Further drawing attention was the fact that the Trylon was by far the tallest structure in the Fair. It was visible from many vantage points on the grounds and even from some miles beyond the Fair. These were the types of intentional but straightforward design choices that helped draw attention to the structure and the futuristic theme.

The exteriors were only the beginning. Visitors did more than gaze upon the Trylon and Perisphere. Ascending on what was then the world's highest escalator, spectators rose high above the ground to a platform that led to the entrance of the Perisphere. They then entered the hollow sphere and stepped onto one of two circular platforms that moved along the interior walls. From this vantage point, they gazed over railings and saw a large, dramatically lit, extremely detailed model of a city from tomorrow and its environs. It was if they were flying high above a real city. The future, it seemed, was right before them.

This model city bore little resemblance to the dusty, chaotic cities that visitors would have known in real life. Democracity, as the model city was called, was much more than just a collection of buildings, streets, parks, and fields. It represented a wholly planned system for living. It was a place where architectural form and function were carefully integrated using the most modern techniques to make life easier and more efficient. In the words of Richard Wurts, Democracity had a "subtle geometric elegance, reminiscent of [director] William Cameron Menzies's breathtaking sets in the 1936 science-fiction film *Things to Come*."[13]

The designers tried to rethink everything they knew about the living and working environments of the 1930s to create a place that would be fit for the bright future they imagined. The city contained a series of zones and communities that radiated in concentric circles around a grand urban center. In some ways, this community of the future was almost self-contained. It included everything from residential districts to areas devoted to manufacturing, farming, and transportation systems. There were designated zones for government, education, sports, entertainment, and religious gatherings, as well.

In other ways, however, this "city of tomorrow" was self-consciously designed to emphasize interrelationships. Its various parts were all laid out to work well together. The idea was that people would be able to get where they needed to go and do what they needed to do quickly and easily. It was planning that would make this possible. Indeed, much planning would be required. To create anything like Democracity in real life would be a vast undertaking. Its designers envisioned it as "11,000 square miles—about 8 million acres" that would be "inhabited by a million and a half people."[14]

Democracity's designers tried to provide everything that a person in 1939 would have thought necessary to live a modern, good life. Careful planning was key. This futurist city avoided the confusion that characterized many real cities and their environs of the day. There would be nothing haphazard or on-the-fly about it.

Democracity was never intended to serve as a literal model for a specific place to be constructed. Instead, it was an idealization. Its creators hoped other people would refine their ideas and then incorporate them into plans for real communities. "Democracity dramatizes the meaning of the Fair," as a brochure for it said. "Consciously or not, we are building the World of Tomorrow; creating symbols of living: not each for himself [sic], but all together."[15]

Democracity embodied idealism that relied on central planning to answer many of America's complicated and sometimes vexing urban issues. It was planning, the exhibit's creators seemed to believe, that would make Democracity such a remarkable place. Indeed, its designers had faith that careful planners could prevent many social ills, including the eruption of petty jealousies and other conflicts. Documentation for the exhibit went so far as to predict that there would be practically no crime in Democracity. They claimed it would be free of "slums, and all the crime that breeds in slums."[16]

One thing that its creators believed was that future life in places such as Democracity would be both enjoyable and relatively easy. "You [will] live in a house of your own ... [in a place] so agreeable that you call it Pleasantville,"[17] stated some of the documentation. "You'll wake up in a cheerful room, on a garden ... in utter quiet ... and the air you breathe will be clean air." More than that, residents would not need to worry about traffic since everything they needed would be nearby.[18] As the planners saw it, this efficiency meant that people would have much more leisure time, or so it was predicted.

Despite lofty expectations, Democracity's designers admitted it would not be a Utopia. Still, they saw it as a significant improvement over the cities that people knew, which, in 1939, were still places that had not fully recovered from the onslaught of the Great Depression. In looking at their plans from a vantage point many years later, it is easy to see that their ideas for a near-idyllic future largely remained rooted in a 1939 mindset.

Another section of the Fair, which was called the "Town of Tomorrow," took a more pragmatic view of the future, though it had a similar message in some ways. The Town of Tomorrow was the site of full-sized demonstration homes that Fair visitors could tour and see up close. While Democracity presented ideas for a time that would not arrive for some time, the Town of Tomorrow announced that a future was available almost immediately.

It was not a world of flying cars or rocket ships. That still seemed many years in the offing. Instead, it was a more down-to-earth future that was ready to be made—or more precisely, purchased—in the very near term. The exhibit was steeped in America's emerging consumer mindset. Overall, it revealed just how much its planners believed that big business would deliver the future. Indeed, in some ways, it was as if the future itself would be a consumer product.

Some of the structures in the Town of Tomorrow were very traditional in design and appearance, but even these had futuristic overtones. Other homes, however, left tradition far behind. Their designs abandoned familiar design aesthetics, and they looked like houses from a world that had not quite arrived.

The House of Plywood was one of these latter kinds of exhibits. That may seem surprising since plywood is hardly a construction material with

In this artist's rendering of the interior of the Perisphere at the 1939 New York World's Fair, visitors are seen standing on twin walkways along the interior edge of the domed structure. As they gaze from above, they see a highly detailed model of a city of the future called Democracity (Theodore Kautzky [1896–1953] and Henry Dreyfuss [1904–1972] for New York World's Fair [1939–1940] Corporation, courtesy Museum of the City of New York).

a futuristic aura. In 1939, however, the thought of using it so boldly and as a defining feature was unexpected and even slightly jolting.

As with all the structures in the Town of Tomorrow, the House of Plywood was a testament to its corporate sponsors. (Among contributors to its construction were Douglas Fir Plywood Association, General Electric,

Johns-Manville, National Better Light-Better Sight Association, and the New York Telephone Company.) The house itself had a modern, geometric design that was quite striking. It had smooth surfaces, wrap-around windows, and a curved exterior wall. Although the house broke with tradition in many ways, its sponsors seem to have believed it would appeal to typical, if young, American families. A brochure produced for the home House explained that it "was primarily designed for a married couple with one child" and could be built for "about $4,000 to $5,000."[19]

More futuristic in conception was the House of Vistas, which was sponsored by a dozen major companies. (Contributors included the Edison Electric Company, Fiat Metal Manufacturing Company, National Chemical and Manufacturing Company, and the Truscon Steel Company.) It was a two-story, flat-roof structure that had the appearance of irregularly stacked blocks.

Then there was the "Small Home of Brick," with sponsors such as the Edison Electric Company, the International Nickel Company, the Structural Clay Products Institute, and several others. It aimed to provide "simplified living for the family with a limited budget."[20] Tellingly, although the house was forward-looking in design and construction, its sponsors did not envision that life within it would be very different from what 1939 World's Fair visitors already knew. It would be a life in which "the wife does all her own housework, and the husband keeps the exterior tidy and in repair in his leisure time," according to press materials.[21]

Other homes in the Town of Tomorrow, such as the "Electric Home," possessed very traditional outward appearances. Even these, however, incorporated many futuristic electrical appliances and gadgets. The Electric Home included an "entertaining and amusing Magic Kitchen that moves, talks, and tells a timely story," all of which was possible because of "constant research and manufacturing magic."[22] Indeed, as its documentation added, "electric servants with economical efficiency have taken over the tasks and time-consuming domestic drudgery of the old order."

It all probably sounded expensive, but visitors were told not to worry. They would be able to outfit the house with the latest General Electric equipment with "a single long-term mortgage loan." The future could be purchased using an installment plan, apparently.

Overall, the Town of Tomorrow foretold a future that could be on the immediate horizon for those who wished to invest in it. In other words, through modernistic homes, large corporations were making the future available as something that could be purchased. The homes applied many of the latest ideas about design and construction, and from one perspective, they were a distinct break from the past. However, the Town of Tomorrow—and indeed, much of the World of Tomorrow as the

Fair envisioned it, overall—would have much that was not very different at all.

The implication was that although people could expect a very modern domestic environment and more leisure time, they would mostly continue to live as they already did. Indeed, the Town of Tomorrow's creators seemed to presume that little would change socially. Women would continue to do the housework; it was just that it would be easier. Men would go to work somewhere else and then return to a home where they would relax and take care of an occasional chore involving the home's exterior upkeep. Meanwhile, the issue of race seemed not to enter into the future much, if at all. The whiteness of the Town of Tomorrow appeared to be an unstated presumption.

The Town of Tomorrow was as much a corporate showcase as it was a demonstration of an abstract idea. Other exhibits at the Fair focused on the corporate side of things even more. Undoubtedly, the company that made the biggest impression was General Motors (GM). Its massive facility at the Fair covered seven acres and housed an expansive exhibit called Highways and Horizons, within which was Futurama. A genuine crowd-pleaser, Futurama was described as "easily the smash hit of the Fair"[23] by one newspaper reporter, who added, "Believe me ... Futurama must be seen to be appreciated."

A press release revealed one reason for the rave reviews and long lines that formed as visitors waited to see the exhibit. GM had created a spectacle of overwhelming proportions, extending a third of a mile.[24] In ambition and scale, it topped even what the Trylon and Perisphere had to offer. A tour-de-force that many people regard as the Fair's most memorable exhibit, it showed a future world in vivid detail.

Futurama was the vision of Norman Bel Geddes. A colorful set designer, he has been described by writer James Mauro as "a man who never let financial considerations get in the way of this vision."[25] Bel Geddes had a keen interest in predicting the future and had even written an article about it for the widely circulated *Ladies' Home Journal* magazine. He lobbied for the job of creating the GM exhibit at the Fair and finally won over skeptical executives who at first balked at the potential cost. Eventually, however, GM went all-in, spending a whopping $7 million on its New York World's Fair exhibit.[26] For something that presumably would only be open to the public for a limited time, it was a significant commitment of resources.

The price tag may have been expensive, but Bel Geddes delivered a breathtaking exhibit. The viewing experience was as ingenious as the diorama was immense. Visitors saw the presentation from individual seating compartments that moved along the length of the display. From the comfort of their moving chairs, a narrator, whose voice was piped in via advanced audio equipment, explained the wondrous world before them. What they saw was incredible. GM's depiction of a future city was even grander than Democracity.

Futurama showed the world as it might appear in 1960, then two decades into the future. It showed off a "magic 35,738 square-foot" model that publicists boasted was "the largest and most lifelike model ever constructed."[27] It possessed astonishing attention to detail and minutiae, a result of Bel Geddes' perfectionism. Futurama included more than "500,000 individually designed buildings and houses, [and] a million trees." It even included "lofty, snow-capped peaks" as part of its immersive depiction of a lifelike world.

As would be expected given its sponsor, Futurama placed the automobile front and center. The exhibit included 50,000 futuristic, individually painted model cars, thousands of which moved on a complex multi-level, multi-lane model highway system.[28]

Interestingly, a press release for the exhibit seemed to suggest that future roadway systems could play a part in solving social ills. "Whenever possible ... express city thoroughfares have been so routed," it said, "as to displace outmoded business sections and undesirable slum areas."[29] The 1939 press release did not say what would happen to the people and businesses whose lives were uprooted by the highways of the future. (In this respect, the exhibit probably did accurately predict, if only partially, the world that was coming. In many cities, the interstate highway system that was begun in 1957 did displace disadvantaged residential and business areas.)

Futurama also showed other aspects of the future, including farms that would be "perhaps startling because of the strip-planting and terraced fields" as well as a "tree orchard ... housed under an individual glass dome" and "glass vats filled with green chemicals."[30]

The detailed dioramas of the Perisphere and GM's Futurama and the forward-looking model houses in the Town of Tomorrow presented visitors with some specific ideas about what their homes and communities might look like in the future. People already imagined that the automobile would play a big part in the future. It was not surprising, therefore, that the Ford Motor Company also staged an elaborate exhibit. It was housed in a massive building and included the "Road of Tomorrow," a raised highway on which visitors could ride in Ford cars along a curving, half-mile course.

Elsewhere, a "focal exhibit" at the Chrysler Motors building presented a "whole drama of transportation" that was even more futuristic. It consisted of a large display created by Raymond Loewy, who was known for his futuristic industrial design work for airplanes and railroad cars.[31]

Like its main rivals, the Ford Motor Company mounted a lavish pavilion at the 1939 World's Fair. Considering the extent and expense of the auto manufacturers' displays, it was clear that these companies presumed that America's future would largely be centered on the automobile and the values of freedom and consumerism that were associated with it (Library of Congress, Prints & Photographs Division, Gottscho-Schleisner Collection).

The main exhibit was housed under the Chrysler building's imposing dome. There, an imaginative display focused on the transportation of tomorrow. It included the mock-up of a rocket that would take passengers of the future from New York to London with fantastic speed. The rocket-oriented idea was very much of the future, but some aspects of the exhibit were heavily dependent on old ideas, including the notion that a passenger-carrying rocket would be shot from a huge gun. (This proposed technology already seemed outmoded. Exhibit designers seem not to have considered more realistic concepts, such as the rocketry proposals of Robert Goddard.)

Regardless of the science underlying the exhibit, the display created a remarkable effect. As described by the *New York Times*, the rocket-port dazzled visitors with "startling effects of speed, light, and sound and distance."[32] As Andrew F. Wood has noted, "Like many of Raymond Loewy's designs, the rocket gun portrayed a streamlined future of steel transformed into art."[33]

Elsewhere, Westinghouse Electric Company's exhibit was just as futuristic. Visitors to the company's Hall of Electric Living encountered a gleaming metallic figure more than seven feet tall. It was none other than Elektro, the so-called "Moto-Man," a hulking humanoid robot that Westinghouse engineers had programmed to walk, speak, and—somewhat curiously—smoke cigarettes.[34] Created using an ingenious combination of technologies that included vacuum tubes, motors, pulleys, and an electronic "brain" composed of 48 electrical relays, Elektro was a functioning, if rudimentary, robotic unit.[35]

By later standards, Elektro can seem like not much more than an assemblage of materials that did very little. After all, it could only perform a few simple tasks, one of which—regardless of one's views on smoking—was gimmicky, at best. More than that, Elektro did not do very much on its own. Most of the robot's actions required the direction of a human presenter who managed the robot's performance. Elektro was very obviously designed to be an entertaining showpiece and was probably not much more than that. As a reporter noted some years later, the robot was "an incredible oddity."[36] But it sparked more than enough curiosity to draw huge crowds to the Westinghouse pavilion.

Elektro may have been a new creation, but it reflected ideas that had been floating around in popular culture for some time. The robot had a shiny, box-like body with tubular legs and arms, comparatively tiny hands, and cartoonish facial features. The result was an appearance that could have served as the model for a comic strip character of the time.

An advertisement for the Elektro exhibit appeared in *The Saturday Evening Post*. The ad made it clear that the imposing robot was intended to be "lots of fun," especially for children in the audience. The goal of entertaining children probably explains why a mechanical dog named Sparko was added to the exhibit.[37]

The whole idea of robots was still mostly the stuff of fiction at the time. Even the word *robot* was relatively new. It only came into widespread use after the success of *R.U.R.* (*Rossum's Universal Robots*), a 1920 drama by the Czech playwright Karel Capek.

The word was new to Americans, but the concept was not. Marvelous automatons, capable of replicating human appearance and motion, were familiar in the 19th century and earlier. Versions of robot-like machines also had long appeared in popular literature, as well, dating back to at least the turn of the century. Consider, for example, that the L. Frank Baum children's novel *The Wizard of Oz* (1900) included the robot-like Tin Man character. It is probably the most remembered of such mechanical creations in U.S. fiction, but the idea also appeared elsewhere. (One interesting example was *Percy, the Mechanism Man*, a short-lived syndicated comic strip that launched in 1912.)

The idea of a functioning mechanical person may have seemed far-fetched in the century's early decades, but it soon became firmly established in popular culture. Several films based on Baum's *Oz*, which were produced beginning as early as 1910, helped circulate the idea. (The most famous *Oz* movie adaptation was director Victor Fleming's beloved classic starring Judy Garland. It premiered in the summer of 1939, a few months after the New York World's Fair opened.)

Other films occasionally picked up the robotic theme, too. The most famous of these was undoubtedly Fritz Lang's dystopian *Metropolis* (1927), which prominently featured Maria, a quasi-robot character. The film was an international sensation. ("Nothing like *Metropolis*, the ambitious Ufa production that has created wide international comment, has been seen on the screen,"[38] wrote a reviewer in the *New York Times*.) Its fame probably helped popularize the robot concept, helping to set the stage for Elektro 12 years later.

On closer inspection, Elektro was more than just an amusement. Beneath the entertaining exterior, there was some serious science. Manufactured at the Westinghouse plant in Mansfield, Ohio, it was the realization of a bold idea, and, in the words of a recent science writer, it had "electrical controls that were remarkably advanced for the time."[39]

Although Westinghouse's robot had minimal functionality, it did hint at the potential that robots could have in the future and especially at the idea that robots could do much of life's hard and unpleasant work. In that way, Elektro, though clunky and imperfect, clearly pointed to a World of Tomorrow in which life would be more comfortable and more convenient. It was an idea that was entirely consistent with the Fair's overall thematic emphasis and with the viewpoint that American consumerism had been promoting since the 1920s.

Over at the American Telephone and Telegraph (AT&T) building, things were more down to earth. AT&T showcased a device called the Voder, the Voice Operation Demonstrator. It was an electronic system for artificially synthesizing human speech that worked with the assistance of a human operator.[40] The technology was in very early stages and had minimal capabilities. But it was a foretaste of the electronic marvels that would materialize in later decades.

AT&T also offered visitors the chance to win a free long-distance telephone call at their pavilion, which served as serve souvenirs, of sorts, for the people who had come to the AT&T exhibit. Many people entered the drawing for the chance to make such a call, which likely seemed like a rare opportunity since the service was then prohibitively expensive for many family budgets. The winners did receive the opportunity to place a call at no charge, but there was a different kind of transaction taking place for those who participated. The calls were free, but they were not private since they were part of the AT&T show. In addition to other visitors being able to listen in on the calls, company representatives also monitored them, supposedly to gather information about "human hearing" and "the content of the phone conversation."[41] Although there is no way of knowing for sure, it seems reasonable to think that most people who won the opportunity probably did not mind the intrusion. To greet family or friends from a great distance at no cost was likely more important to the winners of the free calls than the loss of privacy.

Another remarkable new technology that was to have a significant impact in the near-future was also on display at the Fair. Television was a tantalizing idea with a forward-looking and futuristic aura, consistent with the Fair's theme of the "World of Tomorrow." Only a few years earlier, the transmission of moving images and sound seemed like the stuff of dreams. Now, those dreams were starting to become a reality.

When the World's Fair first opened, some people in the greater New York area saw President Roosevelt's dedication speech via the startling new medium of television. Although it was not a new technology in 1939, television remained relatively unfamiliar to most Americans at the time. Few had seen it first-hand.

It was not a wholly alien concept, however. Television, or something very much like it, had already developed a reputation dating back many years. British engineer Archibald M. Low, for example, had talked about the possibility of "seeing by wire" as early as 1914. Newspapers at the time reported about his remarkable new creation, which he called the "Televista."[42]

Low saw the promise of what would become television, but there were substantial technical difficulties inherent in the way he was thinking about it. Further development of Low's technology was slow. (In fact, in an article he published in 1920, Low wrote that "tele-vision," as he called it by then, "would not be perfected for a very long time."[43])

Subsequently, other people attempted to develop a workable system—most using the same kind of technology that Low had envisioned. Their efforts did not meet with much success, either. Eventually, however, a different technological approach brought some answers. In 1927, a television system that used beams of electrons was shown in San Francisco by a young man named Philo Taylor Farnsworth. After additional development and refinement, this approach proved to be successful.

RCA was one of the first major companies to see the promise of the new technology. As the owner of the National Broadcasting Company (NBC) subdivision, it had televised Roosevelt's remarks as the World's Fair opened on April 20, 1939. It was an eagerly anticipated display of technological prowess. The company had informed shareholders about plans for television as early as 1935 and noted that "public interest" continued to be "unabated" after those plans were made public.[44]

Despite all the fanfare it received, the televised signal only reached about 50 miles. As few as a thousand people outside the Fair may have seen it since it was estimated there were only 200 television receivers in the broadcast area.[45] Still, it was the start of something important, even if it was only a tentative beginning.

With the president's broadcast providing much free publicity for the technology, NBC soon began broadcasting television programming regularly, at first in New York and then elsewhere. Other companies then followed NBC's lead, albeit at a modest scale at the time.

The World's Fair broadcasts established that television in America's future was not a question of if, but rather when. The technology caught the public's eye, but it was far from perfect. Television pictures were small, grainy, and often blurry. The sets were expensive, especially at a time when the nation was only beginning to recover from the economic woes of the Great Depression. Still, it was not hard to imagine how wonderful it would be to have television programming beamed into the home. However, the social implications of television were not as widely understood in 1939. "Nobody seems very certain of anything about television," wrote O.B. Hanson in a magazine essay.[46] As a vice-president and chief engineer for the National Broadcasting Company, Hanson was in a position to know. He had a sense that television's impact would be much broader than most people realized. "Television is bound to have profound effects on our social order," he continued. It was among the most prescient of statements made about the future to come out of that era.

The Fair's fantastic representations of the future suggested that coming waves of scientific discovery and technological breakthroughs would be distilled into imaginative consumer products. This would bring a miraculous new life to an American public that was weary from the travails of the years of economic crisis. In overlapping messages, the exhibits most closely associated with the Fair's World of Tomorrow theme drove home one central idea. Big businesses, along with other American institutions, were ready, willing, and able to deliver a bright future. It would come to those people—presumably consumers—who richly deserved it.

The Fair recapped the state of progress and staked out the position that the United States was ready to lead the way into such a future. It had the know-how, industriousness, perseverance, and wisdom to create a new world of shining tomorrows. The American people would need to do their part, of course. However, that part could be fulfilled by Americans doing the things that came naturally to them and by doubling down on the growing culture of consumerism. The future, as it were, would come when Americans decided to choose it by spending their hard-earned dollars on making it a reality. Of course, there were at least two factors that held the potential to influence how well this might work out.

First, the 1939 World's Fair representations of the future tended to envision the world of things more accurately than it envisioned the world of people. It was relatively easy to see that scientific developments might help solve practical problems and that new technologies might yield all sorts of amazing gadgets and products. It was also relatively easy to develop a visual style—a "look"—with futuristic associations. The aesthetic could be translated into sleek industrial designs, modernistic architectural elements, unusual surfaces and lighting, and more. All these things tended to give a veneer of the future to innovative inventions, real or imagined, so that new things looked new. Indeed, the stagecraft of designers such as Norman Bel Geddes was not just for show. It created a break with the current and the traditional, and it inspired people to look at the objects of the imagined future from a new perspective.

Second, there was another vital factor that received even less attention. The Fair's visions of the future often seemed to imagine new technologies, household gadgetry, and other innovations as if they would happen in a vacuum. It was as if the science, products, and material world would evolve, but the social world would stay the same.

Looking back at the World of Tomorrow, it is not difficult to notice that the future it imagined for women was not exactly pathbreaking. Said more bluntly, the future it envisioned for women was not much of an improvement over the state of things in 1939. For the most part, the corporate visions of the coming world implied that women would continue to fulfill extremely stereotyped and traditional roles.

In discussions that the Fair prompted, however, there were at least some hints of a different point of view. In an essay published to mark the occasion of the World's Fair, Helen Astor, chair of the Fair's Women's participation Committee, wrote an optimistic essay. In it, she concluded that modern "engineering and scientific developments had opened 'the portals of economic opportunity'" for women. She also noted that many women had already entered the professional workplace in increasing numbers, especially in fields such as nursing and clerical work. "Certainly," she said, "every woman should be interested in the World of Tomorrow because women have an opportunity to take their part in this world according to their ideals, on a scale that was not dreamed of in the World of Yesterday."[47]

Astor's attitude, though prevalent in years since, would very likely have seemed progressive to many people at the time. It was not necessarily a view that was embraced enthusiastically by Fair organizers overall. At best, Fair exhibits sent inconsistent messages regarding the full equality of women.

For one thing, in laying out a picture of future life, many corporate exhibits envisioned the social order in the world of tomorrow as very similar to that of 1939. The presumptions and attitudes of the then-present day, which had restricted women mostly to a life of household work, heterosexual marriage, and child-rearing, were presumed and reinforced repeatedly in these exhibits. The future might be a time when menial domestic tasks would be easier. However, the implication was that a woman's "place" in the world of tomorrow would mostly be in the kitchen of tomorrow.

Interestingly, some women were involved in several aspects of planning the Fair, even though their influence was generally limited. A prominent example of women's influence seems to have been in the Fair's Advisory Committee on Consumer Affairs, which began meeting two years before the Fair opened. The group included both women and men, but women served in some of its most prominent positions. Blanche W. Hendrickson was the original chair of the group, and one of its two vice-chairs was Katherine Fisher, the director of the Good Housekeeping Institute.[48]

The fact that a group focusing on consumers might include many women members was not altogether unusual at the time. Women of that era played an essential and often prominent part in emerging efforts to promote consumer interests. Various women-led organizations championed policies to safeguard consumers, intending to make sure products were safe, effective, and economical.[49] Newspapers and magazines regularly reported about the activities of the groups, bringing increasing public awareness of them. Arguably, such organizations were the place where women's leadership was most visible and significant at that time in U.S. history.

The Fair's Advisory Committee on Consumer Affairs included people with this background, as well as members from industry, and perhaps it was inevitable that a conflict of purposes and orientation would emerge. After some months, it became clear to some Committee members that the Fair would emphasize a corporate rather than a consumer point of view. That realization rankled many committee members. An article in the *New York Times* noted that some members believed their names were "being misused to promote commercial exhibits at the exposition."[50] Finally, just weeks before the Fair was to open, the situation boiled over. Twenty-one members promptly quit.[51]

Between Fair exhibits that forecast limited roles for women in the future and Fair planning activities that seemed to mostly marginalize women, a traditional and male-centric mindset was very much on display. That mindset was equally on display, perhaps unwittingly, in some attractions at the Fair, which reflected more flagrant sexism. Despite Fair organizers' overarching interest in promoting what they must have believed was a picture of the future that reflected significant progress, this was hardly the case with some of their decisions.

The Entertainment Zone contained the most glaringly sexist and exploitative part of the Fair. Amid innocent attractions, the Entertainment Zone also hosted more than a half-dozen suggestive, adult-oriented shows featuring women in various stages of undress. One of the racy shows had even been the work of Futurama designer Norman Bel Geddes. His "Hall of Mirrors" show featured an optical illusion in which "a single dancing girl [sic] appears to be rows of several hundred girls visible from every possible angle."[52] Unsurprisingly, the exhibits sparked much controversy.

The scandalous nature of the shows drew protests from religious organizations and others, as might be expected, but the shows themselves were not discontinued. A "Miss Nude of the World [sic] Fair" contest in June, however, was the last straw for some people.[53] New York police raided the competition and arrested two women performers on charges of indecent exposure. New York mayor Fiorello Henry La Guardia subsequently ordered an investigation to see "if the shows injured public morals."[54]

It was hardly the kind of publicity that the Fair needed. Grover A. Whalen, the Fair's president, "denounced the 'so-called beauty contest' as a 'cheap publicity stunt,'" according to one contemporary account, but still, "he defended the regular shows, several of which feature showgirls bare from the hips up."[55]

Many reports conclude that the Fair's organizers tolerated these shows because of their success in attracting paying customers. Income, then, was the primary consideration in including them. On this matter, many discussions of these shows note that though millions of visitors attended the Fair, the overall attendance figures were lower than had been projected. Under these circumstances, Fair leaders may have rationalized the shows as something akin to a necessary evil—a less-than-ideal element to be tolerated for economic reasons.

To say that such rationalizations seem unconvincing is an understatement. These exploitative "girl shows," as they were sometimes called, are difficult to reconcile with the supposedly nobler purposes of the Fair, regardless of their supposed economic contribution to its bottom line. What they were doing in a Fair dedicated to the "World of Tomorrow," especially in the moral climate in the United States of the 1930s, is hard to fathom and certainly evidence that attitudes about women, as expressed in the Fair's content, were mired in the sexism that held sway in the era.

The World of Tomorrow, as the Fair presented it, was also not a world that was imagined as very diverse in other ways, too. To the extent that African Americans and other people of color were represented at all, that representation was marginal. The presumption seemed to be that the American future would be a white future.

Even in the most basic ways, African American representation at the Fair was minimal. Most exhibits neglected to include them at all. Nor did African Americans fare much better in a more immediate arena—employment opportunities at the Fair itself.

Economic hardship was especially acute among African Americans in years of the Great Depression, and that situation was as severe in New York as it was elsewhere. Fair organizers had pledged to keep employment practices free from discrimination. At first, there was some optimism that African Americans would be well represented, at least among the Fair workforce. It soon appeared that hiring practices fell well short of that standard, however. African American leaders protested what they saw as inadequate measures to open employment to members of their community.

In April of 1939, the Greater New York Coordinating Committee for Employment picketed Fair offices in protest. Then, on the very day that the Fair opened to the public, the Rev. Adam Clayton Powell—a future member of the U.S. House of Representatives—helped organize a demonstration of 500 people. The assembled protesters marched just beyond the Fair's gates.[56]

Media attention was focused mainly elsewhere, however, especially since Franklin Roosevelt was giving his widely publicized television address at the same time. In the end, however, this protest, along with other resistance activities that included picketing by the Negro Youth Association, seemed to work. Job prospects for African Americans at the Fair improved, at least to a modest extent.[57]

Powerful institutional interests promulgated the idea of a positive future. They marketed it to the public, and these interests were represented by people who were either oblivious to diversity issues or else chose to ignore them. The issue did not gain traction, and it seems to have had little influence on most fair-goers. In retrospect, however, it is evident that the Fair's overall lack of diversity across many dimensions was a significant shortcoming.

In presuming that women, people of color, and others would remain in the restrictive roles available to them in the 1930s, the Fair's World of Tomorrow presented an incomplete picture from the start. Furthermore, as much as the Fair may have helped generate excitement for the inventions and gadgets that would have an impact, assumptions of social stagnation and a persisting status quo limited the visions of the future that the Fair tried to present.

Many visitors to the Fair probably took the assumptions that were part of the exhibits at face value. While some people of the time may have noticed the lack of representation and the prejudices that may seem obvious today, probably few expected the Fair to present a picture that was otherwise. After all, this was the World of Tomorrow as conceptualized by the most powerful institutions in American society—the same institutions that largely framed and reinforced how Americans looked at the world and themselves.

As much as the 1939 New York World's Fair painted a bright picture of what could be called a techno-consumerist future world, dire international conditions had cast shadows over the event from the very first day. Even as newspapers reported about the Fair, Adolf Hitler grabbed headlines with menacing declarations that Germany had become among the "most heavily armed nations in the world."[58] Indeed, rising tensions and the winds of the coming war were of grave concern. Such concerns grew over the summer months. When Germany launched an invasion of Poland in September of 1939, the level of anxiety rose even more. From an international perspective, it suddenly seemed questionable that a rosy future would materialize anytime soon.

2

From War to Renewal

"To the scrap heap of discredited but once-popular theories, please add another, the immediate Post-War Dream World."[1] That was the conclusion Raymond Loewy, the once-optimistic futurist, reached in 1943.

Just a few years earlier, Loewy had played a prominent role in creating visions of bright tomorrows for the 1939 New York World's Fair. Since then, however, his enthusiasm for the future had faded. America's entry into World War II saw to that. It was a dire conflict, more terrible than any war the world had seen, and Loewy worried about the times to come, even if the United States prevailed in the war.

Just three years earlier, in 1940, the New York World's Fair permanently closed after a downbeat second season. By then, the war in Europe had been raging for months, and Japan's military conquests in Asia were raising concerns in Washington. These tense world events dampened the spirit of optimism that the World's Fair had championed.

Nevertheless, even in February of 1941, some voices kept the hope of a positive future alive. Among them was Henry Luce, the influential publisher. He declared that regardless of international conflicts and complex new challenges, the world was already in the midst of what he called the "American Century."[2] It was probably not a label that seemed obvious when it first appeared in an editorial in Luce's popular *Life* magazine. However, it was a term that would be broadly accepted and used for many years.

Luce was candid about where the country stood at the time. "We Americans are unhappy," he said. "As we look to the future—our own future and the future of other nations—we are filled with foreboding."[3] However, he was far from pessimistic about the nation's long-term prospects. On the contrary, Luce believed that the United States and its system would thrive. Indeed, he left no doubt about his abiding "faith in the good intentions as well as in the ultimate intelligence and ultimate strength of the whole American people."[4]

As Luce saw the situation, the nation was in a unique position. "It now becomes our time," he wrote, "to be the powerhouse from which the ideals spread throughout the world and do their mysterious work of lifting the life of mankind from the levels of beasts to what the Psalmist called a little lower than angels."[5] It was a vision in which the future and American exceptionalism were intertwined. Accordingly, he called for Americans to take charge of the situation in order "to create the first great American Century."[6]

Luce's faith in the nation's future notwithstanding, most Americans soon had other priorities. That became crystal clear when the United States was finally drawn into war after Japan attacked the U.S. naval base in Pearl Harbor on December 7, 1941. In the aftermath of that attack, the dream of an idyllic, consumer-oriented future—the kind of future that the 1939 World's Fair and other sources had vigorously promoted—suddenly seemed irrelevant.

The new realities of war dictated that America's view of the future would change. Almost overnight, America redirected its brawn, brainpower, and resources toward one overarching goal: winning the fight for democracy and the survival of the nation. Bright, carefree days of consumer-oriented wonder would have to wait.

Finding themselves plunged into war, Americans were forced to adapt to a very new and challenging set of realities. Most obviously, the war necessitated a military effort that involved millions of men and many women in uniform. Along with immense demands on the military, however, circumstances also required careful coordination of the nation's labor, industry, and resources on a massive scale. Officials recognized that the war presented not only a complex military problem. It also created a great new challenge to the U.S. economy, which had yet to recover fully from the Great Depression.

The pressing needs of the military generated a vast increase in the demand for labor. The war effort put many more Americans to work than at any time in then-recent memory. But a generation of young men was called to military service and was therefore unavailable for civilian work. Industry's hiring practices needed to change to meet production demands.

Out of necessity, the war created new opportunities for women and people of color. Many of them gained access to well-paying jobs of the type that previously would have gone to the young white men who were now serving in the armed forces. Thus, the American workplace diversified as the nation scrambled to fill the jobs that were necessary for the war effort. The cultural icon of Rosie the Riveter, the subject of a famous 1942 song and a 1944 movie, symbolized the millions of women who contributed to the war effort by working in factories and businesses.

The war effort called upon a wide-ranging set of enterprises—farms, factories, research labs, businesses, educational institutions, and more, all of which provided essential goods and services. Although production to support civilian life also needed to continue, this was no time for civilian frills. Accordingly, America's nonmilitary economic output focused on essential consumer products. As a result, many civilian products were rationed or even discontinued to ensure that raw materials and industrial capacity remained squarely focused on the military's wartime needs. Americans almost universally accepted these new hardships, believing they were necessary sacrifices for victory against enemies who seemed genuinely evil. At a time when young soldiers in combat were dying for

We Can Do It! During World War II, the need for labor in American factories and businesses opened up many opportunities for women and others who previously had limited access to these well-paying jobs. This famous government poster, a harbinger of the future, encouraged women to contribute to the U.S. war effort by joining the workforce in roles that had previously been mostly limited to men (National Archives).

their country, giving up non-essential things in this way probably seemed like a minor sacrifice in comparison.

It did not take long for these changes to materialize. Soon after the Pearl Harbor tragedy, the government began to implement policies aimed at assuring that nothing stood in the way of military needs and the war effort. The U.S. Office of Price Administration (OPA), for example, began a rationing program very soon after the Pearl Harbor attack in1941. Initially, the OPA only mandated the rationing of automotive tires for civilian vehicles. Soon, however, more items were added to the list. Eventually, a wide range of consumer goods came under rationing orders, including gasoline, cars, sugar, shoes, coffee, various food items, typewriters, and many other items.

Along with rationing, the government instituted other policies intended to control the economy, aiming to keep it in working order as the war progressed. One of these was the Emergency Price Control Act of 1942. In that same year, the Office of Economic Stabilization instituted wage controls as part of its mandate. By 1943, then, a collection of government policies harnessed the economy to focus on the war.

These and other measures undoubtedly contributed to the eventual Allied victory, but in the meantime, wartime economic policies also had other consequences on the American home front. Interestingly, one side-effect was mostly positive. The ramp-up in the labor force generated steady paychecks for many workers throughout the war years. It was a welcome development, especially considering that the Great Depression, which at times had seen an unemployment rate of around 25 percent, had only recently ended.

But the domestic employment situation created a new issue. How, given these circumstances, were home-front American workers to spend their steady paychecks? Since the wartime economy led to rationing and shortages in consumer-oriented production, workers had limited opportunities to spend the money that their hard-work generated. American industry was busy turning out jeeps, uniforms, ammunition, airplanes, and a plethora of other supplies for the military. Relatively few products were available for consumer purchase. All of this helped push the bright world of tomorrow, as it had been envisioned just before the war, to the periphery.

In some ways, however, maybe it did not matter that consumer goods were in short supply during the war years. The massive scope and scale of the war, the tremendous loss of life, and the ferocity of the fight weighed heavily on the American psyche. Under such dire and uncertain circumstances, it would be reasonable to ask if the public was even thinking about the optimistic future as they had a few years earlier. With the nation immersed in the most massive and most deadly war the world had ever seen, the American mindset mostly shifted to the here and now, leaving little time for daydreaming about a bright world yet to come. Getting to an idealized world of tomorrow—the kind of world that many people envisioned in the 1930s—would require winning the war first. Given the situation, it was not surprising that the war largely refocused American thinking about the future to the very near term. After all, the future that mattered was the future in which America won the war. There would be time to think about what would come after that later.

Still, as the war raged on, some American leaders began to think ahead. In 1943, more battles and uncertainty were yet to come. By then, however, some American officials and business leaders concluded that it was time to prepare for what would happen after the conflict. U.S. political leaders took the lead in projecting ahead, but American business executives were also keen to shift at least some consumer attention to a postwar future.

Already, industry leaders and government officials knew that the transition to a peacetime economy, whenever it came, would be fraught with dangers and complexities. One thing that no one wanted to see was a relapse to the economic woes that had plagued the nation in the decade leading up to the war. So, even as government and business leaders continued to devote much attention to finishing the war, they also began to plan for life beyond it.

In early January of 1943, a prominent New York real-estate magnate spoke about the postwar future. He concluded that it would not be long before the hostilities would end. After the expected American victory came, he said, "the great industrial machine which produced ... the greatest value of manufactured goods, the highest levels of employment and the largest national income ever recorded in history [for the war effort] will be required to divert its energies to the production of civilian peacetime commodities."[7]

These comments were an indication that some leaders were returning to the prewar idea that a world of plenty would soon be at hand. Still, others warned that the road forward might be difficult to navigate. In March 1943, for example, Leo T. Crowley, the chair of the Federal Deposit Insurance Corporation, noted the urgency of preparing for peacetime. "If past experience is any guide," he said, "we can anticipate that in the post-war future American banking will face the most critical period of its entire history."[8]

The caution that was apparent in Crowley's remarks was hardly surprising, and indeed, the recent experiences of the Great Depression were reason enough to be concerned. Winning the war was regarded as essential, but that alone would provide no guarantee that the economy would not sink back into lethargy and crisis. There was much uncertainty about New Deal policies, which were still very recent. The government's New Deal approach to the economic crisis had not had much time to prove its long-term viability before the war came along. Complicating matters, the sheer scale of the war, and the dramatic impact that it had on employment and production, created a very unfamiliar scenario, unlike anything ever seen before. In the postwar era, then, the United States would be entering uncharted territory, at least to some degree. It seemed possible, perhaps probable, that previous experiences might be of limited usefulness as a guide for future actions.

Perhaps the most worrisome matter looming before the policymakers who were looking ahead to a postwar future was a fundamental one. How should the government handle the demobilization of the millions of soldiers who would be returning to civilian life? If military demobilization was too abrupt, would that negatively impact employment? Would too rapid a demobilization push the economy into a tailspin? These were vexing questions that spurred much debate.

A study that was prepared for President Roosevelt and released in early 1944 warned that military demobilization was a "gigantic issue" and that "nothing comparable has ever been known before."[9] For that reason, the authors of the study urged caution, advocating a careful transition from a wartime economy to a peacetime one when the time came. They concluded, for example, that in the postwar future, the government should pay special attention to how it ended price controls. They were also nervous about a scenario in which taxes might rise to "excessive" levels.

Despite these genuine concerns, however, the authors did not dwell on the uncertainties of the postwar economy. On the contrary, their report, though sober in tone, was mostly optimistic. In fact, after examining it, a writer for the *New York Times* concluded that it pictured "the nation's economic future ... in bright colors."[10] There would be much to oversee, the report suggested, and in that situation, the government and industry would need to take the lead. Overall, however, there was much reason to be hopeful for the times to come.

Thus, conventional wisdom held that as long as the government carefully managed demobilization and the economy, American soldiers could return to civilian life without disrupting economic progress. The demobilized soldiers and their families would be able to enjoy the fruits of an expected and hard-won victory. A consumer paradise, it seemed, was on the horizon.

In the postwar economy, other Americans would presumably benefit, too—or so it was sometimes said. For example, many women found new employment opportunities during the war. But some people wondered whether those opportunities would remain available when young men re-entered the civilian workforce. Eric A. Johnston, president of the U.S. Chamber of Commerce, was confident that a positive outcome would carry the day on this issue. "People who foresee grave difficulties for women industrial workers after the war," he said in 1944, "are just conjuring up ghosts that will never arise." Indeed, Johnston predicted the opposite result and said, "Women will be able to keep almost every gain they have made in industry—in numbers employed, in better types of jobs, in higher wages."[11]

Perhaps unsurprisingly, given the nation's long and troubled history concerning race, less seems to have been said publicly by U.S. political and business leaders about the modest employment gains made by some African Americans and other people of color during the war.

The race issue remained problematic during the conflict, perhaps more so than is sometimes recalled. The nation's focus on the war had not erased long-standing racial tensions, and at times the situation boiled over. When a riot erupted in Detroit on June 20, 1943, and seemed out of control, Franklin Roosevelt responded the following day by sending thousands of heavily armed federal troops to quell the disturbance. Other race-related troubles, not directly related, also broke out in a few cities scattered across the country. So, regardless of any progress on the race issue that America may have made during the conflict, the matter of race relations remained unresolved in U.S. society throughout the war.

Writing in the *Opportunity: A Journal of Negro Life*, Lester B. Granger surveyed the situation. He predicted that in the future, people "will look back upon the present phase of our racial relationships with unbelieving wonder. They will find it hard to understand that a great nation, fighting for its very existence in the bloodiest war of all time, should have been forced to depend upon leaders so dismally incompetent in solving a fundamental problem of national unity and civilian morale."[12]

Indeed, American leaders were still reluctant to confront racial bigotry and inequality directly. Despite this trepidation, however, wartime experiences and rising expectations among African American workers had set the wheels of change in motion. Meaningful changes in American racial policies and attitudes would take some time to materialize, but the process was underway.

Meanwhile, the consumer was on the minds of American leaders. The general thinking before the war was that a consumer-oriented economy was the road to a bright future, and that view had not significantly changed. U.S. leaders presumed that for the United States to be prosperous in the postwar future, the consumer would need to be the engine to power that outcome.

Despite some uncertainty about what the labor situation would be when the war ended, American businesses began talking directly to consumers about a wondrous postwar future even as the conflict continued. The media gave many Americans—mainly white Americans—the impression that when the United States won the war, they would be the beneficiaries of a bountiful future. They would find many opportunities and a vast array of consumer products and services to make their lives better than ever before. Such possibilities, according to this line of thinking, would be the key elements that would restore America's path to a bright and shining tomorrow.

A full-page magazine advertisement for the Prudential Insurance Company of America from 1943 drove home that point. The ad directed its optimistic message squarely to young women on the home front. "Take heart, Little Lady," the headline read, "America's future is safe."[13] The ad then elaborated on its message with soothing, hopeful words:

> Fear not for the future—for America is more than a land of promise. It is a land of fulfillment—where promises come true.... Look beyond these dark wartime days into the bright future that is not so far away. A future in which your courage in starting a family in these trying times will be repaid a thousand-fold—a future of better things, of better living.[14]

This notion that coming victory would usher in the long-sought and idealized consumer-oriented world of plenty was a standard message. In a 1943 article, *The Nation* boldly announced that America's hard work during the war would yield "post-miracles" for consumers after a successful conclusion to the war.[15]

More recently, Lizabeth Cohen, a historian of U.S. consumerism, reviewed the evidence and concluded that even as the war raged on, Americans "were promised that wartime research, particularly in electronics, would pay off in miraculous consumer products after the war."[16] Thus, in the final two years of the war, the business community promoted the idea that a resurgent consumer-driven future was waiting for Americans once victory came.

In a specific example, wartime needs had already pushed the development of plastic, a lightweight material that could be molded and manufactured to serve many purposes. As early as 1942, people envisioned plastics playing a significant part in the world that was on the horizon. In a speech to plastics industry leaders on May 4, 1942, Harry S. Truman, then serving as a senator from Missouri, said so directly:

> It has been prophesied that the post-war period will be an Age of Plastic—an age in which plastics will become an increasingly essential and commonplace

commodity of our everyday life. And you, the members of the plastic industry, can, by your pioneering and industrious application today translate this prophecy into the reality of tomorrow.

Although marked progress has been made in the development of plastics in the past few years, we all know the industry is still in its infancy. Great things are expected of it. And our war effort presents an unexcelled opportunity for you to develop one of the basic industries of the future.[17]

The view that plastics would be an essential building block for the astonishing new products that future life was to offer was already well established. Enthusiasm for the material seemed almost limitless, and people seldom considered the potential downsides to its use, at least not publicly. "The minds of scientists are filled with the wonders that will emerge from the war-bound laboratories for use by ordinary civilians when peace comes," wrote Mary Madison for the *New York Times* in the summer of 1943. "Designers' drafting boards are covered with plans for such amazing and unfamiliar things as plastic automobiles...."[18]

The war pushed the development of modern plastics forward at a dizzying pace. It proved useful in many military equipment and hardware applications. Industry leaders concurred with the view that Truman expressed some months earlier. It was increasingly apparent that they were already thinking about the enormous possibilities for the material when the peacetime economy returned.

A plastics industry spokesperson predicted, with some degree of accuracy, "a post-war world in which some form of plastic will be encountered in almost every aspect of life."[19] Indeed, businesses had already come up with many possible uses for the revolutionary material. They imagined "shock-proof tableware," "a Lucite cake or fruit knife with serrated edges that cut like a buzz saw," "hoses and sprinklers made of pliant, indestructible plastic," and "glass that doesn't crack."[20] The idea that plastic was a material, perhaps *the* material, of the future became entrenched in the American imagination.

In these and other ways, American industry leaders looked ahead with confidence at a time that was well before the end of the war. Of course, the conflict continued to produce hardship. The immense sacrifices made by so many people—military and civilian—continued to weigh on the minds of the public. Moreover, although U.S. leaders were gaining confidence that America and its allies would win the war, there was still uncertainty. The public remained anxious as the conflict wore on. Despite prodding from government and business, thoughts of the future proved to be difficult to reconcile with wartime conditions in the public's mind.

Indeed, some people were very reluctant to go along with the re-emerging talk of a bright future while the war continued. Raymond

Loewy, the once-optimistic designer, was one of them. In an essay he wrote for the *New York Times* in 1943, he claimed that "the public is being misinformed systematically about the wonders that await them."[21] By his reasoning, the scope of the war effort meant that this was misguided thinking, at best. "Advertising and publicity," he continued, "seem to be dedicated to proving that nothing—absolutely nothing—stands in the way of unlimited industrial possibility except this war, and the minute it is over—look out boys!'" He was skeptical that it would be quite that easy.

Still, Loewy correctly identified one factor that would have significant implications in the postwar world as it materialized. "War, we know, has compressed much research into an abnormally concentrated period. Miraculous progress has been made in producing the instruments of war, and sparks have been thrown off in the process which have been bound to kindle the imagination."[22] Those sparks would play a critical role in the postwar consumer world that was soon to arrive.

Loewy was aware that some research, especially in the areas of technology and production methods, was likely to have enormous implications after the war. Of course, he was in no position to realize the full extent of war-related research and just how groundbreaking some of it was. The most critical development that Loewy did not know about was also the most impactful and arguably, the most important scientific and technological breakthrough of the modern era. That development was the atomic research that was underway in the classified Manhattan Project, a far-flung research effort that harnessed immense resources for a particular purpose: to develop an atomic bomb.

The startling new technology of the atomic bomb gave the United States the decisive edge in the final weeks of the war. The U.S. dropped an atom bomb on the Japanese city of Hiroshima on August 6, 1945, and then a second bomb on the city of Nagasaki three days later. After the second bombing, the Japanese high command finally relented and agreed to surrender. At last, some three months after Germany's defeat in May, the war was finally over—the end coming in a blinding display of atomic fury.

Government scientists created the atomic bomb covertly under the auspices of the Manhattan Project. Even Harry Truman, who, as president, ultimately decided to use the bomb, had been left in the dark about it during the time he was vice president. He only learned of the advanced state of atomic bomb research when he assumed the presidency after Roosevelt's death in April of 1945. Most officials were unaware of the project, and the general public knew nothing of the bomb at all. As a result, the atomic devastation in Hiroshima was as much of a shock to Americans as it was for the rest of the world.

The atomic bomb represented an unfamiliar technology with enormous consequences for the future, both good and bad, and its power was undeniable. It was a reality that was hard to comprehend fully. It upended many of the understandings that people had about the world and humankind's place in it. Overall, the bomb's psychological impact would be difficult to overstate. It not only abruptly ended the most global war the world had ever seen. It launched a startlingly new and daunting era—the Atomic Age—in the process.

The Manhattan Project had been a vast, far-flung undertaking. At its height, it involved 130,000 people. The operation cost $2 billion. That such a massive operation was kept secret for many months was an astonishing feat. After Hiroshima and Nagasaki, however, the secret was out. U.S. officials realized that something would have to be said publicly to explain the surprise appearance of a weapon with such awe-inspiring power.

As it turned out, a few government officials with very high-security clearance had planned for these circumstances in advance. As work on the bomb was progressing, officials running the program realized that eventually, their ultra-classified atomic-weapon program would become public knowledge. After all, if the United States used the weapon, which they thought was a distinct possibility, then the veil of secrecy would be lifted. In such an event, there were still some aspects of atomic research, especially those related to specific military applications, that they wished to keep classified. Exactly how, in such a scenario, the government would manage to reveal some information about the bomb while still maintaining a level of secrecy was a puzzle.

According to a history compiled by the U.S. Department of Energy, by 1944, government planners already "began a carefully designed public relations program in anticipation of when they would have to announce the news [of the atomic bomb] to the world."[23] The idea was to "'release some selected information' to satisfy public curiosity when the time came, while still keeping more sensitive information classified." The government assigned General Leslie Groves the task of developing a press-release program along these lines. Groves, in turn, quietly enlisted the help of William Laurence, a *New York Times* science writer. Laurence was expected to funnel government-crafted information about the atomic program to the public in newspaper articles at the appropriate time.[24]

Harry S. Truman announced limited information about the bomb in a press release that was issued just hours after the Hiroshima blast. He acknowledged both the sobering power of the new weapon and the unusual circumstances surrounding its development. Truman aimed to be reassuring. However, he did not want to "divulge the technical processes of production or all the military applications [of the bomb], pending further examination of possible methods of protecting us and the rest of the world from the danger of sudden destruction."[25] Still, he tried to put a positive face on the existence of the terrifying new military technology. The power of the atom, he said, would be a "powerful and forceful influence towards the maintenance of world peace."[26]

A few days later, after the Nagasaki bombing, the U.S. government released a more substantial report explaining the Manhattan Project and its role in the development of the bomb. A physicist named Henry D. Smyth compiled the 182-page document.[27] He had been working on the report for months. He aimed to provide enough information to be a reasonably informative account of the project while still maintaining secrecy about some aspects of the program, especially those relating to the military.

The atomic bomb was a shocking development, but the basic idea that atomic energy could be harnessed with new technology was not new, even in the public realm. Predictions about atomic power had been made at the beginning of the century, albeit without a full understanding of what that might entail. In a 1914 novel called *The World Set Free*, for example, the famous writer H.G. Wells wrote of "atomic bombs," "atomic energy," and "atomic engines." The science behind his speculations was incomplete, and his imaginary creations were far less powerful than the Manhattan Project atomic bomb. However, Wells helped introduce the public to ideas that would be filled out later.

In subsequent years, the inherent power of the atom remained an intriguing, if only partially understood, concept to the general public. It occasionally surfaced in various feature stories and articles. "Atomic force—what a world of as yet undreamed of energy and power," read a 1919 article in *The Evening World*, which also said, "This is the 'atomic force' we have been reading about. Radium on your watch dial, disintegrated in one hour, would drive your railroad train home. One ounce would liberate energy sufficient to propel 189 Mauretanias [ocean liners] across the Atlantic."[28] The topic also appeared in numerous other publications of the era, often discussed in sensationalistic language. A full-page story in the *Tulsa Daily World* in 1922 had the headline: "Tinkering with Angry Atoms May Blow Up the Earth."[29] A painting of the Biblical apocalypse illustrated the article.

It is difficult to know how seriously the public took such material. In any case, speculations that it would become possible to unleash the awesome power of the atom continued to appear occasionally. Even into the 1930s, however, scientists remained uncertain about when they could put advances in atomic research to practical use. It seemed that humans would eventually harness the power of the atom, but that day might be a long way off.[30] So, despite occasional and usually vague public discussion of atomic energy in the future, there had been little to prepare the

When Japan did not surrender after Hiroshima was destroyed by America's new super-weapon, the United States launched a second atomic attack on the city of Nagasaki three days later on August 9, 1945. When Japan subsequently surrendered, it was clear that the terrifying power of the atomic bomb not only ended World War II; the new weapon heralded the beginning of a brand-new era—the Atomic Age (Library of Congress).

public for the abrupt appearance of the atomic bomb on the world stage in 1945.

The government carefully orchestrated news media explanations about the atomic bomb. *New York Times* science writer William Laurence, the journalist selected by the War Department "to explain the atomic bomb to the lay public,"[31] wrote of it in lofty, almost mythological language. In one piece he offered an account of the atomic test he had seen on July 16, 1945, in a remote region of New Mexico:

> At this great moment in history, ranking with the moment in the long ago when man first put fire to work for him and started on his march to civilization, the vast

energy locked within the hearts of atoms was released for the first time in a burst of flame such as had never before been seen on this planet, illuminating the earth and sky for a brief span that seemed eternal with the light of many super-suns.
...
It was like the grand finale of a mighty symphony of the elements, fascinating and terrifying, uplifting and crushing, ominous, devastating, full of great promise and great forebodings.[32]

The way Laurence spoke of the blast made clear that he regarded it as a development that forever altered the trajectory of human history. Laurence concluded that this display of atomic power was nothing less than "a new era in the life of man."[33]

The complex, high-level scientific principles that were central to the development of the bomb were far beyond what was understood by most citizens. However, if the science was obscure to the general public, the potential implications of the bomb were not. It did not take long for the public to realize the nightmarish possibilities that atomic weaponry introduced. Previous weapons were powerful, but they paled in comparison to this new, apocalyptic weapon. The destructive potential of the bomb seemed unbelievable by previous standards. It had an immense influence on how people thought about and conceived the future.

It was evident that the bomb had the power to change the course of humanity, which was the kind of statement that in prior experience would have seemed hyperbolic. However, this was a new reality. The bomb was frighteningly powerful, and it was something that had to be reckoned with, like it or not.

Mentally processing the bomb's horrific toll in Japan was a challenging task. As more details about the attacks on Hiroshima and Nagasaki became known, the picture of what had happened became increasingly more apparent and more horrifying. The journalist John Hersey wrote a bleak and sobering account of the bomb's devastation in a piece he called *Hiroshima*. In the essay, Hersey put a human face on a faraway event that otherwise seemed to defy understanding. It was first published in *The New Yorker*, where the editors devoted nearly the entire August 31, 1946, issue to it. Shortly after that, Alfred A. Knopf published the essay in book form, and the work quickly assumed its place as one of the most influential documents to have been written about the bomb.

The atom bomb did more than end the war and alter the international political landscape, of course. The blasts at Hiroshima and Nagasaki signaled the creation of a whole new world with implications, unlike anything that had come before. The very existence of such weapons under the control of frail and fallible humans was deeply concerning. It did not take much of a leap of the imagination to realize that the weapons that destroyed

The world had seen the development of increasingly powerful weapons since the beginning of the 20th century, but nothing could match the horrifying devastation that resulted from use of the atomic bomb. This photograph shows the remnants of Hiroshima shortly after the atomic bombing (National Archives).

Hiroshima and Nagasaki were only the beginning. Should such weapons be mass-produced and strengthened, the result might be truly cataclysmic. Unsurprisingly, the atomic bomb ushered in an era in which some degree of anxiety was never far from the surface of American cultural life.

In 1945, however, Americans took solace in the fact that only their nation possessed the atomic bomb. Although American leaders foresaw the coming rivalry with the Soviet Union, they did not expect the USSR, or any other nation, to develop an atomic bomb in the immediate future. That judgment turned out to be very wrong. In 1945 and for a few years after the war, however, Americans allayed some of their fears with the realization that only the United States had the power of the atom on its side.

Still, the very existence of the bomb was unsettling. To say that the atom bomb was a two-edged sword would be an enormous understatement. Any weapon that could obliterate an entire city and its population in an instant was a weapon that gave its possessors immense military might. In a time of war, Americans believed that the bomb gave the United States a decided advantage. Still, many people realized that the weapon also posed some threat, even to the nation that owned it. A world with the bomb was a world in which near-apocalyptic catastrophe might be around the corner at any moment.

Soon after the Hiroshima blast, talk about the dangers of living in a world in which any nation possessed an atomic bomb began to surface. "It is easy to see how atomic power could be used to destroy most of mankind," said the writer of one newspaper article.[34]

Another person who worried about the bomb was Harold C. Rey, a scientist from Columbia University who had won a Nobel Prize in 1934 and later worked on the Manhattan Project. Speaking at an event in October of 1945, Rey called for the end of atomic weapons. He feared that the weapons would spread to other nations and that a full-fledged atomic war could emerge within a few years. In his opinion, the very existence of the atomic bomb posed a "dreadful threat" to humanity.[35]

In the following months, fears caused by atomic weapons continued to surface. "We are today very near the edge of an abyss," wrote Oxford University professor E.L. Woodward in the *New York Times*.[36]

Thus, even though the bomb was initially a source of American confidence, it was also a source of unease and even anxiety. When the Cold War emerged in the postwar period, atomic weapons (and later, nuclear weapons) added a degree of uncertainty to the American experience over time. When the Soviet Union unexpectedly exploded an atomic bomb in a 1949 test, those underlying fears and anxieties became even more pronounced.

In the early years of the atomic era, many perceptions about the world changed in profound ways. The atom simultaneously held the power to destroy everything and to bring about a brave, new world that would be fueled by its now-revealed secrets. It is not surprising, then, that the Age of the Atom greatly influenced how Americans thought about the future. Winning the war seemed to have secured the nation's immediate horizon and helped the cause of democracy. However, the atomic bomb and the psychological impact that it exerted over society often caused significant stress. Evidence of how U.S. culture tried to cope with that stress and maintain a sense of security could be found in many places.

Interestingly, some of the first treatments of these themes appeared in comic books, a cultural form that had risen in popularity over the years. Comics existed mostly at the margins of U.S. popular culture of that time, and most people regarded them as little more than "kids' stuff." Few people took them seriously. Some of the stories that comic books told and some of the heroes they portrayed, however, are revealing. They give some indication of how U.S. culture was processing the realities of the Atomic Age.

Comic books had become a familiar part of the popular culture shortly before the war. Offshoots of newspaper comic strips, which had helped widen audiences for mass-marketed daily newspapers at the turn of the century, comic books extended the narrative possibilities of the form. By the 1930s, the creators of comic books increasingly began featuring adventure and crime-fighting stories—stories that were not unlike those in popular pulp magazines of the time. In 1938, the industry took a dramatic turn when the costumed hero *Superman*, a character created by Jerry Siegel and Joe Shuster, appeared in the inaugural issue of *Action Comics*.

Superman was an instantly popular character, and most comic book publishers quickly created costumed superhero titles to compete. By the time the United States entered World War II, stories featuring a wide range of superheroes were ready to join the fight for democracy in fictional exploits.

After the war, a few comic books picked up on atomic themes. They still received little scrutiny, and adults were generally unaware of what, exactly, was in them. However, some of the topics and storylines that appeared in them more directly confronted the world situation than might be expected. In any case, with comic books' quick production schedules, the first stories with atomic themes appeared soon after the end of the war. In the November–December 1945 issue of *Headline Comics*, for example, a character named Adam Mann is shown inadvertently consuming a radioactive substance and gaining the power of an atomic bomb as a result.[37] Then there is the cover of the October 1946 issue of *Action Comics*, which shows Superman in an atomic blast.[38]

Another atomic-inspired comic book from the same era was *Atoman*, which also debuted in 1946. In some ways, the fictional Atoman character exemplified the real-world contradictions of the atomic age. Atomic power could be used for good, but it could also be used for evil. Atoman represented the positive aspects of atomic power at a time when American society was still grappling with the atomic bomb's destructive nature.

The first issue of *Atoman*, which was dated February 1946, introduced the character with dramatic, hyperbolic language:

> Out of the turmoil and horror of war, a new age is born—the atomic age! And with the new era, a new man appears on the stage of the world! Who is this new man whose body generates atomic power, whose muscles give him the colossal might of the universe? It is Atoman! [p. 4].

From the first issue of the short-lived publication, the storyline revealed a distinctly postwar worldview. Although the stories unfold in the new era of optimism, the hero's adventures show that the world remained very dangerous. Enemy spies in the stories come close to stealing

America's atomic secrets, threatening the security of the entire world. Like America in the real world of 1946, Atoman possessed the power of the atom. Also like the real world of 1946, other people with sinister motives wanted that power, too.

The atomic theme appeared elsewhere in comic books, in science fiction novels, and elsewhere in U.S. popular culture in the late 1940s. Indeed, the Atomic Age penetrated American life in wide-ranging ways. When it did, the co-existing good and adverse implications of the new atomic world cast the world in an uncertain and confusing light. As seen from that time, if the future were to be an atomic future, it remained unknown what, exactly, that meant. Coming to terms with the atomic age's dangers and promises would be a long process that unfolded as America's speculations about the world of tomorrow continued to evolve.

Despite the mix of optimism and anxiety that the Atomic Age presented, one of its effects was clearer to see. The unlocking of the atom's secrets powerfully symbolized humankind's increasing ability to control nature through the instruments of science and technology. Indeed, in the postwar world, Americans—like many people around the globe—gained increasing confidence that human intelligence and ingenuity had reached new heights. They believed that confounding problems could and would be solved, that science and industry were poised to make good on past promises to deliver a remarkable and wondrous, consumer-oriented future. To some, it may have seemed as though humans were playing God and toying with forces not meant for them—forces they did not fully understand. To many others, the Atomic Age was a new age of progress. Humankind, from that point of view, had just opened the door to tomorrow.

Brimming with confidence, Americans looked to a future in which the possibilities seemed nearly endless. So, with peace achieved, American culture largely, though not entirely, refocused on the bright future. The optimism that found expression in the 1939–1940 World's Fair and other corners of society had been interrupted by the war. However, victory seemed to re-open the door to the idealistic life of ease and plenty that the business sector had promoted before Pearl Harbor.

Of course, the world was different, not only because of the atomic bomb but also because the sheer horror of the war had unnerved many people. The human toll of the conflict, which included genocide on a terrifying scale, was staggering. Coming to terms with all that happened was challenging. Thoughts of tomorrow's world, it seemed, now needed to include the possibility, however remote, that humans might cause their own annihilation.

Optimistic futurism and fears of a darker future, in which the atomic age would go wrong, remained opposing but co-existing cultural impulses for many years to come. The Cold War rivalry with the Soviet Union and other communist nations (including China, after 1949) provided Americans with the context into which they projected these positive and negative visions of the future. At various times and crisis points, views of a gloomy future gained much traction.[39] (These included such developments as the Soviet acquisition of atomic weaponry, the rise of McCarthyism, and more.) Despite this, from the late 1940s until the early 1960s, a positive view of the future remained a powerful draw. When fear did emerge, it never wholly overwhelmed a persistent optimism that the best years of the nation were ahead, at least in the eyes of many Americans.

The powerful allure of a bright future may also have been partially the result of a cultural inclination. For centuries, Americans had seen their country as a special place, uniquely gifted and qualified to chart a positive course for humanity. This predisposition, which is often called "American Exceptionalism," had a long-standing history in U.S. political culture, dating back to Colonial-era talk of a chosen "city on a hill."

However, there was probably more to the resilience of the idea of a bright future than merely the pull of ideology and cultural tradition. Indeed, throughout the postwar era, the idea of America's positive future was deeply intertwined with beliefs about consumer consumption. In promoting the idea of a consumer's world, U.S. businesses were also promoting an idyllic vision of tomorrow.

To that way of thinking, much of the consumer-based economy depended on the continuing growth of consumer spending. Visions of a positive future were undoubtedly genuinely held by many people, including those in business and industry, but these visions were also a strategy. They were a significant part of consumer-focused advertising and marketing of the era. It came from the belief that if Americans fell into a long period of pessimism and despair about what the future held, that might disrupt their spending habits. That could place the nation's economic health and future in jeopardy. With these assumptions firmly entrenched, U.S. businesses continued aggressively selling the idea that the world of tomorrow was secure. For apparently, only when Americans did not doubt that wonders awaited them would they be induced to spend their way to achieving that outcome.

In the years immediately following the war, American culture grappled with such impulses. There were legitimate concerns about international politics, but the optimism that had started to emerge in pre-war years gradually returned. Consider, for example, the hobby magazine *Popular Science*. Since Pearl Harbor, every cover of that monthly magazine had featured a military or war-related illustration. Within a few months of Japan's surrender, however, the magazine returned to a focus on civilian topics and scientific wonders, often with futuristic themes. The December 1945 issue addressed the atomic issue and emphasized the potential for the peaceful use of atomic technology in a way that was reminiscent of articles from well before the war. Rather than speaking of the atom's capacity for destruction, the author wrote, "You will soon see mobile engines running on U-235 and cities heated by steam from graphite panels."[40]

By 1946, *Popular Science*'s focus almost entirely reverted to civilian science and peacetime technology. Cover stories that year addressed topics ranging from astronomy (January 1946 issue) to rocketry (May 1946), as well as more down-to-earth topics of interest to middle-class citizens. If the magazine was any indication, the implication was that peace restored hope for a positive future.

At this time, talk about the future often focused on the circumstances of everyday life. There were hopes for more plentiful consumer goods, new patterns of living, new opportunities for higher education, and significantly improved transportation systems. The latter subject was a popular topic. By this time, companies such as General Motors and Ford were among the mightiest on the American scene. If anything, their power had even strengthened during the war years when they helped fulfill the needs of the U.S. military.

In the postwar years, the U.S. automobile industry continued production at a rapid pace. Americans widely perceived it as a bellwether of the American economy. The often-repeated phrase "What's good for General Motors is good for America" summed up the widely held perception that the automotive industry, and that company, in particular, was central to the nation.[41] America's future often seemed bound up with the future of the automobile. Indeed, cars became a powerful symbol of American might and freedom.

Given the importance of the automobile industry and the renewed cultural emphasis on a bold, technological future, it was perhaps not surprising that the idea of flying cars resurfaced in these years, as well.

Despite a widespread belief that flying cars were the product of post–World War II imagination, the idea was already quite old by then. For many years, inventors had worked on the concept, but real-world implementations of the concept achieved only limited success. One somewhat workable version of a flying car, for instance, was shown in a 1922 air show in Paris, France. That version of the "flying automobile" had folding wings that allowed the vehicle, which was basically a biplane, to "run in the streets under its own power," according to one article.[42]

By the 1930s, several people and companies tried to make flying cars a practical reality. Indeed, the last few years of that decade saw efforts to bring the concept to life in such vehicles as the Windmill Autoplane, the

Waterman Arrowbile, and the Autogiro. None was particularly practical or without problems.

Although little attention was devoted to making civilian vehicles of this sort during World War II, when the conflict ended, flying cars again attracted attention. In the new Atomic Age, when almost everything seemed possible, the idea seemed, if anything, closer than ever to realization.

In 1946, the Southern Aircraft company proposed a new contender: a flying car with folding wings and a detachable tailpiece. The prototype required some effort to operate, but its design made it possible to convert the vehicle from an airplane to a drivable, if somewhat odd-looking, automobile.[43] Around the same time in 1946 and 1947, another firm, Convair, also developed flying car designs—the Model 116 and the Model 118. Convair even managed to conduct more than 60 test flights. Then, a few years later, Moulton Taylor introduced the Aerocar. This model went into production in 1949, albeit on a small scale. The company even sold a few.

The search for a viable flying car design continued into the 1950s. New companies entered the race, but the results were mixed, at best. Flying cars remained a compelling idea, but it was an idea that was never successfully implemented on a large scale. Ultimately, for all the enthusiasm and ingenuity devoted to it, the flying car concept never worked out. The engineering aspects were probably within grasp. Issues of practicality, cost, safety, and other concerns, however, proved to be insurmountable roadblocks.

Decades later, the flying car concept of the postwar era would be fondly recalled by many people who expressed nostalgia for the futurism of the early postwar period. Flying cars never did emerge as a successful technology in the following years. Many people later saw that as a disappointment—as a piece of evidence that the wondrous future they had once imagined did not materialize as they expected.

However, in the early postwar period, flying cars symbolized a future of miraculous possibilities. The idea of flying cars brought together dreams of cars, flight, technological prowess, and consumer satisfaction. Therefore, it is not difficult to see why the idea was much more successful than the few actual vehicles produced. Although the personal flying automobile would remain a tantalizing symbol of the future, it was the earth-bound automobile that would command the public's attention for the time being.

Meanwhile, several new developments jolted America's confidence in the future. The Soviet Union's development of an atomic bomb, China's transformation into a communist state, and other world events fueled a sense of foreboding and anxiety that boiled over at times. Despite these developments, however, Americans retained hope for a promising future.

The 1950s were to be a decade in which ideas about the future often would play off against these opposing viewpoints. There were moments of dread, but there was also much optimism. Americans seldom questioned one fundamental assumption, however. They were brimming with confidence in the science and technology that were transforming their world. Few doubted that the United States possessed the tools that were necessary for unlocking more of nature's secrets. Confidence that the nation could develop new and more effective solutions to the problems remained relatively steady. So, despite the anxieties that some world events prompted, such confidence was a central presumption in mainstream American thinking. The question of whether such confidence was always a good idea was a question that people could and arguably should have asked more often than they did. Given the realities of the day, however, such introspections would have to wait. The world was rapidly changing. Keeping up with its breathtaking developments, while keeping an eye on the future, would prove to be a consuming task.

3

A Consumer's Future

In the early years of the Atomic Age, it finally seemed that all the hardships and sacrifices of the Great Depression and World War II would yield a spectacular payoff. A bold, new life appeared to be at hand. It would be a life in which people would be freed from everyday burdens and could enjoy the fruits of scientific discoveries and innovations. Undoubtedly, it seemed, a bright future—a consumer's future—was in sight.

Of course, the American public also knew there was a scenario in which the future might be considerably bleaker than they hoped. The nation had survived two world wars, and no one needed reminding that another was conceivable. Lest anyone forget that grim possibility, America's emerging rivalry with the Soviet Union and international communism provided a reality check.

Still, many people mustered hope for a less conflict-ridden world. World leaders realized the dangers, and they took some measures to reduce the likelihood of a new and potentially catastrophic war. One major step was the creation of the United Nations (UN) after the war. Its 1945 charter stressed the importance of securing a better future for all of humanity. The founding member states agreed that, henceforth, they would act together to reach that goal. The UN would "develop friendly relations among nations" and foster "international peace and security" while reaffirming "faith in fundamental human rights, the dignity and worth of the human person, [and] in the equal rights of men and women" across the globe.[1]

After deciding to locate its headquarters in New York City, the UN built an impressive new campus along the shore of the East River. The towering building's sleek and gleaming façade soon became a powerful symbol of the UN's aspirations for a future in which humankind would live together in harmony and be free from the scourges of war.

The UN's mandate and promise heartened many people. Admittedly, the League of Nations, which the United States never joined after its establishment following World War I, had failed when it tried to do much the same. However, the postwar world was different, or so many people thought, and the founders of the United Nations hoped to succeed where the League of Nations had stumbled. Of course, not everyone shared an optimistic opinion of the new organization. Even in the United States, some people were skeptical about the UN's chances of accomplishing its goals.

Regardless of differing views about it then and now, however, the creation of the United Nations presented the world with a sign that things were different from before. As a symbol of international cooperation, the UN pointed to a hopeful future. It was an aspirational institution on the world stage, and it provided some reason for optimism.

The world situation was not quite that simple, however, and unfolding events sometimes dampened the mood. Indeed, fits of anxiety and foreboding punctuated the immediate postwar years. At crisis points, a dark view of the future sometimes threatened to overwhelm more optimistic expectations. However, Americans never wholly succumbed to fears of gloom and doom. Instead, visions of a bright future, a future of consumer wonders, retained a place in American thinking.

After a destructive war that had killed millions, the creation of the United Nations signaled a renewed sense of urgency about maintaining world peace and security in the future, especially in light of the new Atomic Age. Shown here is the organization's headquarters in building in New York (National Archives).

There is no denying, however, that the nation's general sense of optimism was sometimes severely tested. The mid-century excesses of McCarthyism and the Red Scare are well-documented examples. For several years beginning in the late 1940s, many Americans succumbed to a deep fear that approached existential dread. The future seemed very precarious, especially to those who thought America stood alone, as if on a small boat of democracy in an angry sea of communist despotism.

Among the many reasons for this development were dramatic changes on the international stage. Americans were shocked when the Soviet Union unveiled its atomic bomb in August of 1949. It was a rattling new complication that set the nation on edge. Not long after, in October of the same year, Mao Zedong's long struggle to install a communist government in China succeeded, which further stoked American fears. Only a few months later, in June of 1950, the Korean War broke out, again threatening world peace and security. Events such as these, coming in rapid succession, added fuel to Americans' anxieties about the Atomic Age and the escalating Cold War.

Congressional hearings reinforced these fears. Even before the Soviet Union's development of an atomic bomb, Americans held grave concerns about the spread of communism. The House Un-American Activities Committee generated alarming headlines in the late 1940s, for example, when it examined the influence of communism in Hollywood. Widely reported 1947 hearings on the topic resulted in the infamous "Hollywood Ten" blacklist, focusing much national attention on the issue of communism in America in the process.

Not long after, when the Senate's Subcommittee on Investigations began looking into communism in the United States in earnest, the situation seemed increasingly dire. From 1950 to 1954, the Subcommittee held high-profile hearings. Its chair, Wisconsin Senator Joseph McCarthy, grilled many witnesses in its exhaustive search for communists, especially in government. As McCarthy's hardline tactics intensified, fear also seemed to rise.

Hollywood, meanwhile, was eager to show it held no sympathy for communism. It inadvertently helped fuel the already-tense situation with the release of many melodramatic films with communist conspiracy themes. Films such as *Red Menace* (1949), *I Was a Communist Spy for the FBI* (1951), *Invasion USA* (1952), *My Son John* (1952), and *Big Jim McLain* (1952) pushed the idea that communism was secretly seeping into American life.[2]

The escalating climate of fear may have emboldened McCarthy, but his aggressive style and grandstanding eventually went too far. McCarthy's accusations and harsh treatment of witnesses during an investigation into communism within the U.S. Army caused an uproar. It soon led to his downfall.

The growing new medium of television undoubtedly hastened McCarthy's fall from power and grace. Indeed, television news organizations extensively covered the Army hearings, and the medium's spotlight cast McCarthy in a particularly unflattering light.

Television's role in McCarthy's political demise was one of the strongest pieces of evidence yet to emerge of the new medium's astonishing cultural power. Although it made a big impression at the 1939 World's Fair, television had not been much of a factor in the U.S. cultural scene during the war years. All that changed after the conflict as industry refocused on the consumer economy and television technology became cheaper and more widely available.

As the number of broadcast stations increased and the price of television sets fell, television's popularity exploded. Within a few years, it began to play a dominant role in American life, helping to shape the entire culture—including ideas about the world of the present and the future. By mid-century, the once-futuristic technology of television not only became a present-day reality for many Americans; it quickly assumed a significant place among competing media of both news and entertainment varieties.

Television in the late 1940s and 1950s meant broadcast television. The unique characteristics of this business model should not be underestimated. It had stark differences from later options, such as home video, cable, internet streaming, and time-shifting recording technologies. Significantly, in the early years of television, the broadcast model resulted in minimal viewing options, which had significant ramifications.

From the broadcasters' perspective, the television business presented challenges and complexities. For one thing, the costs and regulatory hurdles in establishing a local television station were substantial. As a result, even large cities had only a few broadcast stations, which was the primary reason that viewers had such limited programming choices. Indeed, within any television market, there were few channels from which to choose. That meant that viewers typically had only three or four different program options at any one time.

The types of programming available were also limited. One reason for this was that the business model for television relied upon reaching as many potential viewers as possible. The technology limited how far a television signal would extend, so in the literal sense, a television station's reach was only 30 or 40 miles.

Attracting viewers' attention was another matter entirely. To do that, programming, for the most part, was intentionally designed to appeal to a broad, generalized audience. The system was straightforward. Advertisers paid the most for ad spots on shows that generated the best viewership numbers, and they paid less—sometimes much less—for shows that did not attract enough viewers to meet their advertising goals. Since viewership numbers were what mattered, television looked for material that would please most people. A result was that content seldom challenged viewers' presumptions or expectations. It was the only way broadcasters thought the system could work. From their perspective, since they made their money by selling advertising time, their revenue streams—and hence, profitability—depended on creating content with mainstream appeal. Niche programming, when it aired, appeared in out-of-the-way timeslots that had limited appeal to advertisers due to low viewership numbers.

The desire to aim widely, which was not necessarily always at a conscious level, led television to replicate the status quo on many levels. One result was pervasive sexism. Indeed, television programs almost entirely portrayed women according to the patriarchal attitudes of the time. Television typically presented women as housewives, mothers, servants, secretaries, nurses, or in some other traditional roles. That was regrettable, but it was not surprising. The medium was reflecting standard (if by then, weakening) assumptions that retained much cultural power in those years.

So, television programming generally reflected the viewpoint of the majority or at least the majority as understood by broadcast executives and advertisers. Furthermore, just as women appeared in stereotyped roles, television presented racial and ethnic minorities as stereotypes, as well. Minority points of view received very little attention or representation. Instead, television programmers played it safe and repeated the interests—and often, the prejudices—of the dominant voices of the society at the time. As a result, most shows on television possessed a look that bore little resemblance to the actual make-up of the U.S. population. Indeed, viewers encountered a bland, monotone, homogenized portrait of America—a far cry from the nation's actual diversity. It was as though traditional social, political, and institutional forces cast an exclusionary spell, which resulted in television rarely acknowledging the nation's diversity at all. Instead, the white, middle-class, male perspective remained dominant and domineering.

Contributing to this unfortunate situation, the sharp economic inequality that separated white families, on the one hand, and the families of African Americans and other people of color, on the other, undoubtedly played a significant role in television mostly ignoring almost everyone except white viewers. Since white viewers on average had more money than others, they were more attractive to advertisers who were looking for viewers with ample disposable income. Income and wealth inequality between and among racial and ethnic groups was a persisting problem, and it continued to shape how institutions of many kinds imagined the nation's future overall.

In 1955, the numbers painted a particularly dire picture. According to the Bureau of the Census, the median family income of white families was $4,613 (not adjusted for inflation). Meanwhile, the reported annual income for African American families was $2,544—or about 45 percent below white income. Unfortunately, rather than promoting change, this discrepancy seems to have reinforced long-standing prejudices. Feeling that this was just the way things were meant to be, much of white America continued to ignore the economic plight of African Americans and other people of color. That had the significant effect of excluding people who were not white from the picture of the future that consumer corporations were creating.

During the 1950s, advertising spending rapidly increased. At the beginning of the decade, ad revenues in the U.S. were $1.3 billion. By 1960, that figure rose to a staggering $6 billion.[3] Despite this explosive growth in advertising overall, however, most ads continued to address a target market composed of middle-class whites. So, at the very time that advertising was helping to establish ideas about what the future would bring, a sizable segment of the U.S. population was left out of the picture. The future was conceived in the image of the white majority—in the image of the consumers who had the most money and who therefore mattered most to corporate America and its advertisers. Other people, if represented at all, mostly appeared as little more than window dressing. The blindness of this approach ignored social realities, as would become increasingly apparent in later years.

It was no accident, then, that visions of an optimistic future were mostly aimed at and embraced by white America. The legacy of past racial attitudes lingered, and members of white, middle-class society mostly saw the future through the lens of their own identity. As a result, the picture of tomorrow that was crystallizing in 1950s America was not just a bright future; it was also a white future—a future that was straight and male-oriented, as well.

The world outside America's borders influenced how the future was envisioned, too, though in different ways. The shadow of the Cold War represented a potential obstacle to the image of a consumers' paradise that U.S. businesses were trying to create. The spasms of fear that sometimes threatened the American psyche created a genuine problem. Americans already thought communism posed a significant threat. With the added existential dread of the atom bomb, which by the early 1950s had been joined by the even more powerful hydrogen bomb, the situation seemed particularly dire.

Not long after assuming the presidency in early 1953, Dwight Eisenhower decided that some action needed to be taken to help lower the anxieties caused by the existence of nuclear weapons. The new hydrogen bombs were even more destructive than either of the atomic bombs used against Japan, and the arms race between the United States and the Soviet Union resulted in ever-increasing production. It now seemed increasingly possible that there were enough nuclear weapons to wipe out life on the planet. It was a very new and terrifying realization.

In this context, Eisenhower searched for a way to maintain public perceptions of American nuclear superiority while also allaying growing apprehensions of potential nuclear war. The solution that he and his assistants arrived at was a policy called Operation Candor. In it, the president aimed to be reasonably forthcoming about the real dangers of the world's nuclear situation, on the one hand, and to be a messenger of hope for a peaceful future, on the other.

There was another layer to the policy, as well. Beginning early in Eisenhower's presidency, the private sector lobbied the administration intending to gain approval for the commercial use of nuclear power, which was not allowed at the time. Eisenhower was sympathetic to this view, and prominent industry leaders liked the idea, too. Indeed, leading corporate heads, such as the president of the Monsanto Chemical Company, Charles A. Thomas, as well as some members of the Atomic Energy Commission, strongly favored opening nuclear research for civilian corporate use.[4]

Eisenhower believed the issue was significant within the context of the overall international nuclear situation. He was eager to permit the use of atomic research by private enterprise. However, the president was also aware that the Soviets had quickly developed a powerful nuclear arms program and that the issue of proliferation was growing. The public was particularly rattled and uneasy about the rapid pace of atomic development in the Soviet Union. As an article about Operation Candor in the *Washington Post* reported, the program aimed to be frank, within limits, about "the danger which confronted the nation" and to "help them [the American people] understand" the situation.[5]

Candidness was one thing, but that would only go so far without some way of de-escalating public fears. On December 8, 1953, President Eisenhower made a public pronouncement that was intended to have that effect. Speaking before the General Assembly of the United Nations, Eisenhower delivered a speech known as "Atoms for Peace." In it, he continued to talk about the dangers of the nuclear world. He could hardly have done otherwise. However, he also made a plea for the United States and the Soviet Union to scale back their arms race. And perhaps just as importantly, he encouraged "world-wide investigation into the most effective peacetime uses of fissionable material ... [and to] apply atomic energy to the needs of agriculture, medicine, and other peaceful activities. A special purpose would be to provide abundant electrical energy in the power-starved areas of the world."[6]

Several writers had revised the speech during its preparation, but Eisenhower personally added some significant changes to it. As scholar Shawn J. Parry-Giles has noted, the final draft had "shifted away from the more strident 'rhetoric of fear' [that characterized early drafts] and highlighted the theme of peace."[7]

The speech aimed at the worldwide audience that the United Nations' platform provided. However, coming in late 1953, at a time when Joseph McCarthy was still searching for hidden communists in America, the "Atoms for Peace" speech played a significant role in bringing a positive and reassuring message back to the American people. Eisenhower's remarks reasserted the idea that the power of the atom could ultimately be a source for progress and a better future, even if the danger had not yet passed.

Days of worry about nuclear destruction were far from over, of course, and they would continue for many years to come. However,

In an effort to promote peaceful use of atomic energy and quell fears in the tense atmosphere of the Cold War, the administration of President Dwight D. Eisenhower promoted a new philosophy called "Atoms for Peace." Eisenhower outlined his vision in a speech at the United Nations on December 8, 1953 (National Archives).

Eisenhower had effectively offered at least some hope that the world could avoid catastrophe. It would take keen judgment, courage, and vigilance, according to the conventional wisdom, but many, probably most Americans continued to believe that their nation would successfully meet the challenges ahead. Accordingly, while national anxieties remained, visions of a wondrous, rather than a disastrous, world to come remained powerful. The scientific community and the government helped perpetuate an optimistic picture of America's future.

As the nation looked forward to what it hoped would be a peaceful world, large parts of the society were in the process of transformation. Two intertwined developments led the way in these large-scale changes: the emergence of a new kind of suburbia, and the rise of what came to be called "car culture." The new-style housing that was the basis of postwar suburbs and the increasing dependence on (and idealization of) automobiles created a nearly perfect accompaniment for the consumer culture. As such, they played a critical part in shaping ideas about the future.

Developers aggressively marketed newly constructed, tract-home suburban communities to young families who were eager to start life anew. The affordable, mass-produced suburbs were marketed in much the same way as many consumer products. The idea quickly caught on. The implication was that this was the way of the future.

Indeed, in promoting tract housing, the message to consumers was that the new suburbs represented a clean slate. Developers marketed these suburbs to potential residents as opportunities to start fresh and to build new communities in innovative and even futuristic ways. The suburbs contrasted with America's aging industrial cities, which many younger Americans increasingly regarded as tired and unappealing. Even the best cities, one line of thinking went, included large swaths of old and decaying buildings and tenements. The aging metropolises were packed with too many people and had too many problems—or so it was commonly thought.

In contrast to this were the sparkling new suburbs. Often built on previously pristine farmlands outside city limits, they offered an alluring escape from the drudgery and claustrophobic environs of urban life. That, at least, was how developers sold the idea of the suburbs to the many Americans seeking to achieve the American Dream of home ownership.

The new suburbs were not exactly the perfect solution to the problems that plagued cities, however. Racial segregation, for example, very much thrived in postwar suburbia. This segregation was no accident. Due to discriminatory government housing policies and prevalent banking practices in that era, many of the supposedly idyllic new suburban communities blatantly excluded racial minorities. African Americans, especially, discovered that obtaining home mortgages was extremely challenging. Added to that, provisions in the fine print of suburban sales contracts often disallowed sales to persons of color.[8] As a result, the new suburbs were almost exclusively white in many areas. If suburban living represented life in tomorrow's world, then the future looked to be overwhelmingly white.

Suburban living quickly gained popularity among its white target audience, however. The explosive growth of suburbia pulled many people out of cities and into previously rural areas. However, the rise of suburbs brought new issues. This new lifestyle required a way for residents to travel from their suburban enclaves to the places where suburbanites worked, shopped, ran errands, and participated in all sorts of activities. There was little availability or interest in public transportation. Instead, the automobile stood as a pre-existing solution, of sorts, to this new problem. Indeed, widespread car ownership and the cheap gasoline of the era helped make it possible for people to live at distances that were remote from their workplaces.

If cars were to be the answer, however, then there was one other requirement: a modern series of highways on which to drive them. The old system of roads certainly was not up to the task. They could not handle much volume, and they were inefficiently laid out. Rising suburbs and growing car use generated an increasing need for high-capacity, well-designed, and well-laid-out highways that would provide relatively uninterrupted routes.

The creation of the interstate highway system was an attempt to solve such issues. An outgrowth of the Federal Highway Act of 1956, the new web of high-speed, multi-lane motorways made long commutes faster and more effortless than ever, which facilitated suburban living. At the same time, the modern highways added to the psychological allure of the open road, a development that automobile manufacturers found useful in their extensive marketing and advertising campaigns.

In the rising world of suburbia, cars were essential for commuting to shopping and workplaces. Indeed, the growth of suburban living was only possible because of widespread car ownership.[9] Public transportation as it existed was inadequate, and government leaders seemed mostly uninterested in significantly expanding it. So, if the stereotypical suburban consumer represented the future, then the automobile, which by the 1950s was rife with futuristic associations, apparently would be a significant part of that future.

Henry Ford had died in 1947 at the age of 83, and in some ways that represented the end of a historic era in the automotive industry. However, a new era of the automobile was already beginning. Indeed, in the years after Ford's death, cars took on more cultural significance in American society than ever before. Cars possessed enormous symbolic value and were strongly associated with American freedom, success, and prosperity—all of which were crucial elements in how Americans imagined the future.

The case of automotive design reveals how futurism and cars became bonded in American thinking. Long-time General Motors designer and car stylist Harley Earl was fascinated by aerospace technology. Earl was overseeing GM's style work on the 1948 Cadillac when he decided to approve the addition of a new feature to that high-end luxury car's appearance. Drawing inspiration from the Lockheed P-38 fighter plane and its twin-boom design, Earl's design team added tail fins to the new Cadillac model.[10] The fins were based on the same design principles that gave the P-38 aircraft a sleek, futuristic appearance. They immediately gave the car a striking and unusual new look. They underscored GM's intended message that the '48 Cadillac was a distinct break from the past.

Although tail fins served no useful function, they immediately gave GM cars a futuristic feel. Customers responded positively, and the company quickly added the feature to many of its other models. The tail-fin feature became so popular that other manufacturers followed suit and added them to many of their models, as well. Ford, for example, added them to many of their designs throughout the decade. Meanwhile, at rival Chrysler, designer Virgil Exner took the fin idea and pushed it even further. In his "Forward Look" design, he added larger fins and an even greater aerodynamic appearance to the 1955 Chrysler model. The company soon incorporated these design principles into other models, too.

In borrowing from aerospace, car designers helped establish a natural association between cars and the world of tomorrow. The companies were well aware of this connection. With the addition of such aerospace-inspired design elements to 1957 Plymouths, the company's advertisements announced, "Suddenly, it's 1960!" The car of the future—or at least of the near future—had arrived, at least according to the marketing campaign.[11]

The increased application of chrome detailing to cars, which occurred at about the same time, was another nod to the future, though it was not an entirely new practice.[12] (Some GM cars included strips of chrome as a decorative feature beginning in the 1930s.[13]) The use of the material in the 1950s, however, was far more pronounced and striking than before. Glistening chrome bumpers, door handles, trim, and other details added a fresh, modern look. The polished metal, with its extremely reflective appearance, seemed to be something taken straight out of the world of jet fighters, missiles, and rocketry. Indeed, chrome's clean, bright, and shiny surface was evocative of a coming world with the same characteristics.

3. A Consumer's Future

American "car culture" was at its height in the 1950s, and during these years, automobiles were strongly associated with the future. U.S. car manufacturers actively promoted this sense of futurism in their automotive designs and marketing campaigns. Many cars, including this 1959 Cadillac Eldorado from General Motors, even included tail fins, a distinctive but merely decorative feature that originally was inspired by aerospace designs (iStock.com/Anton_Sokolov).

Many American cars of the era elicited these same kinds of associations. The 1956 Dodge was noted for its "twin-jet taillights" and "gleaming band of chrome," as one news account said.[14] Writing about a 1957 Pontiac model, another report praised the car's "Star Flight styling," while adding, "A missile outline trim of stainless steel sweeps the entire length of the car on each side."[15]

Tail fins, chrome, stainless steel, and other elements added visual cues that helped establish the idea that modern automobiles represented the future and that new models were a break from the prewar past. Chrome detailing declined decades ago and is now much more limited. Automobile tail fins can now seem odd, superficial, and even slightly bizarre, especially to people unfamiliar with them. In the late 1940s and 1950s, however, such features were powerful, hard-to-mistake symbols of the future. They provided a quick and easy way for consumers to declare that they, too, were not stuck in the past. Instead, they were zooming ahead to meet the bright world of tomorrow head-on.

Even more dramatic and futuristic automotive design appeared in experimental cars—what later would be called "concept cars"—during these years. One striking example was exhibited to the public by General Motors in 1954. Even the name of the car, the XP-21, made the vehicle sound as if it were coming straight out of an aerospace lab. The striking appearance of the vehicle borrowed much from the world of aeronautics.

The driver's seat was in a "cockpit, beneath a plastic bubble," and the car was powered by an oversized gas-turbine engine that looked as though it had been modeled after a jet fighter.[16] The XP-21 never went into production, but that did not matter. The prototype helped further establish the automobile industry's futurism and modernity in the public mind.

As the case of automobiles in both their production and experimental versions demonstrates, the ramped-up consumerism of the 1950s often relied on creating demand for the new and the revolutionary. In some ways, advertisers tried to convince the public that the future—or at least some of it—could be taken home today. In other words, if they wanted to live the life of tomorrow today, consumers were encouraged to seek out the new, forward-looking products that American business and industry marketed to young, upwardly mobile consumers in the present.

Some aspects of the future would have to wait for science and technology to catch up with imagination, of course. But consumers could have many things that seemed like the future immediately. Importantly, consumers would know a product represented the future when they saw it because it would look like the future. Indeed, advertisements, marketing material, and popular culture had invented a distinctive, futuristic look—a look that is still recognized for this association decades later.

Like the future it represented, this look was usually shiny, sleek, and aerodynamic, often emphasizing clean lines, simple geometric forms, and modern materials. Plastics and gleaming steel, aluminum, and chrome ruled the day. Compared to products with these futuristic design and production elements, everything else suddenly seemed quaint and old-fashioned.

The future was not the only marketing approach used in ads during the 1950s, but it was one of the most distinctive ways that advertisers appealed to the public. Many types of businesses viewed it as an effective way to reach customers. For example, the National Motor Bearing Company was probably not the kind of enterprise that most people associated with the future. However, a 1954 magazine ad for the company featured artwork that looked like the cover of a science fiction novel. The detailed illustration showed a colossal machine at work on the Martian surface while an astronaut in a spacesuit looked on. Its headline declared, "When atomic machines man the iron mines of Mars.... National oil seals will protect their performance."[17]

An advertisement for another firm, the U.S. Cast Iron Pipe Company, featured an illustration that depicted a futuristic undersea tractor working on crops as sharks and fishes swam around it. The ad copy said, "100 years from now, we'll 'farm' the sea to feed a hungry world."[18] Then there was a 1957 print ad for Hughes Products, a company that had the tagline "creating a new world with electronics." One of their ads depicted an aerospace-themed illustration and asked, "How soon can you ship by missile?"[19]

These and countless other advertisements with futuristic orientations bombarded the public in national, regional, and local ad campaigns. They established not only visual impressions of what the future might hold. They also were evidence of the U.S. business community's keen interest in being associated with that future.

In the eyes of corporate America, the future would be surprising in some ways, but it would not be wholly different from the present. Tomorrow's world, as corporate America and advertisers promoted it, still embraced traditional values and the everyday lifestyles of white, upwardly mobile, middle-class consumers. The future would be somewhat like the world in which consumers lived. The main difference was that it would be more relaxed and more comfortable. There would be much more free time and much less work.

Idealized thinking about emerging 1950s suburban lifestyles correlated with the picture of the future that businesses and advertisers painted. As much of the focus of modern life shifted away from old industrial cities to pristine new quarters on the outskirts of urban areas, and beyond, suburbia came to represent the new, unexplored frontier—one filled with sparkling new homes and shiny new things—to America's mostly white middle-class.

Indeed, the consumer frontier of the future was decidedly not the frontier of old. In this new world, ease of living, convenience, conspicuous consumption, and planned obsolescence—all ideas that flourished in the 1950s—were central to the way life in the future was being conceived. These ideas came together in a very particular vision of future lifestyles, in which people would endlessly want the newest, most labor-saving products, and American businesses would happily supply them.

The mindset of middle-class America in the 1950s played an essential part in reinforcing this view of the future world. The emphasis on conformity at the time played a significant role in this. Sociologist David Riesman, the author of the influential book *The Lonely Crowd* (1950), noted that American society was in the process of radical transformation.[20] Peer pressure and rising social expectations were creating a new situation. More than ever before, he suggested, Americans were feeling pressure to "keep up with the Joneses." In that environment, many people saw conspicuous consumption as a good thing. It demonstrated to others that they had arrived—that they had achieved the kind of success that allowed for the acquisition of desirable consumer goods.

At a time when mass media, and especially television, were shaping beliefs about how people should live, a constant stream of marketing messages for new products and services peppered consumers. The implication was clear: Why would a person choose to live in the past and not select the bold, new future instead? There was only one viable way to answer that question in the 1950s: A person must choose the future. Only by doing that would people stay current, keep up with society's winners, and find the life they sought. The consumerist future *was* the future from that point of view. This mindset provided nearly perfect conditions for advertising the many new and new-looking consumer products that were coming to market.

Many visions about the life of tomorrow from this era focused on the home, where consumer goods would be the ticket to the good life. Indeed, advertisements and marketing materials suggested that modern, future-oriented life would be made possible by a wide range of products. These ranged from vacuum cleaners that seemed to have design elements borrowed from rocket ships, to "TV dinners" that made cooking meals unnecessary, to television sets that provided a new kind of hearth for the home, and beyond. Such things brought the future, or some of it, into the world of today.

What the emphasis on consuming did not do was change anything about existing social roles or family relationships. Indeed, visions of the future 1950s-style nearly always replicated existing patterns of living. Eventually, it turned out that the future, as pictured in the 1950s, would not only continue to be influenced by the damaging effects of racism; it would also be as sexist as ever. Men would remain the unquestioned heads of households and metaphorical lords of their futuristic manses. It would be men who would venture into the modern workplace, and it would be men who would occupy the most significant positions there.

Meanwhile, conventional thinking held that women would greatly benefit from many of the exciting innovations that the future had to offer. This version of future life looked a lot like existing middle-class life, in which many people presumed the most appropriate roles for women were as wives and mothers and that women should direct their lives toward maintaining and managing households. So, the lives of women in this futuristic setting were mostly like their lives in the past. Women would be responsible for domestic chores and for looking pretty and being ready to soothe their husbands' frayed nerves after a long day at the office. Technological innovation and modern gadgetry, it turned out, would not lead to much rethinking about deeply ingrained social assumptions.

Among the many examples that could be cited to make this point is a 1956 promotional film called *Design for Dreaming*. It was produced for the General Motors Corporation and represented its vision for a future life of easy living and leisure, or, as the film says, "a journey to the place where tomorrow meets today."

The nine-minute film is in the style of a musical and features a modern woman who sings and dances her way through the production. A mostly off-camera male voice provides commentary in the form of songs. Although the woman is presumably the film's star, her role is subsidiary to a male point of view. Overall, the film's sexism is hard to miss, as is the endorsement of a conspicuous-consumption lifestyle. At one point, the woman longingly gazes at new Corvettes and Pontiacs. The male then reassuringly sings, "We'll have the usual two-car garage," words that take for granted that successful suburban families will need space for not just one, but two automobiles.

Design for Dreaming mostly focuses on cars, but there is also a brief section about the home of the future, in which life will require less toil, especially in the kitchen. Indeed, the film supports the sexist stereotype that the kitchen is the proper place for women. With a punch-card computer system and appliances controlled by "push-button magic," the future will be a world in which women "don't have to be chained to the stove all day." The obvious implication is that futuristic technology will free women from this drudgery. After seeing all this, the woman sings, "The kitchen of tomorrow is calling me!" There was no indication that it was also calling her presumed husband.

The story then reverts to a focus on General Motors' futuristic automobiles—the "dream cars of tomorrow," according to the film. The production concludes with a depiction of the woman and her presumed husband as they happily speed along an automated highway and into tomorrow. The future, it seems, was to be a life of comfort and luxury, overseen by men.

If the imagined future as envisioned in the 1950s sometimes seems like something out of a Disney movie or theme park, there is a good reason. Walt Disney played a central role in bringing visions of the future to public attention. He did this by using his considerable influence to champion specific future-oriented projects and combining them with his personal and business interests, primarily as related to television and amusement-park projects, which were new additions to his business portfolio in the 1950s.

In some ways, Walt Disney may seem like an unlikely person to have filled such a role. After all, by the 1950s, he was already seen as a somewhat old-fashioned, avuncular type. He had a friendly, slightly conservative image and seemed a bit set in his ways. Ironically, however, it may have been precisely those perceived qualities that helped make him an effective spokesperson for the future—or at least of a specific type of future.

Disney's strong familiarity lent an aura of assurance to the images of the future that he and others offered. As with much of corporate America's oft-implied view, the future would be new and wondrous, but it would retain the traditionalism that many Americans knew and loved. When Disney presented visions of tomorrow, therefore, it could all be taken in stride.

Indeed, Disney's ideas about the future were always somewhat anchored in the affection he had for traditional American values. Disney grew up in the Midwest, surrounded by traditionalism. His generally conservative way of seeing things is evident in the short cartoons and animated feature films that had brought him fame and made him into a cultural force.

In some ways, however, Disney set off on a new trajectory after World War II. Although his familiar animated cartoons remained popular and a reliable source of revenue, Disney had ambitious visions that he wanted to fulfill. Two of these have particular bearing on how the concept of the future developed in the cultural landscape of the time. These were Disney's plans to create a new kind of family-oriented amusement park in Southern California and his plan for the Disney studio to branch out into the exciting world of television, which seemed to be the medium of tomorrow. The two projects were highly interrelated, and both played a significant role in articulating specific ideas about the future.

The decision to create an amusement park was a major turning point in Disney's career. For some months, Disney thought about developing an exhibit or a traveling roadshow of amusements. By 1952, his ideas evolved and crystallized into what eventually would become Disneyland.[21] It was to bring together many of Disney's interests, including characters and settings from his many animated cartoons and new attractions having that same sort of spirit, all of which would delight children and their families. The project was vital to Disney on a personal level, and he used as many of his creative resources as he could muster to make it a reality.

At the time Disney proposed to enter the amusement park business, it was by no means clear that the plan would succeed. One potential stumbling block was that amusement parks tended to have sullied reputations. Why would the wholesome Disney operation want to get involved with those? Even if Walt's vision could be fleshed out and brought to life in a way that would attract a respectable audience of paying customers, there was first the problem of how to get it built. One thing was sure: it would be costly. From the outset, Disney faced an uphill battle to attract the necessary finances. The venture was so different from Disney's tried-and-true film productions that it seemed too risky in the eyes of most potential investors.

3. A Consumer's Future 75

Fortuitously, perhaps, Disney's passion for the amusement park idea added extra encouragement to his interest in producing programming for television. Those two activities may seem unrelated, but Disney soon latched onto the idea of securing funding from a television network to help finance the park. Although the biggest networks of that day—CBS and NBC—showed little interest, the fledgling American Broadcasting Network (ABC) saw an opportunity. In the plan that emerged, Disney would provide the network with a weekly television program and sign over to ABC a minority share of the amusement park operation, as well as various rights and royalties from the proposed park. In return, ABC was to provide $500,000 in cash to build the park, and to back an additional $4.5 million bank loan for that purpose.[22]

With funding falling into place, Disney pushed ahead with planning and construction. As he envisioned it, the park would have several separate parts, each organized around a theme. One of those themes would be "the future."

After kicking around several ideas, the decision was made to call the park Disneyland. Not by coincidence, that was also the name selected for the weekly television series that began airing on October 27, 1954, on the ABC network. However, the *Disneyland* television series was more than just a television series. The show ended up being just as much a weekly advertisement for the amusement center of the same name as it was a regular TV show.

It took enormous effort to ready the park for its opening day on July 17, 1955. When that day arrived, however, there was keen public interest that was no doubt aided by vigorous marketing efforts.

The future-oriented section of the park was called Tomorrowland. In a way, it was somewhat reminiscent of the 1939 World's Fair in New York City, which was called "the World of Tomorrow." The inclusion of corporate-sponsored exhibits was one similarity. Indeed, Tomorrowland benefited from contributions from many corporate sponsors. The companies represented included Dutch Boy Paint, Monsanto, American Motors, and more. All of them had strong affiliations with the American middle class.

Planners solidly based Tomorrowland on the types of futuristic concepts that U.S. businesses and advertisers had been creating for some time, and this approach was an integral part of the overall Disneyland concept. As always, Walt Disney did not veer from his traditionalism and generally conservative outlook on life, but that did not mean he was not legitimately interested in innovation. Like many people, then, he embraced new visions for the coming world even as he remained committed to the kind of society and social fabric that he had always known and loved. The point of progress, in this way of thinking, was to retain the basics of American life and to use revolutions of science to enhance what people already knew.

Upon entering Tomorrowland, visitors encountered a full-size rocket located at the center of the attraction. Balancing on three metallic legs and towering seven stories above ground level, it was an imposing sight. As visitors gazed up at its gleaming exterior, they looked to a world in which space travel would not only be possible but maybe even commonplace. Visitors may also have noticed a prominent marking on the rocket—the famous TWA logo of the renowned Trans-World Airline company.[23] The future, it seemed, would not only be a marvel of scientific discovery; it would also have corporate sponsorship.

Most of Tomorrowland featured down-to-earth exhibits that were both imaginative and entertaining. In 1957, some months after it first opened, a new attraction was added—the House of the Future. It was an innovative, full-scale prototype that represented what future homes might offer to the public.

The major theme of the House of Tomorrow was plastic, which was not surprising given that its primary sponsor was the Monsanto Chemical Company, one of the nation's most significant plastics manufacturers. Indeed, plastic was used extensively throughout the house, especially in the interior.

In terms of design, virtually nothing about its exterior was reminiscent of traditional home architecture. Its facade was striking and futuristic. The structure's exterior shell, fabricated with robust and lightweight fiberglass, featured curved U-shaped modules. As one reporter wrote, "The house 'floats' in the air; the wings are five feet or more above the ground, cantilevered out from a central column."

Although Monsanto was the main sponsor of the house, it was a cooperative effort that brought together many firms. The list of companies that contributed to the House of Tomorrow reads like an honor roll of U.S. business in that era. Among the prominent companies included were American Motors Corporation, Bell Telephone System, Crane Company, Libby-Owens-Corning Fiberglas [sic] Corporation and Sylvania Electric Products, to name but a few.

The result of three years of specialized research and an investment of over $1 million, the House of Tomorrow exhibit offered a look into the future that seemed reasonable and within reach. It brought together in real space many of the ideas and concepts that Americans already knew from advertisements, television shows, and mass-market publications.

By the late 1950s, then, a keen cultural interest in the future blended with the consumer world that American business had been promoting since the end of the war. While dreams of the future always were varied and addressed many aspects of life, the consumer-oriented future assumed a prominent place in the cultural landscape by that time.

In the campaign to build public enthusiasm for its amusement park, Disney used the *Disneyland* television series to help create interest and demand. Although the campaign aimed to promote the park overall, the futuristic section called Tomorrowland received some specific attention. Part of this last effort involved several high-profile episodes in the television series that were devoted to space travel, arguably the most exciting aspect of the future in the public mind at the time. These few Disneyland episodes fulfilled their intended purpose, but they turned out to also be significant for building American support for the developing real-life space program.

Stories about space travel and interplanetary exploration had circulated in American culture for years. As much as these stories sometimes captured the public's imagination before World War II, people remained skeptical about actual space travel. After the war, however, things that previously seemed impossible looked much more achievable. Finally, many people began to take the idea of space flight more seriously.

Such thoughts were likely affected, at least to some degree, by a wave of unidentified flying object (UFO) sightings that garnered extensive media attention in the late 1940s. Most notable were the news reports surrounding an incident in 1947, when civilian pilot Kenneth Arnold spotted a UFO near Mount Rainier, sparking the public's imagination.

Before long, many other accounts of "flying saucers" appeared in the press. The military and government officials investigated many of these reports, and at least some people took them seriously. UFO reports became so frequent and created so much of a stir that in the late 1950s, famed psychiatrist Carl Jung even wrote about the phenomenon in a book called *Flying Saucers: A Modern Myth of Things Seen in the Skies*.[24] Meanwhile, the public's fascination continued, and UFOs also inspired many stories in popular fiction, movies, and comic books.

At the same time, other types of stories about rocketry and space travel also appeared in the media regularly. Some of this material was pure fiction, but other accounts aimed to be realistic and looked at space travel as a scientific possibility that was achievable in the near term.

In 1949, for example, a book by science writer Willy Ley called *The Conquest of Space* argued in favor of the idea. Ley took the possibility of space flight seriously and made a strong case. His case was bolstered by futuristic illustrations that were created by the artist Chesley Bonestell, which evocatively pictured space and other worlds. Bonestell's visuals were stunning, and his depiction of space proved to be very influential in the coming years.

Then there were films such as director George Pal's *Destination Moon* (1950). Though nominally science-fiction, Pal's movie was more or less a procedural account of what space travel could be like, with an emphasis on its presumed hazards and peril. It was the first of several space exploration films that Pal would make, and it helped push the idea of space travel to a broad public.

The following year of 1951 saw the publication of Arthur C. Clarke's nonfiction book *The Exploration of Space*. Clarke was already well known for his science-fiction stories, which drew respect because they often were grounded in real science. His sober new book on space travel helped establish the idea as a real possibility in the American consciousness.

These and other media accounts of future space travel helped push the topic into mainstream thought. Increasingly, authoritative voices seemed willing to state on the record that space travel was more than a remote possibility; it was something achievable in the near term. With this point of view regularly appearing in the media, the public became, as writer Marina Benjamin has written, "space-hungry."[25] So, when *Collier's*, a popular magazine with a good reputation, began a series of stories on space travel, there was an enthusiastic, ready-made audience waiting for it.

Probably the most influential article in *Collier's* space series was a 1952 piece called "Man Will Conquer Space Soon: Top Scientists Tell How in Fifteen Startling Pages." It was based on the vision of the brilliant but controversial Wernher von Braun. Among the most famous scientists of mid-century, von Braun was at one time an arch-enemy of the United States. After all, he led Nazi rocketry efforts during the war, and his work resulted in much devastation.

At the end of the war, von Braun was brought to America, where, after some rehabilitation of his reputation, he became a leading—perhaps *the* leading—force in the U.S. military's missile program at the time. Von Braun, it is usually said, had always been more interested in human space exploration than in politics, or in the military applications of rocketry. Now, with this article, he made a bold pronouncement of just how wondrous space flight could soon become.

In 1954, Walt Disney's drive to launch the *Disneyland* television show and make the Disneyland park a reality came together with von Braun's campaign to raise public support for a formal civilian space program. Indeed, after the influential *Collier's* article, von Braun and Disney decided to work together to promote their mutual interests. The plan, which would support both space travel and Disney's park, called for the production of a series of futuristic documentaries on space travel for the *Disneyland* television series. Von Braun's ideas would serve as the basis

3. A Consumer's Future

It is generally agreed that the U.S. rocket program benefited greatly from the services of Dr. Wernher von Braun, who had previously led German rocket research during World War II. Brought to the United States after the war, the famed scientist was as much an advocate for space travel as he was a brilliant engineer and technologist. A well-known public figure in mid-century America, von Braun worked with Walt Disney to create several documentaries about space travel in the 1950s. In this 1956 photograph by Thomas J. O'Halloran, von Braun (right) and Major General J.B. Medaris are shown with a model of a Redstone guided missile (Library of Congress).

for these, providing an authoritative voice to the episodes.[26] The episodes would further the cause of space travel that von Braun championed, and it would also be an excellent way to promote Tomorrowland. Disney liked the idea.

The *Disneyland* series eventually aired three such documentaries. They were educational, speculative, and entertaining. Disney had even assigned one of his top animators, Ward Kimball, to the project—a sure sign of how important it was to Disney.

The first of these episodes, "Man in Space," aired on March 9, 1955, just a few months before the theme park was to open. The program drew much attention, just as Disney and von Braun had hoped. Building on the interest the first program generated, a follow-up, "Man and the Moon," was broadcast on December 28 of that year. (The final entry, "Mars and Beyond," was not broadcast until two years later, on December 4, 1957.[27]) Whatever their role in helping move the American space program forward, the *Disneyland* episodes brought von Braun's ideas to an even broader public than the *Collier's* articles. Of course, the *Disneyland* space episodes were also useful for marketing the amusement park, just as Walt Disney had hoped.

Consumerism was central to American conceptions of the future, but it was only one factor in play. That vision pictured a world of convenience, ease, and modernity, and it required confidence in those things. From roughly 1945 to the early 1960s, that confidence was interwoven with trust in science and technology—the things that were critical in giving America the atom bomb and victory in World War II. Technology and science also launched the new era that was in the process of unfolding before Americans' eyes.

Indeed, the consumerist world of tomorrow depended on research and innovation to propel the country toward the long-sought "good life." So, as more and more of nature's secrets were revealed, many Americans thought that humans finally seemed poised to become masters of the universe, or something close to it. Things that were once only dreams—flying cars, travel into space, living undersea, eradication of disease, and more—now seemed possible.

This general feeling also seeped into other areas of life. Even with ongoing Cold War fears and a briskly changing society, by the late 1950s, Americans were brimming with confidence. For in the 1950s, it often appeared that even though problems abounded, a systematic and scientific approach guided by American moral principles would yield nothing but positive results. That was the formula that would solve problems and deliver them into a bright, shining future and possibly even into space. The Cold War persisted, but an enticing world of tomorrow—a techno-consumerist future—seemed to be visible beyond it.

4

A New Frontier

This is the President of the United States speaking. Through the marvels of scientific advance, my voice is coming to you from a satellite circling in outer space. My message is a simple one. Through this unique means, I convey to you and all mankind, America's wish for peace on earth and good will to men everywhere.[1]

The radio signal was scratchy and intermittent, but the voice of Dwight D. Eisenhower was reassuring. When this message was transmitted from the U.S. Army's Project SCORE (Signal Communications by Orbiting Relay Equipment) satellite and then rebroadcast by news outlets around the world on December 19, 1958, a new era had already begun. At long last, the much-anticipated age of rocketry was now a reality. The new Space Age loomed large in the American consciousness as it suddenly seemed that the future was wide open and filled with possibilities.

With the longtime dream of space travel finally within reach, a new wave of excitement and anticipation swept over the cultural landscape. From the halls of power to the main streets and sideroads of the nation, the topic of space was in the air. "It's pretty hard to visualize the awesomeness of outer space, the literal infinity that exists in every direction beyond Earth's atmosphere," wrote an editorialist for a pulp magazine at the time. "Yes, it's a big universe we're tapping," the writer continued. "Like children putting our first foot outside the protective walls of a cradle, we've first got to learn to stand up, then walk, and finally run."[2]

To an extent, space was a familiar topic that people had been talking about decades, of course. After World War II, however, enthusiasm for the subject had grown dramatically. Numerous rocket enthusiasts, filmmakers, science-fiction writers, artists, rocket scientists, and technologists—Walt Disney and Wernher von Braun among them—tirelessly championed the cause of rocketry and, by extension, space travel. These people tended to have a positive and aspirational outlook, and to them, rockets and space travel suggested a wide-open arena for human discovery. They looked hopefully at the possibilities that rockets and space research presented.

The influence of popular culture in promoting the topic, specifically, should not be underestimated. At mid-century, the regular appearance of space themes in pulp magazines, science fiction novels, movies, television, and comic strips kept the topic fresh in the minds of the American public. The continuing adventures of fictional characters, such as Flash Gordon and Buck Rogers, gave space an exciting public image.

By the mid–1950s, an informal group of serious science-fiction writers had been promoting space travel and exploration through imaginative short stories and novels for some time. Later dubbed "astrofuturists" by scholar De Witt Douglas Kilgore,[3] this group included such science-fiction luminaries as Isaac Asimov, Arthur C. Clarke, Robert Heinlein, and others. These writers may not have been taken as seriously by the publishing world as mainstream authors of their day, but they attracted the attention of many space devotees.

The astrofuturist writers usually portrayed space in epic terms, as a vast stage upon which to enact the next phase of human history. In the best of their works, their speculative stories incorporated—albeit loosely, at times—actual science. In that respect, astrofuturist writing pushed the science-fiction genre beyond boundaries that typified many of the swashbuckling science-fiction stories from comics, movies, and pulp magazines of earlier years.

It was this connection between highly fictional speculation and real scientific possibilities that gave this wave of science fiction its power. Still, the astrofuturist writers displayed extraordinary imaginations, and their thinking often zoomed far ahead of scientific reality in the 1950s. In the context of the era, their visions sparked excitement, and their works had a strong influence on their readers. Their writings especially appealed to young people thinking about the new age of science and especially to curious minds thinking about the world of the future. As Emily S. Rosenberg has written, the astrofuturists "offered especially powerful images and narratives about a new 'age of discovery' in which brave individuals would guide interplanetary explorations."[4] Indeed, the stories and novels produced by the astrofuturists fueled the imaginations of readers in America and across the globe. Years later, many scientists, technologists, and others interested in space professionally would note with affection the inspiration that science-fiction stories had provided them earlier.

More traditional news and academic-oriented sources sometimes addressed the space topic at this time, too. World War II had shown that rockets were a reality, the full capability of which had yet to be unlocked. After the war, the topic was broached publicly by an increasing number of respectable scientists, science writers, and journalists. The public generally knew that the military was working on harnessing rocket power, but the civilian possibilities for travel to space remained a matter of speculation.

Within this context, the public seemed ready for some bold, new development. The combined effect of astrofuturist science fiction and clear-eyed technological commentary helped fuel interest and the creation of what Witt Douglas Kilgore describes as a "constant evocation of a 'sense of wonder.'"[5] Increasing interest in reaching outer space, he said, "promoted the belief that only by escaping its terrestrial cradle will the American experiment realize its full potential."[6]

The event that finally pushed such speculative dreams to the forefront of the American agenda came on October 4, 1957. On that date, which was only months before President Eisenhower issued his message via space, the USSR had shocked the world by successfully launching its Sputnik satellite. It was surely not what Americans had expected. No doubt, given U.S. leadership in atomic research and other sciences, most Americans likely presumed that their nation would take the lead into space when the time came. However, the reality was that the Soviet Union was the first nation to send a satellite into space. Indeed, Sputnik left no doubt that the long-predicted Space Age had finally arrived and that the Soviet Union had taken the lead.

The tiny Soviet satellite heralded not only the excitement of a new technological epoch but also a renewed sense of political anxiety. In reality, at less than two feet in diameter and weighing only about 200 pounds, Sputnik's short time circling the earth posed little real threat to the United States. However, in its brief time in space, Sputnik flew over the United States several times at a speed of 18,000 miles per hour. That was more than enough to prompt concern. It took little imagination to figure that if a Soviet rocket could send a satellite into space, then eventually, the Soviets would be able to swap the satellite for a nuclear weapon. Moreover, the mere thought of a nuclear weapon as the payload of a Soviet rocket, which presumably could reach almost any target on earth with lightning-fast speed, was terrifying.

The public was understandably anxious, and U.S. military officials were concerned, too. One report indicated that in reaction to Sputnik, "defense officials listened anxiously this week to the mysterious beeping from the Sputnik and to the strident Soviet boasts about intercontinental ballistic missiles ... [that could] speed to the edge of space and hit targets thousands of miles away."[7] Sputnik's successful flight, however short, represented more than merely a challenge to America's presumed scientific edge and its national pride. In the context of the Cold War, Sputnik also signaled a possible threat to the very existence of the United States. Indeed, Sputnik was a proverbial warning shot that rattled the American psyche. The very fact of its successful launch seemed to assure the new Space Age would never (or at least, never in the foreseeable future) be solely about space travel, science, and exploration. Instead, from the earliest days, the Space Age also would be about the contest for military superiority and the roles that rockets and space would play in that context.

Whatever the reaction in the Pentagon, Sputnik shocked the American public. The Cold War, though no longer new, continued to rage on so that even before Sputnik, many Americans felt extremely threatened. They sometimes imagined themselves as being surrounded in a sea of communism that threatened to envelop the free world. With Sputnik, the Soviets seemed to have upped the ante and tipped the balance of power in their direction. As NASA historians have said, Sputnik had a "Pearl Harbor effect" on the American public, and it created the "illusion of a technological gap."[8] It caused many Americans to believe the United States had fallen behind the Soviet Union in important defense technology. Soon, with the talk of a "missile gap," and American fears increased.

To the dismay of many people—including some members of his own political party—President Eisenhower gave the impression that he did not think Sputnik presented much cause for alarm. He acknowledged the Soviet achievement, but he urged a calm and measured reaction from the United States. It was a carefully thought out and logical response, but it alarmed many people in and out of Washington.

Of course, there was much more to the story than most Americans knew—even most of those in high places. Although almost all Americans and officials were surprised and shocked by Sputnik, Eisenhower certainly was not. He had no reason to be taken aback. Only a select few people at the time knew, but U.S. intelligence officials had been briefing him regularly about the Soviet rocket and missile program. They had given Eisenhower top-secret information about Soviet plans to launch an orbital rocket very soon. Intelligence officials had even predicted that this would likely happen by late 1957.[9] The Sputnik launch fell comfortably within this timeline. Eisenhower and a few top government officials expected something like it. Most Americans, however, did not.

Eisenhower also knew the United States missile program was making progress behind the scenes. His preference for a cautious, steady approach made sense for anyone in possession of all these facts. Since the Sputnik satellite did not seem to represent any revolutionary new achievement, there was little reason to think the Soviets had jumped as far ahead of the United States as was feared by many Americans. Still, as the authors of a recently declassified intelligence analysis have written, the "Soviets achieved a political and propaganda triumph because Eisenhower had believed a rush into space was unwarranted and that a Soviet arrival

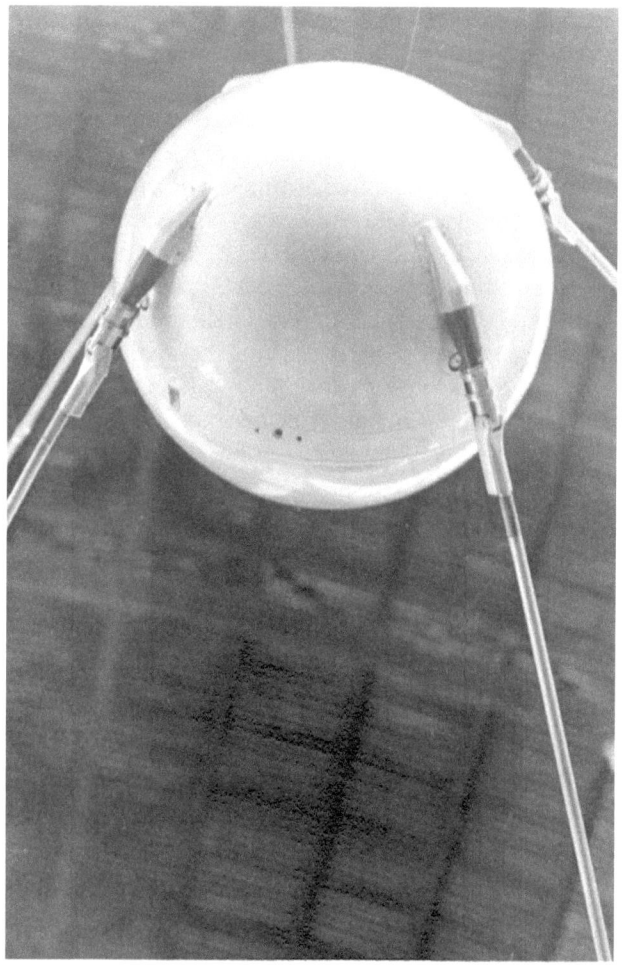

On October 4, 1957, the Soviet Union successfully launched its Sputnik satellite and shocked the world in the process. The satellite was tiny and had limited capabilities, but the historic and game-changing nature of this event was immediately recognized by all. Sputnik sparked fears among Americans that they were falling behind in the race toward the future. Soon after the launch, the United States ramped up its space program in earnest. This NASA close-up photograph, which was taken at the Paris Air Show in 1975, shows a full-scale model of the original Sputnik satellite (NASA).

there first would have little meaning. For Eisenhower, there was no 'space race.'"[10] Of course, since the public and most officials did not have access to the intelligence briefings that informed Eisenhower's reaction, they lacked enough context to understand it fully.

However, some aspects of the Soviet Union's rocket plans were out in the open, even though many people did not notice them. Before the Sputnik launch, many observers possessed general awareness that the Soviets were working on something, even if they were not sure what. U.S. officials widely presumed that the USSR was interested in rockets, if only for potential military applications. Some months before Sputnik, in fact, American officials publicly speculated what this might mean for the future. In one instance, an American military officer, who was speaking at a 1957 conference sponsored by the United States Air Force and the General Dynamics Corporation, told an audience of "300 of the foremost scientists and engineers in rocketry and related fields" about the USSR's space plans. "Our safety as a nation [in the future]," he warned, "may depend on our achieving 'space superiority' over the Soviets."[11] In this era, it was also no secret that the Soviets were keen to upstage the United States on any technological front that would deliver a public relations advantage for the communist giant.

For people paying very close attention, there were hints of an impending Soviet rocket just before the Sputnik launch. Indeed, just a day before, a small item in the *New York Times* by science writer Walter Sullivan suggested something big was imminent. Reporting from a scientific conference in Washington, he wrote:

> An astonished audience of Western rocket specialists listened last night as a Soviet scientist gave design and performance details of a Soviet rocket.... Western experts said it was the first time the Russians had made public details of any of their rockets. They added that several features seemed new and ingenious.[12]

It is worth noting that 1957 was also the so-called International Geophysical Year (IGY), a multinational initiative that encouraged scientific projects leading to a greater understanding of the earth. Regardless of its intended purpose, many nations saw the IGY as a stage upon which they could show off their scientific prowess. Even in the United States, many people saw IGY as a way to promote space science. Groups such as the small but vocal American Rocket Society championed the idea. Members of that group, as well as academics and people from other walks of life, became "increasingly vocal," in the words of aviation and space writer William E. Burrows.[13] Their efforts to persuade decision-makers and the public-at-large about the importance of a space program would increase in the coming years.

However, despite this pressure, neither presidents Truman nor Eisenhower had been enthusiastic about moving ahead with a public space program at any great speed. Eisenhower, especially, was not eager to mix a military missile program, which involved classified research and development, with a civilian space program, which would presumably be more open to public input and scrutiny. Since the military program was not one that the government wished to be completely forthcoming about for understandable national security reasons, Eisenhower's initial reaction to Sputnik was to leave American space policies mainly as they were.

In retrospect, it appears that Eisenhower correctly assessed the situation overall. Of course, these were circumstances in which the Soviet Union did have some advantage, if it can be called that, of not having to deal with public opinion or the free press that existed in the United States. Since the USSR was a closed society, Soviet officials could shape public perceptions without fear that journalists or questioning officials would throw light on any aspect of their nation's space program. Its leaders could push forward with space projects without public debate and without fearing domestic criticism or media backlash. In the United States, the situation was radically different, of course, and Eisenhower was in some ways stuck with having to make an assessment that he could not fully explain to the American people for reasons of national security.

The weeks immediately following Sputnik were tense. The success of the first Soviet satellite had delivered a major psychological blow to American confidence and morale. In many ways, appearances were deceiving, however. Behind the scenes, the U.S. rocketry and missile program was beginning to make strides and would soon equal and even overtake what the Russians were able to accomplish. But many Americans did not know or believe that.

Then, on November 3, 1957, Sputnik 2 exacerbated that situation by carrying a dog named Laika into space. While the feat was not as impressive as sending a human into space would have been, Laika proved to be public relations gold. She was hailed as a national hero in the Soviet Union and generated much positive attention to the world, further establishing the perception of Soviet space superiority.

Although Laika's mission seemed heroic and straightforward, there was an element of deception involved as the Sputnik 2 flight unfolded. The Soviet plan had always been that Laika's would be a one-way mission, glorious though it would be. They knew in advance that her life would be sacrificed to advance the Soviet push into space. Oxygen in the tiny capsule would eventually run out, and there was not yet a way to return the spacecraft safely to earth. The Soviets planned for this eventuality, and reportedly, they took precautions to assure Laika's death would be as painless and as comfortable as possible.

As things unfolded, however, this aspect of the mission soon devolved into Soviet deception. Due to an equipment malfunction, Laika perished very soon after reaching space instead of surviving until later in the spaceflight. Laika's early demise from what has been called "overheating and panic"[14] would have given the impression of failure were this to become known, so the Soviets pretended otherwise for several days. Eventually, Soviet officials issued the false cover story that Laika had given her life peacefully at the end of her mission as had always been planned. The true story of Laika's abrupt and painful death, had it been known, would have cast a very different light on the status of the Soviet program. As it was, the public did not learn the full story about Laika's early demise until many years later.

Meanwhile, the United States was scrambling to assuage the public's concern by launching a satellite-carrying rocket of its own. To move things along, it chose one of the several rocket technologies that were already under development for military purposes. Unfortunately, this proved to be a hasty and ill-advised decision. On December 6, 1957, a Vanguard rocket carrying a small satellite lifted only a few feet into the air before stalling and crashing on its launch pad, generating a massive explosion in the process. It was a spectacular and embarrassing failure that further stoked American fears that the United States was falling behind as the Russians were extending their lead.

Despite this public relations setback, within a month, the United States finally did have a success to counter the Soviets. *Explorer 1* traveled to space on January 31, 1958. The scientific instruments relayed data, including information about the Van Allen radiation belt, back to earth for several months.

Over the next few years, the ramped-up American rocket program made significant advances. Meanwhile, the U.S. political world undertook a furious response to the Soviet Union's initial space victories. To address concerns that the nation was falling behind Soviet space and missile capabilities, Congress soon authorized a major increase in "spending for aerospace endeavors, technical and scientific educational programs, and the chartering of new federal agencies to manage air and space research and development."[15] American space officials expanded the U.S. space program in the following months. They reorganized the existing program and folded its longstanding National Advisory Committee for Aeronautics—an organization with 8,000 employees and a $100 million budget—into a brand-new agency, the National Aeronautics and Space Administration (NASA).[16] With much fanfare, this new agency began operations on October 1, 1958.

Within days of its creation, NASA quietly approved a bold new initiative. The plan remained secret until December 17, 1958, when the world finally learned of Project Mercury, NASA's ambitious plan to send humans into space. Not long after, on April 9, 1959, NASA introduced the seven astronauts who had been selected to prepare for Mercury space flights.

The group, which was dubbed the Mercury Seven, included John Glenn, Alan Shepard, Wally Schirra, Gus Grissom, Gordon Cooper, Scott Carpenter, and Deke Slayton. Members of the Mercury Seven soon became household names across America.

NASA and the mostly unquestioning news media extolled America's first astronauts as new heroes for a new age. When the newly appointed NASA astronauts instantly became celebrities, the agency quickly capitalized on the public relations opportunity that the astronauts provided. The astronauts became an essential tool in shaping public attitudes about human space flight—or "manned" space flight, as reports tellingly described it the time. Indeed, from the earliest days of NASA, the public was sold on the idea that the Space Age was the next logical step of the human adventure, not merely a project for gathering scientific data by remote means. As James Kauffman's analysis of NASA's early public relations efforts concludes, agency officials encouraged the public to view human space flight as "indispensable to the conquest of outer space."[17]

As part of its public relations work, NASA officials orchestrated public appearances by the astronauts. The agency also helped to arrange a $500,000 contract between the Mercury Seven and *Life* magazine, ostensibly giving the publication exclusive rights to the astronauts' "life stories." The idea that the *Life* contract was little more than public relations was downplayed, and contract payments probably did really help the astronauts in their private lives. After all, these were young, married, family men, but their average salary was reportedly only $11,311 per year.[18] That was above the average income in that era. However, it was still pitifully low, considering the inherent dangerousness of their work. Still, whatever the personal benefits the astronauts received from the *Life* contract, the benefits to NASA and the U.S. space agenda were also significant. The popular magazine ran at least 28 stories about the astronauts between 1959 and 1963, beginning with a splashy cover story on the issue dated September 14, 1959.[19]

Although it may not be apparent in retrospect, NASA's use of public relations to further its agenda is understandable. Despite much public enthusiasm for the Mercury program and the Space Age, in general, NASA funding was not guaranteed, and the whole U.S. space initiative was not free from politics. The emotional American reaction to Sputnik had kicked the space agenda to the forefront. However, as a new federal agency, NASA was subject to the same inquiries, hearings, debates, and other potential controversies as other parts of the government, all of which were also competing for funding.

As NASA was ramping up in the final months of the 1950s, a presidential election was in the offing. Eisenhower's second term was ending, and that meant someone new would soon occupy the Oval Office. At the time, there was still some residual unhappiness about how Eisenhower had handled the Sputnik crisis. Some people could not forget his response, which they regarded as inadequate and out of touch. Fears that the Soviet Union might lurch ahead in its space program and military technology were all that was needed to propel the space program into the political arena.

The Space Age always had such political aspects, even if this was not apparent at times. In the late 1950s, one high-profile public figure who brought these themes together was the ambitious young senator from Massachusetts, John F. Kennedy. As Kennedy prepared a run at the presidency, the shadow of Sputnik was one of the influences in his growing interest in space policy. Unlike President Eisenhower and Vice President Richard Nixon, it seems that Kennedy believed that Sputnik and the USSR's space program posed a significant threat to the United States. That, at least, was the implicit message that voters heard when Kennedy spoke about space. Indeed, as his campaign unfolded, Kennedy strongly advocated for more attention and resources on space development for national security as well as national prestige considerations.

Upon receiving the Democratic Party's nomination for the presidency, Kennedy prominently included the topic of space in his famous acceptance speech. As articulated in these remarks, his vision for a "New Frontier" brought together and rhetorically merged the Space Age with longstanding American traditions. A section of the speech illustrates this point:

> Franklin Roosevelt's New Deal promised security and succor to those in need. But the New Frontier of which I speak is not a set of promises—it is a set of challenges. It sums up not what I intend to offer the American people, but what I intend to ask of them. It appeals to their pride, not to their pocketbook—it holds out the promise of more sacrifice instead of more security.
>
> But I tell you the New Frontier is here, whether we seek it or not. Beyond that frontier are the uncharted areas of science and space, unsolved problems of peace and war, unconquered pockets of ignorance and prejudice, unanswered questions of poverty and surplus. It would be easier to shrink back from that frontier, to look to the safe mediocrity of the past, to be lulled by good intentions and high rhetoric—and those who prefer that course should not cast their votes for me, regardless of party.
>
> But I believe the times demand new invention, innovation, imagination, decision. I am asking each of you to be pioneers on that New Frontier. My call is to the young in heart, regardless of age—to all who respond to the Scriptural call: "Be strong and of a good courage; be not afraid, neither be thou dismayed."
>
> For courage—not complacency—is our need today—leadership—not salesmanship. And the only valid test of leadership is the ability to lead and lead vigorously.[20]

4. A New Frontier

Kennedy's endorsement of the Space Age continued after he won the presidency in November 1960. By then, NASA was making significant progress. Rocket technology advanced rapidly, and the United States soon equaled most aspects of the Soviet space program.

Still, the Russians remained adept at promoting its space program to a worldwide audience. On April 21, 1961—just weeks after John F. Kennedy was sworn into office as the 35th president of the United States—the Soviets successfully launched a Vostok spacecraft carrying cosmonaut Yuri Gagarin. As a result of his 108-minute flight, Gagarin was glorified as a national hero in the USSR and hailed as the "first man in space" around the world. Eager to get its own human-passenger Mercury space program off the ground, literally and figuratively, NASA sent Alan B. Shepard, Jr., into suborbital flight very shortly after that, on May 5, 1961.

Not long after, Kennedy upped the stakes by making a bold pronouncement. Speaking before a joint session of Congress on May 25, 1961, he said that it was "time for this nation to take a leading role in space achievement, which in many ways may hold the key to our future on earth." The way to do this, he announced, would be for the United States to commit that "before this decade is out," the nation would succeed in "landing a man on the moon and returning him safely to earth. No single space project in this period will be more impressive to mankind...."[21]

Meeting Kennedy's challenge would be difficult. However, in setting such an ambitious goal, the president assured that space would remain a national priority at a time when there were many other pressing situations. In some ways, the space program was not the most obvious focus of American attention at the time. The disastrous Bay of Pigs invasion of Cuba just a few weeks before Kennedy's space announcement had already raised international tensions and a new situation to manage. When the USSR-backed East Germany constructed the ominous Berlin Wall that summer, there was still more added to a quickly overloading American agenda. Still, the space race continued even as such events unfolded.

NASA sent Gus Grissom into space for a short, suborbital mission in July of 1961. Then, a month later, the Soviets countered by sending another of its cosmonauts aloft on a mission that resulted in 17 earth orbits.

From the U.S. public's point of view, the most prominent American breakthrough in the American space program came the following year. On February 20, 1962, NASA astronaut John Glenn orbited the earth three times in NASA's Friendship 7 space capsule. That was still fewer orbits than the Soviets had managed a few months earlier. However, Friendship 7's successful flight was enough of an achievement that it finally seemed as though the United States had mostly, if not wholly, reached parity with the USSR. In fact, it now seemed that NASA was poised to move ahead in the space race.

With Friendship 7's success, NASA's prominence rose to ever greater heights in the American cultural landscape, and Glenn, who was bright and articulate, soon emerged as a media darling—a compelling figure in the American propaganda war with the Soviets. It was no wonder that the American public embraced him as a space hero—even more than Shepard or Grissom, both of whom had gone to space before him.

Kennedy's thinking in establishing the moon-landing goal had always been that it would help galvanize America's resolve and enhance national unity. For him, the moon mission served symbolic purposes, in addition to whatever tangible benefits it might deliver. In a famous address given at Rice University on September 12, 1962, he further explained just how important it was for the nation to remain focused on its intentions to go to the moon. Consider, for example, the lofty and aspirational language in these extracts from his remarks:

> Those who came before us made certain that this country rode the first waves of the industrial revolutions, the first waves of modern invention, and the first wave of nuclear power, and this generation does not intend to founder in the backwash of the coming age of space. We mean to be a part of it—we mean to lead it. For the eyes of the world now look into space, to the moon and to the planets beyond, and we have vowed that we shall not see it governed by a hostile flag of conquest, but by a banner of freedom and peace. We have vowed that we shall not see space filled with weapons of mass destruction, but with instruments of knowledge and understanding....
> We set sail on this new sea because there is new knowledge to be gained, and new rights to be won, and they must be won and used for the progress of all people. For space science, like nuclear science and all technology, has no conscience of its own. Whether it will become a force for good or ill depends on man, and only if the United States occupies a position of pre-eminence can we help decide whether this new ocean will be a sea of peace or a new terrifying theater of war. I do not say that we should or will go unprotected against the hostile misuse of space any more than we go unprotected against the hostile use of land or sea, but I do say that space can be explored and mastered without feeding the fires of war, without repeating the mistakes that man has made in extending his writ around this globe of ours....
> We choose to go to the moon. We choose to go to the moon in this decade and do the other things, not because they are easy, but because they are hard, because that goal will serve to organize and measure the best of our energies and skills, because that challenge is one that we are willing to accept, one we are unwilling to postpone, and one which we intend to win....[22]

By this time, Kennedy's vision for a "New Frontier," which he had announced a few years earlier, had become intertwined with the Space-Age goal of an American moon mission. The combination presented an intriguing view of America's future. From one point of view, the space program was already framed to somewhat distance it from the politics of the progressive social reforms that were beginning to take a significant role in American life. Kennedy may have had lofty goals for society at large, but in some ways, the NASA agenda often seemed apart from these broader aims.

NASA astronaut Walter "Wally" Schirra became the fifth American to fly into space aboard the Sigma 7 in the Mercury-Atlas 8, shown here at its launch on October 3, 1962. The flight came at a tense time, just two weeks before the Cuban Missile Crisis threatened to plunge the United States into an open military conflict with the Soviet Union. By then, the U.S. space program was making great strides in its quest to send humans on a round-trip mission to the Moon (NASA).

While it is true that Kennedy's "New Frontier" was a vision of the future, it also harkened to the past. The very word "frontier" rhetorically connected the president's dreams of the future with the Frontier Age of the 19th century. Simultaneously looking forward and backward was hardly anything unprecedented, and so in some ways, Kennedy was not breaking new ground. Americans often gazed ahead and in the rearview mirror at the same time. One example was the future-oriented 1939 World's Fair, where an emphasis on the "World of Tomorrow" was tempered by elements of nostalgia for an idealized, largely sanitized past.

Throughout the 1950s, these kinds of contrasting impulses of future and past played out across popular culture. At the time, Americans took it for granted and saw it as nothing unusual. In 1954 and 1955, for example, the popular *Disneyland* television series aired a five-part series about the 19th-century folk-hero Davy Crockett, who was called "King of the Wild Frontier" in marketing materials. Starring the amiable actor Fess Parker, the series was at the center of a craze that swept across 1950s America. Thus, even in the early days of the Space Age, when the very same *Disneyland* program was preparing to air futuristic "Man in Space" episodes, it was part of an American culture that still held onto a mythic past.

That the Space Age should coincide with an apparent cultural longing for long-ago times was a noteworthy phenomenon. In addition to Disney's prominent role in promoting Frontier themes, other trends in American popular culture of the decade had also revisited the Frontier Myth, most often in that myth's iconic Old West incarnation. That decade saw a resurgence of Western films and the beginning of a crossover of Westerns to television, for example. Indeed, the era of astronauts was also an era of renewed interest in cowboys. Films such as director Fred Zinnemann's *High Noon* (1952) and John Ford's *The Searchers* (1956), among others, presented updated versions of the Frontier mythology even as the Space Age was gaining momentum.

As with earlier films, the era's Western movies were open to allegorical interpretation, and so in some ways, they easily fit into the modern age as symbolic representations of a traditional American narrative. However, the main thrust of the familiar Frontier mythology remained. Just as many people regarded space as a *tabula rasa*, Hollywood Westerns continued to present the American West as though it had been a blank slate that was waiting, as if to be saved, for the arrival of American civilization. The historical Old West was no such thing, of course, since various Native American cultures and their civilization had been thoroughly ensconced there for centuries. But this fact, obvious though it should have been, was mostly downplayed. Instead, the movie and television version of the Frontier Myth that appeared in Westerns usually reinforced the idea of the

4. A New Frontier

rightness, if not the inevitability, of American extending its dominion over this expansive territory, spreading its vision of morality throughout the world as it did so.

This way of thinking about the 19th-century Frontier fit congruently into American political culture of the 1950s and early 1960s. This impulse is evident in the realm of international politics of the era. At the time, the United States and the USSR were consumed in the Cold War, and each superpower sought to bring nearly every corner of the world—the frontier beyond American borders, in other words—into its fold. For the United States, this meant bringing new realms into the ranks of American-style democratic societies. Thus, in what was perceived as a life-and-death confrontation with communism, U.S. foreign policy saw the whole globe as a kind of frontier. That frontier was always deeply connected to ideas about the future—a future in which the world would be saved from communism and reshaped it into a brighter, happier place. The world on the horizon, as America saw it, would either be about the triumph of democracy across the globe, or it would be a dark, ruinous end of civilization as Americans knew it. Under these circumstances, it was a small step from applying the Frontier Myth to American politics to also applying it to the vast openness of outer space, where the earthly struggle to re-create the world in an American image continued into the heavens.

The New Frontier was about American power to shape how the world would be. It was a way of picturing the future in a manner that viewed humankind's coming ventures into space as a new opportunity that would help lift America and its society to new heights, figuratively and literally. It would open a future that would also be an era in which technology would solve problems and improve life on earth.

Again, however, this New Frontier would not be entirely new. Indeed, if the space-oriented New Frontier of the future was to be revolutionary in some ways, this did not necessarily mean that the envisioned Space Age would change everything. In fact, in its social features, the Space-Age future, as embodied in NASA's space program, mostly resembled the existing social order of mid-century America, especially concerning sex and race. In many ways, for example, the carefully crafted image of the Mercury Seven astronauts strongly resembled the stereotypical white male hero that had long held sway in American popular culture and particularly in the Frontier Myth. Many presumed that the people leading humankind's journey into space would be rugged white men in this mold. The thought that this was the presumption of a complex web of patriarchy, to use language from a later period, was not a common idea.

But it is not true that no one had foreseen a significant role for women as the Space Age was getting underway. In fact, even before Sputnik jolted

The early NASA astronauts were national celebrities in their day and none more than John Glenn, the first U.S. astronaut to orbit the earth in space. Acclaimed as a Space-Age hero, Glenn's rugged and straightforward image seemed to be an updated version of cowboy heroes from the mythic Old West. Glenn's life of national service continued after his days in the astronaut corps. He served as United States senator from Ohio from 1974 until 1999. In 1998, Glenn made one last trip into space as a payload specialist aboard the space shuttle *Discovery*. This photograph dates from 1959 (NASA).

the American public and propelled the U.S. space program into high gear in response, members of the American Psychological Association had publicly speculated that it might be women, not men, who would lead humankind into space. An article in the September 4, 1957, edition of the *New York Times*, for example, reported that a panel of psychologists had examined that very issue. Noting the advantages that women possessed in terms of their "size and certain physiological and psychological qualities," the panel "speculated ... that when man [sic] was ready to take off for the moon it would be a woman who would probably make the first flight."[23] That was apparently not a message that many people took at face value, however. True to the prevailing sexism of the era, the same article described the psychologists' discussion of the topic as possessing "certain humorous and even fantastic aspects." So, the idea that women might participate meaningfully, or perhaps even lead America into space did make its way into the public conversation. However, the implication was that people should not take it seriously.

Still, when NASA initiated the Mercury program some months later, the idea had not disappeared entirely. One advocate for women in space was Dr. William Randolph Lovelace, a physician who worked closely with NASA and was instrumental in the testing and selection of the Mercury Seven astronauts. At the time, most NASA officials seem to have been uninterested in pursuing the idea of women astronauts, but Lovelace remained enthusiastic about it. Only a few others from the space community, including a man Lovelace knew, Air Force Brigadier General Donald Flickinger, seem to have shared his interest in exploring the possibility of adding women to the astronaut corps.

In 1960, Lovelace decided to pursue the idea of women astronauts independently, outside of NASA's bureaucracy. Working out of his privately funded Foundation for Medical Education in Albuquerque, New Mexico, he invited Geraldyn "Jerrie" Cobb, a well-known pilot, to undergo a series of tests directly modeled on those that had been used to select the Mercury Seven. Cobb's results were impressive. Lovelace announced this fact in a high-profile press conference in Stockholm on August 19, 1960, which prompted a flurry of media stories and heightened public interest.

Again, however, the language used in reporting this lacked the heroic rhetoric that was apparent in much writing about the men who were in training for space flight. One example could be found in a *Life* magazine article titled "Damp Prelude to Space: A Potential Lady Orbiter Excels in Lonesome Test," which was published in October of 1960.[24] As with much news coverage about the possibility of an American woman astronaut, the dismissive wording of the article probably left many readers thinking that the idea was mostly a curiosity.

Meanwhile, Lovelace's Woman in Space program continued unofficially. About two dozen women were invited to join Lovelace's study, of whom 19 women agreed to participate.

Lovelace soon began a new series of grueling and exhaustive tests. Eventually, 13 of the test subjects passed. This elite group of pilots (later dubbed the "Mercury 13" by some writers) included Jerrie Cobb, Wally

Funk, Irene Leverton, Myrtle Cagle, Jane B. Hart, Gene Nora Stumbough, Jerri Sloan, Rhea Hurrle, Sarah Gorelick, Bernice Trimble, Jan Dietrich, Marion Dietrich (Jan's twin sister), and Jean Hixson.

After completing tests in New Mexico, Lovelace sent members of the group to a Navy facility in Pensacola, Florida, to use some specialized equipment that was needed to continue the process. At this point, however, the program ran into a roadblock. Since Lovelace's program was unofficial, there had been no request from NASA asking permission to use the Navy facility for Lovelace's work. Also, shortly before the women were scheduled to report to Pensacola for the tests, the unofficial program drew the attention of officials, who were not enthusiastic about it. Consequently, just days before the women were to travel there, the Navy denied them use of the facility.[25]

The upshot of this was the abrupt cancelation of Lovelace's program. He had taken it as far as he could go independently, and NASA was not interested in keeping the program alive by making it official. However, at least two of the women in the Mercury 13 were not ready to give up, and they attempted to press forward.

Jerrie Cobb and Jan Hart wrote to Vice-President Lyndon Johnson, who was then serving as vice president, with the hope that he would help revive the program. Cobb was probably the better-known aviator of the two, but Hart was not only a well-regarded pilot; she was also the wife of a sitting U.S. Senator, Philip Hart, a connection that assured the request would at least get some notice.

The appeal to Johnson resulted in little progress. Still undaunted, Cobb and Hart subsequently appeared before a Congressional subcommittee that was considering various aspects of the space program. That, too, was to little avail, however. John Glenn also gave testimony at the hearings, and his statements appeared to bolster the status quo. "The fact that women are not in this field," Glenn said, "is a fact of our social order."[26] As scholar Margaret Weitekamp has concisely concluded, in the face of substantial inertia in Congress, "Cobb and Hart struggled to make a clear case for why, in a political climate that did not value's women's participation, women should be astronauts."[27] Ultimately, the policies were left unchanged, and the question of sending American women into space attracted little support.

That was likely something that some members of Congress later regretted. The following year, the Soviets scored another public relations coup. On June 16, 1963, they launched a Vostok 6 rocket carrying 26-year-old Valentina Tereshkova. To much international fanfare, she became the first woman in space.

The daughter of a Soviet World War II hero, Tereshkova was instantly lauded around the world as she set a new endurance record by orbiting the earth for nearly five days. It was a bitter development for those promoting the U.S. space effort. When *Life* reported about the story, for example, the writer made special mention of Tereshkova's background, noting that the first woman in space "was not even a pilot" and possessed "virtually no technical background."[28]

That the U.S. program, which was maintaining its focus on human travel to the moon, was making good progress at the time, was of little consolation publicly. The news that the Soviets had been the first to send a woman into space was a public relations victory for the communists and made the United States look behind the times. *Life* magazine, with its vested interest in NASA and the existing astronauts, subsequently published a somewhat bitter-sounding story on the subject of women and the U.S. space program. "The U.S. could have been first to put a woman up into space merely by deciding to do so," it read. Citing the "grueling physical examination" that Jerrie Cobb and the other women astronaut prospects had previously undergone in Lovelace's unofficial program, the article added that these American women "were experienced pilots with qualifications far more impressive than Valentina Tereshkova's."[29] None of that, however, changed the fact that the Soviets had already sent a woman into space.

In another article at the time, Clare Boothe Luce, the writer and political figure, assessed the situation more bluntly. "Why did the Soviet Union launch a woman cosmonaut into space? Failure of American men to give the right answer to this question may yet prove to be the costliest Cold War blunder.... In entrusting a 26-year-old girl [sic] with a cosmonaut mission, the Soviet Union has given its women unmistakable proof that it believes them to possess these same virtues. ... [Tereshkova's flight] symbolizes to Russian women that they actively share (not passively bask, like American women) in the glory of conquering space."[30]

Although America had no women astronauts, women had indeed been making significant contributions to the space program all along, albeit with practically no visibility or recognition. While nearly all the critical scientific and technical jobs that made the space program possible remained closed to women at the time, one group of women was essential to NASA's success—the so-called "human computers." They were the people who calculated complex mathematics for NASA manually in the days before electronic computing. Their work was essential in moving research forward.

Women quietly served in such jobs in large numbers since the days of World War II. After the conflict, women "computers" continued to contribute valuable work at places such as the Langley Memorial Aeronautical

Laboratory, a facility that served as the central research center for NASA's predecessor, the National Advisory Committee for Aeronautics. Initially, many young, white women filled the "computer" ranks there. Eventually, in the 1940s, Langley officials also started hiring qualified African American women to help meet growing demand.[31]

Working under conditions of segregation, African American women proved to be essential workers in the fledgling space program. For example, Katherine Johnson, one of the best known and most accomplished members of this group, started at Langley in 1953 and continued her work into the NASA years. By 1958, her talents attracted notice within the agency, and she became a member of the Space Task Force. Later, in the era when electronic computers began to replace humans for this work, her work continued to be well regarded. Indeed, she famously calculated the flight paths of Mercury astronauts Alan Shepard and John Glenn.[32]

The work of the women computers seldom received recognition at the time. It was much later when they and their work finally received well-deserved attention. Unfortunately, even though women made demonstrable contributions to the space program, they did not get credit and were subsequently not taken much into account in the early days of space. They were essential but largely marginalized and invisible contributors to the New Frontier of Kennedy's vision.

As this brief overview of events suggests, the future of the space era that NASA and its overseers envisioned seemed to presume that the so-called place of women would remain mostly unchanged. By 1963, however, the whole social order in the United States was starting to show signs of strain. It would not be long before such assumptions appeared very dubious.

The plight of African American men revealed that significant social improvements had yet to materialize at the leading edge of the New Frontier for them, either. Indeed, African American men were not a substantial part of the conversation when it came to staffing NASA's professional or astronaut ranks, though sometimes there was a glimmer of potential progress.

In 1961, for example, the Kennedy administration seemed to be promoting the idea that a pilot named Ed Dwight soon would become a NASA astronaut. At the time, the African American community lauded him for this apparent achievement. Months passed, however, and NASA never officially named him a pilot. He eventually resigned his commission in the Air Force.[33] By then, Lyndon Johnson had assumed the presidency, and a different pilot, Robert Lawrence, Jr., was named as the first African American astronaut. Tragically, Lawrence died during a training flight just months after the announcement of his astronaut status. It would be some time before NASA revisited the lack of African Americans in its pilot corps and finally addressed the issue.

Behind the scenes, African American men fared little better. As Richard Paul and Steven Moss discuss in a comprehensive examination of unsung African American contributors to the early U.S. space program, African American engineers, such as Julius Montgomery, faced enormous challenges even after admission to professional positions within the NASA organization.[34] It was well into the 1960s before there was any substantial progress on this front. Even at that point, full equality and opportunity had not become a reality for African American men and women, or for that matter, for people of color, more generally.

As things stood, if NASA and its programs were to be an embodiment of what the future held, then the future would not dramatically alter social relationships as they existed in American society of the late 1950s and

Robert H. Lawrence was named to the Air Force's Manned Orbital Laboratory program in June of 1967, making him the first officially designated African American astronaut. His appointment was an indication that the U.S. space effort was finally diversifying. Having achieved the rank of major in the U.S. Air Force and as the recipient of a Ph.D. in chemistry, he was exceptionally well qualified to join America's growing space program. Sadly, Lawrence died in a training accident just months later, in October 1967 (U.S. Air Force).

early 1960s. Presidents Kennedy and Johnson may have hoped to use the space initiative to bring about prejudice-reducing social reforms. But the image of the space program that the public saw mostly excluded women and people of color. The type of future associated with the Space Age and the New Frontier may have been technologically and scientifically advanced. In social terms, however, people had little reason to conclude that the nation's venture into space would significantly change long-established social hierarchies and prejudices in America. On the contrary, the entire space program, in some ways, reassured people that the space-oriented future would replicate the social world as it existed. White, middle-class American men apparently would continue to occupy center stage, while others would be supporting characters.

These conditions were taken for granted while the focus on the future in the space-oriented frontier was directed to the wonders and marvels of space itself and to the technological miracles that would make travels into space possible. The cultural components to create the Space-Age future were mostly in place. There was nearly blind faith that Americans would be successful in using science and technology to create a pathway to the heavens. Concurrently, most of the public firmly believed that science and technology would continue to unlock even more of nature's secrets and would solve all sorts of real-world problems. Thus, while the most common symbols of the Space Age were rockets and representations of human travel to the heavens, the Space Age was a statement about the whole of humanity's future, in space and on earth.

In many ways, the Space Age embodied a cultural perspective—a viewpoint that influenced ideas about how the future would unfold. It was incorporated in an aesthetic sensibility that found broad expression across society. As part of that, potent Space-Age imagery powerfully shaped how people imagined this envisioned future world. The visual aesthetics of the Space Age took cues from the sleek aerodynamic lines that were common to both rockets and jet airplanes and from the gleaming Space-Age materials used by the aerospace industry. This Space-Age "look," which had already found expression in automotive design, continued to expand into many consumer products that filled showrooms and store shelves. It became a decorative element in many household items, such as toasters and other kitchen gadgets, and appliances, which otherwise had no apparent relationship to the Space Age.

In the media world, the sleek, gleaming, futurism of Space Age design and imagery was also very prevalent. Of particular note were those artists who were skilled at translating aspects of the not-yet-realized Space-Age future into evocative pictures that appealed to everyday people. One such artist, Chesley Bonestell, garnered attention as the result of his many illustrations for science-fiction, nonfiction magazine articles, and screen productions. He continued to create many images that made rocketry and space exploration seem wondrous. Many other artists also helped popularize a vision of how futuristic aspects of the Space Age would look.

Among these artists was Robert McCall, a gifted illustrator who began working for *Life* magazine in the 1950s. McCall was already interested in aircraft technology and was sometimes hired to illustrate stories that included that focus. Then, with the advent of Sputnik and the Space Age, his skills were increasingly directed to depictions of rockets and space flight. When *Life* devoted most of its April 21, 1961, edition to space, McCall produced several spectacular paintings for a pictorial essay titled "Wild but Sane Ideas for Space Flight."[35] McCall's vivid work was widely reproduced and imitated, and it was very influential. Later in the decade, he was selected to create production and promotional art for director Stanley Kubrick's stunning science-fiction film, *2001: A Space Odyssey*.

Elsewhere, a futuristic syndicated comic strip that was created in the late 1950s offered newspaper readers across the country with a steady diet of images depicting life in the coming Space Age. Launched in late 1958, artist Arthur Radebaugh's comic strip, *Closer Than We Think*, took themes from the Space Age and looked at the future expansively. Typically, the one-panel comic strips took ordinary aspects of mid-century life in America and then showed how Space-Age technological advances would revolutionize them in the future.

Before creating this comic strip, Radebaugh had worked extensively in advertising for clients in the automotive field and other large industries. In 1947, he had even produced a locally published futuristic comic strip, *Can You Imagine*, for the *Detroit News Pictorial*.[36] With this background making visually striking car ads and comics, Radebaugh had already been dealing with the type of consumerist futurism that the major automobile manufacturers and other large corporations had been promoting for many years.

Radebaugh once said that his illustrations were "halfway between science fiction and designs for modern living."[37] His *Closer Than We Think* comic strip built on those themes and elaborated a fantastical world of gadgetry, convenience, and marvel. Writer Matt Novak has described it as "a madcap American utopia, filled with flying cars and fantastical skyscrapers."[38] Possessing a style that would have been at home in science-fiction comic books of the era, Radebaugh's drawings were flights of the imagination that fit in neatly with the visualizations of the Space-Age future that also appeared throughout late-1950s popular culture. The strip's illustrations of astonishing machines, lifestyles, and gadgets helped reinforce mainstream visual representations of the future. They infused existing consumerist futurism with Space-Age thinking.

Radebaugh presented a marvelous and imaginative portrait of tomorrow's world. His drawings showed houses under giant glass domes, postal workers wearing jet packs, robots in the workplace, farms growing engineered vegetables the size of small cars, satellites controlling the weather, hospitals orbiting the earth, and many other amazing developments. As he showed it, the future would be a paradise enhanced by futuristic inventions. It would be a comfortable and carefree life, apparently free of financial worries or concerns for social ills.

Radebaugh's comic strip constituted a broad, highly positive portrayal of the Space Age that emphasized continuity as much as change. This approach had implications for the future it presented. For example, it reflected the biases of the era and envisioned a white, suburban future that seemed devoid of diversity and in which women remained restricted to traditional roles. It seldom questioned the status quo about anything of social significance, though perhaps this is not surprising since it was an era that valued conformity. It was, after all, the time of "company men" and "keeping up with the Joneses." *Closer Than We Think* also reflected a deep, apparently limitless faith in technology, businesses, and American institutions. The potential downsides of car culture, processed foods, supposedly labor-saving devices, and more were not part of Radebaugh's vision. Perhaps this is also not surprising, given that for years, business, industry, government, and the media had promoted the idea that technological wonders and scientific breakthroughs would deliver a bright, gleaming future.

Acceptance of this oversimplified and arguably sanitized view of the Space-Age future was consistent with the U.S. middle class's psyche of the time. The arrival of the Space Age seems to have further reinforced some presumptions that, in retrospect, may not have been very sound. In any case, Radebaugh's was only one of many voices that articulated a similar vision of the future.

The real scientific and technological advances of the Space Age had launched a new era. As the work of Radebaugh and others shows, it did not take long for U.S. culture to incorporate and build upon these advances and to fuse them with the visions of a consumerist future that were already well-established in American life. By the early 1960s, some people may have thought that the rapid ascent to the heavens, literally and figuratively, would continue without interruption. The New Frontier beckoned, but it would not turn out to be what people had imagined.

5

Peak Future

It was the spring of 1962, and it seemed as though the future had arrived. Space Age enthusiasm, combined with the long campaign to promote consumer-oriented futurism, pushed the world to the threshold of tomorrow. Americans stood ready to step into a brave, new world in which long-held dreams would finally come to fruition. One look at the towering Space Needle in Seattle seemed to confirm that. Unlike anything most people had ever seen, the landmark building, rising high into the air, symbolized tomorrow's promise and potential.

Writer Knute Berger, who lived in the area then, has written about his excitement when he first saw the Space Needle. "It was as if a spaceship from a friendly future had landed in our own backyard," he said. "We were hyped up in anticipation of what the Needle represented: The Space Age had arrived."[1]

The Space Needle was the architectural centerpiece of the Century 21 Exposition—popularly known as the Seattle World's Fair—which opened to the public on April 21, 1962. Several years of intense planning, lobbying, and hard work had gone into making the Exposition a reality, and now it was ready for the world to see. The Fair was a platform from which organizers could boast of the Northwest region's growing importance. However, with science and technology as its focus, it was first and foremost another glimpse into what the future might hold.

The idea to host such a high-profile event in Seattle was by no means an obvious one. At the time, Seattle was hardly the world-class city it later became. Raising awareness of the city was part of the point that City Council member Al Rochester had in mind when he broached the subject in the mid–1950s. His idea was not entirely as outlandish as it may have seemed at first. The state had hosted a world's fair once before, the Alaska-Yukon-Pacific Exposition, in 1909, and that event had attracted over 3 million visitors. Seattle and the world had changed radically since then, and Rochester and the people who supported his vision decided that the time had come to reintroduce Seattle and the Pacific Northwest to the postwar world. They imagined a high-profile event that would top Seattle's first world's fair decades earlier.

It took time to generate interest among the many stakeholders whose backing would be essential. By 1957, however, a special commission and the governor formally endorsed the plan to host a world exposition organized around the themes of science and progress. Initially, planners had hoped to mount the event quickly, so that its opening could coincide with the 50th anniversary of the Alaska-Yukon-Pacific Exposition in 1959. After considering the complexity of planning and funding the exposition, planners eventually agreed to push the opening back to 1962.

As plans progressed, organizers added the tagline, "America's Space Age World's Fair," to their marketing plans for the Exposition. Although there had been no doubt about the event's theme and purpose, the new slogan further emphasized the Exposition's relevance and its futurist orientation.

Work on the site and facilities had already started when organizers received the good news that their Century 21 Exposition had obtained the blessing of the International Bureau of Expositions (IBE) in 1960. With

The iconic Space Needle, shown here in a photograph from 1994, rises 600 feet above the city of Seattle. Its overall silhouette—essentially consisting of a disk-like habitable space sitting atop a supporting column—was repeated in many futuristic building designs (National Archives).

5. Peak Future

this prestigious international body's endorsement, organizers could tout the Exposition as an officially recognized "world's fair." The IBE's seal of approval added an extra layer of prestige to their undertaking.[2]

Over the following months, plans came together, and construction crews raced to transform the grounds and to create new exhibition spaces. With the attention-getting Space Needle as the Fair's centerpiece, organizers wanted to be sure that the event would be an affair to remember—a world's fair that would garner the attention and admiration of people from across the globe. To that end, planners looked for ways to impress those who visited the event.

That, in part, was behind the idea for visitors to begin their trip to the Fair with a ride on a futuristic monorail transportation system that was similar to the much-publicized system at the Disneyland theme park that had opened just a few years earlier. As one journalist of the era explained, visitors are "whisked, in 96 seconds, from the center of Seattle to the Exposition grounds a mile away on a sleek monorail train. Once there they can ascend by elevator to the top of the theme structure of the fair—a 550-foot 'Space Needle' tower topped by a revolving observation platform and 200-seat restaurant that will make a complete revolution each hour."[3]

From a lofty perch atop the Space Needle, visitors were able to get a bird's eye view of the fairground's distinct areas. Each zone had a different theme, though several overlapped. There was the World of Science, the World of Commerce and Industry, the World of Century 21, the World of Art, and lastly, the World of Entertainment. The first three of these contained the bulk of the exhibits that explicitly reflected the Fair's science and futurism themes.

The aura of the Space Age was apparent throughout the Fair. Further emphasizing this connection was an official visit by John Glenn, the famed astronaut who had triumphantly circled the earth three times in Mercury Seven only a few months earlier. He made his highly publicized stop at the Exposition on May 10, 1962, soon after its doors had opened to the public. Visitors followed him, asked for autographs, and crowded around him as he interacted with the press during the visit. Adding to the gravitas of Glenn's day at the Fair, he was accompanied by none other than Wernher von Braun, then heralded as the father of America's space program, for part of the day. Glenn's visit culminated that afternoon with the dedication of the NASA exhibit that had been specially prepared for the Century 21 Exposition. During the ceremony, Glenn shared the podium with Vice-President Lyndon Johnson.[4]

Fair organizers took no chances in reinforcing the core messages that they wanted visitors to receive. They were far less interested in recounting accomplishments of the past than had been the case with some world's fairs, and much more interested in boasting of achievements yet to come. Rather than a celebration of where America had been, therefore, it was a strident statement about where the world was going. Even the official map of the Exposition championed this message. "Welcome to the future," the legend read, leaving no doubt about what orientation the planners had in mind.

The World of Science section clearly emphasized this theme. Arguably, it served as the Fair's centerpiece even more than the symbolic Space Needle. The United States government contributed $9.5 million to the World of Science exhibition, and more than a hundred scientists were involved in planning it.[5] The result was a fascinating experience. Visitors learned about scientific research aiming "to determine human sex before birth; motivate man to do good; [and] give him longer, healthier life." There was even a section about food-production techniques that would be needed to feed "the world's burgeoning population."[6]

The highlight of the World of Science, however, was a multimedia exhibit called the Spacetarium. Constructed by the Boeing Corporation, it was an experience that used sight and sound to simulate a ten-billion-mile voyage "where visitors view the planets as though from a speeding space ship."[7] Standing in a circular theater and watching a film projected onto the 78-feet-in-diameter dome above, which was then the largest such projection surface in the world,[8] up to 750 visitors could experience the imaginary trip at a time.

Over in the World of Commerce and Industry zone, visitors also encountered a Space-Age future. The Ford Motor Company building was a futuristic-looking geodesic dome of the sort popularized by the futurist Buckminster Fuller. Within it, visitors experienced "Adventure in Outer Space," another opportunity to take an imaginary journey to the heavens.[9]

Many exhibits in the World of Commerce and Industry, as well as in the World of Century 21, were more earth-bound than these space-oriented experiences, but they also looked to the world of tomorrow. General Motors and Ford, for example, both exhibited futuristic concept cars. The sense of futurism that informed the overall designs of these automobiles was more pronounced than ever. General Motors, for example, showcased a vehicle called the Firebird III. It had a jet-inspired bubble cockpit and rocket-like fins—five in all—that were so pronounced that it hardly looked like a land-based vehicle at all. Ford, meanwhile, debuted a scale model for a concept car it called the Seattle-ite. Its low-slung and very elongated design also included a bubble cockpit, and it also had fins and taillights that resembled the afterburners of jets. More startlingly, though, the Seattle-ite had six wheels—two on the rear axle and four (two on each side) at the front. Neither car ever went into production, but some of the ideas and less visible technology (including onboard computers) later appeared in consumer vehicles. In any case, these cars suggested that America's highways would soon be traversed in vehicles quite unlike the cars of the time.

Many other Fair exhibits also picked up on the future theme. Among the many corporate presentations were models of futuristic homes as well as displays and prototypes of futuristic gadgetry—all intended to make life more convenient. It was a showcase of the technology that the corporate world thought was most likely to make a significant impact throughout people's lives. And more than in the past, computers figured prominently in some of these displays, as was especially evident at the IBM Pavilion. The net effect reinforced the kind of consumer futurism that had been gathering momentum throughout the previous years. Meanwhile, there was little on display at the Seattle World's Fair to suggest any dramatic reordering of the nation's society. Instead, the presumption seemed to be that technology, science, and consumerism would mostly progress as the society overall remained static.

Although the Space Needle probably remains the most recognized structure from the Seattle World's Fair, the immense Coliseum was also notable for its distinctive visual design. Well-known architect Paul Thiry had been asked to design a structure that would be open and unencumbered, but that would yet provide a canopy over a vast expanse. His ingenious plan used five miles of cabling to support a roof structure so gigantic that it could cover an exhibition area of 130,000 square feet.[10]

The opening of the Seattle World's Fair just a few years after the launch of the hugely popular Disneyland in California invites comparisons to that Disney property and especially its Tomorrowland. At first glance, Disney's influence on the Century 21 Exposition might seem slight. But while it was not always visible, Disney's influence abounded.

From the beginning, Seattle organizers solicited input from the Disney company. The Exposition even retained the services of several Disney staff members to help with planning. The exposition's monorail, which was much like the monorail at Disneyland, was perhaps the most noticeably similar feature between the two venues. Beyond this, however, Disney had a significant effect in more subtle ways. As Stacy Warren concludes, the Disney influence was especially prominent in the Exposition's layout, and operations—in its "vision for a smoothly operating city—a new image of urbanity that can still be seen on the ground today."[11]

Still, despite championing the future, the 1962 Seattle World's Fair was not revolutionary in design or conception. The vision that it presented consisted of refinements and restatements of previous ideas more than new and original insights. That was probably reflective of where mid-century futurism, as a cultural phenomenon created for and

When planning for the 1962 Seattle World's Fair, organizers consulted with Walt Disney to help bring their vision of Century 21 to life. Although much of the Disney influence is subtle, the inclusion of a futuristic monorail system, shown here in a later photograph, much like the one that had been installed at the Disneyland theme park a few years earlier, was visible evidence of the Disney touch (iStock.com/400tmax).

consumed by the general public, stood in the second year of John Kennedy's administration.

One aspect of the future envisioned at the Seattle World's Fair was mostly new, however, at least for public-oriented events of this sort. That was an apparent willingness to question, albeit tentatively, the rosy picture of the future that such events usually depicted. Perhaps the long years of the Cold War were starting to take a toll. Whatever the reason, the anxiety that lurked beneath the surface of American optimism appeared to be strengthening. In that context, some parts of the Seattle World's Fair cast doubt on an otherwise happy and positive vision of the future.

The World of Tomorrow, for example, framed life in the next century as potentially a "threshold" or a "threat," with the scourge of nuclear war regarded as the most likely danger.[12] "The man [sic] of today must earn these rewards ... [of the future]," read a statement in the official Fair guidebook, "otherwise his legacy may be one of human misery and destruction."[13] It was a realistic point of view but hardly one that fit tidily with the generally bright and triumphalist messages that this Fair, like most American expressions of futurism in that era, seemed eager to promote.

5. Peak Future   111

Still, nothing about the knife-edge choices that humankind would face was new. Nor would such questions have surprised anyone visiting the Fair at the time. Americans—and indeed, citizens of the world—had been living with the potential for cataclysmic destruction ever since the atomic blast at Hiroshima 17 years earlier. Since that time, Cold War tensions had often suggested that if humankind was not careful, dire consequences could result.

Even in years when Americans were preparing fallout shelters, and young students were practicing hiding under their school desks in the event of a nuclear strike, the possibility of a near-utopian, consumer-driven world of plenty still held much cultural power. While people knew a dark future was possible, that view seldom overwhelmed the generally optimistic spirit of mid-century America.[14] Aside from some tense moments, such as the Cuban Missile Crisis in the fall of 1962, ominous visions of the future largely remained a subtext to American cultural life. Americans knew that the world was dangerous and possibly even on the brink of destruction. At the same time, however, they mostly managed to set aside fears and anxieties.

The most prominent examples of mid-century American futurism, including the Seattle World's Fair, were informed by a similar mindset. It was as if to say problems exist, but human ingenuity and perseverance will make it possible to overcome them. To some extent, this reflected the confidence that Americans still had in their institutions and way of life. There was also another option: if some visions of the future were to be unthinkable, maybe one choice would be not to think about them. It was defensive avoidance, perhaps. But it also made optimism for the future, as well as a certain sense of innocence, seem possible despite the existence of situations that seemed to contradict that viewpoint.

Despite some wear around the edges, then, the futurism of the early 1960s often retained a remarkably shiny and optimistic veneer that usually persisted even when current events sometimes challenged that perspective. The picture of a positive future remained a dominant cultural narrative, at least for the time being. Something else was also happening, however.

The "future" was starting to look very familiar. Much thinking about the future had begun to coalesce, or even stagnate, around a relatively fixed set of ideas about what was to come. These basic ideas were repeated over and over, often with only the slightest of modifications. Although not in every instance, in some ways, visions of the future became a trope. The American public had internalized frequently articulated ideas about how the future might look and how people might live in it. Many newer versions of the future were just that—versions of established futuristic ideas.

Time was moving forward, but the picture of the future that many people imagined was not.

Visitors to the Seattle World's Fair, for example, encountered one attraction that was futuristic but hardly startling—the Bubbleator. In some sense, an oddity, the Bubbleator was a transparent, globe-shaped elevator that could carry dozens of passengers at a time. Its orb-shape and plexiglass exterior gave it a highly distinctive appearance. It was mostly a gimmick, but it was a crowd-pleaser. As writer Bill Cotter observed, "It may seem silly now, but it was a huge success during the fair."[15]

Passengers of the Bubbleator might very well have daydreamed about future life with amazing new gadgets, lifestyle improvements, and communities filled with towering buildings like the Space Needle. As it turned out, they soon would have a weekly opportunity to see such life. It would be broadcast weekly in a new television show called *The Jetsons*.

In the fall of 1962, the ABC television network added *The Jetsons* to its prime-time schedule. It was a modest series—a cartoon, in fact—that depicted life in the distant future. Produced by William Hanna and Joseph Barbera, *The Jetsons* combined existing ideas about the world of tomorrow and packaged them as a situation comedy. The future appeared in many quarters of the era's popular culture, but few of those depictions resonated with the general public as much as Hanna and Barbera's new series.

The show was nominally about an ordinary character named George Jetson and his family—wife Jane Jetson, children Judy (a teenager) and Elroy (an elementary school student)—as well as their dog Astro and a robotic domestic servant named Rosie. Although set in a world of tomorrow, the stories it told were mostly about the kinds of amusing problems that were common in live-action situation comedies of the era. George gets into trouble with his boss; household appliances need repair; the Jetson children have issues that children everywhere seem to have. Despite the far-off setting, the 1962 audience could easily recognize these types of stories, and the producers thought nothing otherwise. "We were just portraying life as it is and as it will be forever,"[16] Joseph Barbera later said. "I don't care where we live, or what happens.... Human beings will never change.... Your style may change, your cars may change, your clothing may change, but people, I don't think, will ever change."[17]

Hanna and Barbera adopted a simple and straightforward approach for the new series, and for the most part, the futuristic element merely added an unusual and entertaining veneer to the stories. The show was a straightforward comedy, with not a hint of looming disaster or significant problems in the offing. It was the same strategy that Hanna and Barbera had used two years earlier in their prime-time animated series,

5. Peak Future 113

The Flintstones. That series was about an imaginary Stone-Age family. *The Jetsons* was mostly a variation of the same idea with a different timeframe.

When ABC executives added *The Jetsons* to the network's evening lineup, they undoubtedly hoped it would match the surprise success of *The Flintstones.* But ABC scheduled the new series in a difficult spot. Airing opposite popular and well-established shows, it failed to find an audience or high ratings. As a result, *The Jetsons* ended its prime-time run after only one season. With only 24 episodes produced, there seemed to be nothing that would have led anyone to predict it had much potential.

That presumption soon proved to be wrong. After being booted from prime-time, ABC moved *The Jetsons* to Saturday mornings, a programming slot set aside for children's shows. Joining other animated shows on Saturday mornings (and subsequently, in syndication), repeats of the original 24 episodes of *The Jetsons* series reached an ever-expanding audience. (It was only much later in the 1980s that Hanna and Barbera produced two more seasons of the show to augment the original 24.)

An animated television series that primarily aimed at an audience of children may seem ephemeral to an examination of society's thinking about the future. However, the influence of *The Jetsons* was outsized and more substantial than its meager success on prime-time or its relegation to Saturday morning television might suggest. After years of repeats, it emerged as a veritable clearinghouse of previously presented ideas, concepts, innovations, and designs for the future. The series successfully synthesized many futuristic ideas and redistributed them. As writer Matt Novak has observed, "*The Jetsons* was the distillation of every Space Age promise Americans could muster. [It represented a] golden age of American futurism because (technologically, at least) it had everything our hearts could desire—jetpacks, flying cars, robot maids, moving sidewalks."[18]

Though its artistic style was quite cartoonish, the overall visual design of the series was memorable in and some cases striking. The backgrounds, for example, were reductionist and modern-looking, with form and function merged into a satisfying and straightforward visual vocabulary. The resulting look was consistent with much other modern animation, advertising art, and illustration of the era.

Most of the exterior shots featured sky and space in the background. The buildings in which the Jetsons lived, worked, shopped, and went to school were perched on columns thrusting high into the sky. They looked like exaggerated versions of the Space Needle. Rather than utilizing block shapes and straight lines, structures in the Jetsons' world had bold curves and patterns, and an almost aerodynamic look. Joseph Barbera later explained that this architecture of "round buildings kind of on a pedestal" was based, at least partially, on building designs that had been seen at the 1939 New York World's Fair.[19]

From the more immediate past, the architectural environment depicted in *The Jetsons* also showed the influence of the so-called Googie style—an approach to architecture that emphasizes curving, exaggerated shapes, and cantilevered design elements. That style had first emerged in California during the late 1940s and could be seen in architectural plans for coffee shops, gas stations, dry cleaners, and shopping plazas. It soon spread across the American landscape of the 1950s. It was always associated with a very modern design sense, and the use of Googie design in *The Jetsons* helped solidify a further association with the future. It suggested a world in which people would live in the skies and where they would be freed from the restraints of the past, at least metaphorically.

As Barbera said, the idea behind *The Jetsons* had been to create a world of entertaining stories filled with "ways to make our lives easier and to create what we thought was a better lifestyle."[20] It was a vision that presumed gadgetry and technology would solve many of life's problems. Beyond that, the series assumed, as Barbera also said, that people would remain more or less the same.

People may or may not change, but societies surely do. On the subject of social change, however, *The Jetsons*, like most mid-century representations of the future, foresaw very little that did not resemble the middle class of the early 1960s. The social status quo was deeply ingrained and taken for granted. The Jetsons' world was primarily a future version of white suburbia, with all the sometimes-dubious implications that this represented.

By taking many aspects of American society as given, *The Jetsons* could be pure escapism for its intended market. It was a pleasant respite from the news and tensions of the day. The future, as foretold in *The Jetsons*, rocketed past all of that. In their world, there was no Cuban missile crisis, no blossoming Civil Rights movement, no discernible evidence of social injustices, and no corporate wrongdoing. There were only simple problems and simple solutions.

Because of its continuing popularity, the series ended up influencing several generations. Decades later, it is still fondly remembered by many people. It was a cartoon fantasy, and it is highly doubtful that anyone ever took it as more than that on a conscious level. Nevertheless, its depiction of the future made a vivid impression. To many people, the sense of "innocence" that it possessed struck a chord. Although it is probably unlikely that very many people looked to an animated television show for accurate predictions of the future, *The Jetsons* still came to symbolize a bright, optimistic future, in which life's biggest problems and worries would be insignificant. Later, when it became clear that the future would not be nearly so rosy, *The Jetsons* came to represent a lost opportunity. It was a reminder, as writer Matt Novak has suggested, of "a future that never arrived."[21]

The Jetsons synthesized many ideas about the future and packaged them in a form that became widely known, but it was never an attempt to predict the coming world. In other quarters of society, however, people were working up pictures of the future with much more serious intent.

For example, in their 1962 book, Arnold Barach and the editors of *Kiplinger Magazine*'s firmly grounded their discussion of the future in reality. In *1975 and the Changes to Come,* they expanded on previous articles and made specific predictions. Covering housing, work-life, industry, education, communications, medicine, government, transportation, nuclear energy, and other topics, Barach and his associates provided clear, rational reasoning to back up their many predictions.

Plastic houses, some equipped with one-piece bathrooms made of molded plastic, were in the offing, they concluded.[22] Homes of the future would have "movable walls, luminescent ceilings, open roofs, circular rooms,"[23] and other features. Overall, much of what they predicted for housing was very similar to previous ideas. In some ways, their ideas corresponded to elements of the House of Tomorrow, the Disneyland attraction introduced in 1957.

Not surprisingly, the book also foresaw a world of shopping. They predicted that enthusiastic consumerism would continue as it had since World War II. In the future, however, it would be aided by new technologies to make it easier and more convenient. The book explains how grocery shopping might work in the future: "You will ride into a cylindrical building on a covered moving sidewalk…[that] takes you down the spiral ramp of the supermarket past every item on display."[24] All a person would need to do is select the item as it passed by, and then at the checkout point, "Every item you selected is already waiting on the counter before you." A computer would tally the order. Customers would only need to collect their purchases and pay before speeding off to presumably other consumer experiences.

As for education, the book offers much discussion about how technology, and especially computers and television, would become significant components for teaching at all levels of instruction. In one section, the book quite accurately notes the growing pressures on American education that would continue to mount from the country's rapidly increasing population.[25] After all, at the time of the book's publication, the children of the postwar Baby Boom were flooding into American schools, and the system was having trouble keeping up with the demand.

On the topic of transportation, the authors of *1975 and the Changes to Come* realized that the same population increases that were beginning to apply pressure to the educational system would also lead to another problem: increased automobile traffic. They conclude that integrated transportation systems could be possible solutions. One proposal, a rail-based system of Levacars, used vehicles that "would ride on a thin film of air a fraction of an inch above the rails" and at a speed of over 200 miles per hour.[26] Many of their other ideas about future transportation solutions reflected refinements of then-existing transportation technologies rather than startling innovations.

The chapter on communications is especially enlightening. Integrated relay-communication satellites, a technology that was making great strides at the time, receives much attention. (The idea behind this innovation was similar to a proposal that astrofuturist science-fiction writer Arthur C. Clarke, who served in the Royal Air Force during World War II, put forward in a 1945 issue of the journal *Wireless World*.) The chapter also envisions a future technology that somewhat resembles the internet. Elsewhere, the authors sound a cautionary note. Presuming that the time people spend looking at television and other screens will rise, they say, "The sociologists who fretted in the fifties about the demeaning effects of the magic screen will continue to fret."[27]

Other chapters deal with space exploration and travel, "more medical marvels," the spread of nuclear power, and, less predictably, what the authors call a looming "crisis in city hall."[28] They presumed that families would continue to relocate to suburbia, generating budgetary, infrastructure, law enforcement, and educational issues in the process. "Changes," the authors concluded, "will come with bitter political controversies,"[29] which probably is an understatement considering developments that came after that time. The book even ruminates about the strains that population growth would likely place on water resources and the environment, which was a subject often glossed over in many versions of mid-century futurism.

Overall, some of the predictions in *1975 and the Changes to Come* ended up being very much off the mark, but in other instances, its conclusions were mostly accurate. Of course, the book was only aiming to predict ten years, which was not far in the distance. In that respect, Barach and his co-authors provide a useful glimpse into how the future was envisioned in that era. Perhaps more importantly, the book provides evidence that the potential pitfalls and downsides of the future world were being contemplated more directly and more openly than had often been the case. The book still exudes confidence in the American way and in U.S. institutions. However, the authors were also starting to recognize that the

5. Peak Future

road ahead could have more obstacles and prove to be more difficult than had often been noted.

Surely, events in 1962 and 1963 drove home that point. The October 1962 Cuban Missile Crisis was arguably the most dangerous confrontation in the long Cold War between the United States and the Soviet Union. It was a stern reminder that danger was ever-present and that one wrong move could lead to mutual annihilation.

In the following summer, the March on Washington commanded national attention. In delivering his riveting "I have a dream" speech, Martin Luther King, Jr., cast a harsh light on the sorry state of race relations in America. It was more apparent than ever that the nation's long struggle for Civil Rights was poised to upend society as never before.

Then came the biggest shock of all. On November 22, 1963, John F. Kennedy, the youthful president and champion of the New Frontier, was assassinated as he rode in a parade through the streets of Dallas. That event plunged the nation into mourning. If America still possessed a sense of innocence, the assassin's bullet shattered it.

Overwhelming feelings of grief and loss overwhelmed the nation in the days after Kennedy's death. The assassination gravely wounded the national psyche, and it took time to recover. Life did go on, and America slowly picked up the pieces. With the president's passing, however, things would never seem the same. Still, it would be a mistake to underestimate the nation's resiliency after the assassination. The shock and sense of mourning were real, but so, for the time being, was the belief that this was an event the nation could endure.

Five months after John Kennedy's death, New York City hosted an event that had been in the works for several years. On April 22, 1964, more than 92,000 people passed through the gates on opening day of the 1964 New York World's Fair. Built nearly from scratch on the same site that was home to the 1939 World's Fair, it was somewhat an attempt to recapture some of the sense of wonder and enthusiasm of the 1939 event, which was fondly remembered by many people. Indeed, memories of the earlier fair had inspired the people who originally came up with the idea. As explained by Lawrence R. Samuel, a local lawyer named Robert Kopple raised the possibility of a second New York World's Fair in 1958.[30] Kopple, who worked concessions at the 1939 fair as a youth and now was the father of two young daughters, apparently thought a new Fair would benefit the younger generation. It would be a way to demonstrate that "people around the world are basically the same," he said, "and I thought it would be nice to bring the nations of the world together again."[31]

From this simple starting point, the idea gathered momentum. An organizing group began the process of soliciting support, acquiring funding, and securing the necessary approvals. Along the way, organizers selected Robert Moses to be the president of the Fair. A legendary but autocratic New York public official, he had virtually reshaped the city over many years of urban redevelopment.

Interestingly, by the time Moses was on board, the organizers of Seattle's Century 21 Exposition were already well into planning. Beyond that, there was even more competition for a world's fair since interested parties in both Washington, D.C., and Los Angeles were also exploring that idea.

The Seattle event had a head start, and it secured the blessing of the Bureau of International Expositions. Organizers in New York pressed on, however. Things seemed to look up, especially when it became clear that there was some political support for an additional exposition beyond the Seattle event. With its high-profile and international importance, New York seemed like the logical choice.

With momentum for a New York World's Fair building, Moses and the organizers dearly wanted the endorsement of the BIE. However, that organization had already given its official approval to the Century 21 Exposition in Seattle. More to the point, BIE rules strictly forbade issuing a second approval to a country that hosted such an event within the previ-

Possessing a sense of futurism similar to that of Seattle's Space Needle and even buildings in *The Jetsons* television series, the New York Pavilion at the 1964–1965 World's Fair had a striking but familiar design (iStock.com/Gary Brewster).

ous ten years. In the end, even the formidable Moses was unable to secure an exception from the BIE. So, the plan went forward without the BIE designation.

Unlike the 1962 event in Seattle, the 1964–1965 World's Fair opened at a time when the United States was dealing with many psychological and political challenges. The wound of Kennedy's passing was still fresh, and the fissures in American society that were starting to become more visible even in 1962 were increasingly evident in 1964.

It may not have been surprising, therefore, that just as had been the case in 1939, the threat of disruption due to racial issues loomed over the 1964–1965 New York World's Fair in April. At the time, many African Americans and their supporters felt that progress on racial matters was too slow. Accordingly, just before the event's first day, members of the Brooklyn chapter of the Congress of Racial Equality (CORE), a prominent Civil Rights organization, announced their intention to stage a "stall-in" on opening day. The tactic threatened to snarl traffic and disrupt the flow of people arriving and departing the event.

It appears that CORE's protest was not so much about the Fair itself as it was about the opening day speaker, Lyndon Johnson, who succeeded John F. Kennedy in the White House. Although Johnson was a Texas Democrat and widely perceived as liberal, some people thought he was moving too slowly in dismantling the barriers to equality that had long plagued the nation. As journalist Jon Margolis notes, it is not possible to be sure if the threatened demonstration caused the lower-than-expected turnout (fewer than 93,000 visitors) on opening day. However, there is little doubt that it was a contributing factor.[32] In any case, it was an inauspicious start to an event that was, according to its official theme, supposed to be promoting the idea of "Peace through Understanding." Although it aimed to create an idealized world-unto-itself in, issues from the increasingly uncertain outside world, the *real* world, were already seeping in.

Still, Johnson made his speech. And despite some heckling from the audience, the Fair opened on schedule. However, over the next two summers, the event never drew the vast numbers of people that had been predicted by the overly optimistic organizers. Nonetheless, it made a significant cultural impact, creating lasting memories for those who visited or even for people who just read about it in newspapers and magazines or learned about it from stories on television. In some ways, the New York World's Fair even overshadowed the Century 21 Exposition that had been hosted in Seattle just two years earlier. After all, the 1964–1965 Fair was in New York, the nation's largest and arguably most vibrant metropolis and its media and economic capital.

Despite the official theme of "Peace through Understanding," the

Fair squarely focused on the future. That future, however, was increasingly familiar and strongly resembled the type of consumerist, technologically oriented, gadget-driven future that popular culture promoted for many years. Still, this version of tomorrow's world appeared up-to-date and consistent with a vantage point in the 1960s. So, if the Fair's overall picture of the world to come did not seem wholly original by this time, it was nonetheless reassuring, at least for some people. That was significant since creating a sense of safety and security was essential to the type of futurism that corporate America and officialdom were aiming to create. The technology, science, and consumer conveniences were important, but for them to deliver the idealized life envisioned in mainstream mid-century futurism required something more: belief. From one perspective, it was this belief in an optimistic future that was the critical element for thinking about the world ahead. Optimism was the foundation for building the future. Exhibits in the 1964–1965 New York World's Fair suggest that its planners valiantly tried to provide that sense of confidence.

Continuing belief in the positive possibilities of technology and science was at the core of this enterprise. In the Hall of Science, many displays championed this viewpoint. Take, for example, the exhibit mounted by the U.S. Atomic Energy Commission (AEC). The AEC enthusiastically promoted peacetime use of the atom, to the extent that it initially thought about sending a mobile reactor to the Fair for public viewing.[33] That idea was discarded and instead replaced with a plan for two exhibits: one for adults and another exclusively for children.

The adult exhibit focused on the usefulness of atomic energy and on atomic research in medicine, agriculture, and other parts of life. It was overwhelmingly positive in orientation, although it did also touch upon how people could protect themselves from nuclear fallout. (Even that part of the exhibit had the benign, even dull title of "Radiation and Man," an indication of how the AEC aimed to finesse that part of the subject and neutralize it as much as possible.)

Meanwhile, an exhibit called "Atomsville, USA," also sponsored by the AEC, was geared toward children. This exhibit unabashedly "attempted to seed positive feelings about atomic energy and all its possible applications among children by turning the worst-case scenarios into a manageable and even fun exercise."[34] For example, there were hands-on displays that allowed children to pretend they were working with various radioactive materials or controlling nuclear energy devices. It was all part of the effort to present atomic energy in a fun and non-threatening way.[35]

One of the more unusual exhibits mostly geared at children involved a fully functional device called an irradiator. An account published in the *Token and Medal Society Journal* describes how it worked:

The visitor deposited his [sic] dime into a narrow machine with transparent sides. The dime rolled down a chute into the area where the coin was irradiated for a few seconds. It was then ejected via another chute, into a tray at the end of the machine. A Geiger counter nearby demonstrated the radioactivity of the silver dime.[36]

Before returning the irradiated dime to its owner, an attendant placed the coin in a small, bright blue plastic holder. Printed on the holder were the words: "Neutron Irradiated Dime, NY [sic] World's Fair 1964–1965."

It was a fascinating display, and children eagerly gathered around the strange process, waiting to receive a radioactive souvenir. At the Fair, this attraction was a novelty. However, dime irradiators had been a popular attraction in a few other venues (such as the American Museum of Atomic Energy in Oak Ridge, Tennessee) for more than a decade.

The process irradiated the coins at extremely low levels. It only worked because U.S. dimes still had a high silver content at this time. A press release about dime irradiation machines, which was issued by the American Museum of Atomic Energy (now the American Museum of Energy and Science), explained the process:

> A mixture of radioactive antimony and beryllium is enclosed in a lead container. Gamma rays from the antimony are absorbed by the beryllium atoms, and a neutron is expelled by the beryllium atom in the process.... These neutrons, having no electrical charge, penetrate silver atoms in the dime. Instead of remaining normal silver-109, they become radioactive silver-110.... Radioactive silver, with a half-life of 22 seconds, decays rapidly to cadmium-110 (in 22 seconds, half of the radioactivity in each dime is gone, in another 22 seconds half the remainder goes, and so on until all the silver-110 has become cadmium). Only an exceedingly minute fraction of the silver atoms have been made radioactive.[37]

Illustrative of widespread public acceptance of nuclear energy as a safe and secure source of energy for the future, the Atomic Energy Commission's exhibit at the 1964–1965 World's Fair included a device that irradiated dimes, which were then placed in blue holders and returned to visitors as souvenirs. The dimes, which quickly lost any traces of radiation, were popular with children (collection of the author).

The idea of making everyday items radioactive, even at very minimal levels and for a short amount of time, and then distributing them to children as trinkets may seem ludicrous today. However, in the mid–1960s, it proved to be an attention-getting part of the exhibit. The dime irradiator was an unusual gimmick in some respects. However, it probably reinforced the idea that radioactivity was fun and exciting. It demonstrated that point in a very literal way. It suggested that radiation was not something to fear. It was something people could put in their pockets and then continue with their day. That was precisely the point of view that the exhibitors were trying to promote.

NASA was also on site. Its exhibit was in an area of the Fair called the U.S. Space Park. The display included a three-and-a-half story replica of a Saturn rocket engine. Also on hand was a full-scale model of the Lunar Excursion Module, the vehicle NASA planned to use for sending astronauts from an orbiting space capsule to the lunar surface in the much-anticipated moon mission.[38]

Corporate America was also well represented at the Fair. It was clear that U.S. businesses remained very interested in promoting the techno-consumerist futurism that had been building for many years. Of the many companies represented, the American automobile industry, which was then at its zenith, seemed especially interested in making a big impression. General Motors, Ford, and Chrysler all participated.

Visitors seemed eager to visit the car manufacturer exhibits, which was not surprising given that automobiles remained a potent symbol of freedom and mobility in the United States. Indeed, in the mid–1960s, Americans generally loved their cars as much as ever. The new interstate highway system—officially the Dwight D. Eisenhower National System of Interstate and Defense Highways that was established by Congress in 1956—made it possible to experience the open road as never before. The industry had been using futurism to promote its products for years, and it enthusiastically continued along that path. The underlying presumption was that the future would revolve around the automobile.

There were more concept cars at the Fair, too. General Motors showed off a very futuristic looking model called the Firebird IV. Its sleek and silvery appearance made it look like it could easily cut through the air en route to its destination. The design seemed well-suited for a so-called automated highway of the future, where it would use self-piloting capabilities (yet to be developed) to whisk passengers to their destination in safety and comfort. Then there was Chrysler, the smallest of the "Big Three" U.S. automobile manufacturers. It brought a working version of its Turbine Car.

America's two largest carmakers, General Motors and Ford, invested heavily in their respective pavilions. The results were spectacular architectural showpieces that contained dazzling exhibits. Ford executives wanted to provide visitors with "a unique and memorable entertainment adventure."[39] To achieve that end, they worked closely with Walt Disney and his associates. Disney brought in a modernist architect, Welton Becket, whose firm had designed the distinctive Capitol Records building and others in the Los Angeles area, as well as many other buildings internationally. For the Ford pavilion, Welton designed a futuristic homage to the Ford Rotunda, a building originally constructed for the 1934 Chicago World's Fair and then reinstalled in Dearborn, Michigan, where it was destroyed by fire in 1963. Welton's design for the new pavilion, which is often called the "Wonder Rotunda," paid tribute to the recently destroyed structure by incorporating a circular design and centering the building around a ring of hundred-foot pylons.

Inside, Disney designers created the highlight of the company's exhibit, the Magic Skyway. In this attraction, visitors rode along a moving conveyor in Ford convertibles. From their comfortable seats, they witnessed displays showing highlights of human progress. Their brief journey concluded at "Space City," an elaborate model of an imaginary city far in the future.

Meanwhile, General Motors constructed a unique building that was designed by its staff. The building was a massive, rectangular structure. It featured a slanted concave canopy, rising over a hundred feet into the air over the entrance. The other end of the building featured a large dome that looked like a flying saucer. The overall effect was striking at any time of day, but especially at night when the canopy was dramatically illuminated. It set the progress-oriented, futuristic tone for the experience that GM wanted visitors to get when they entered the pavilion.

Inside, ironically, the centerpiece of the General Motors exhibit looked to the past to create an attraction that aimed to represent the future. Turning to Norman Bel Geddes' work that was so prominent at the 1939 World's Fair for inspiration, GM even resurrected the name Futurama for its main exhibit. The 1964 version, Futurama II, featured Tomorrow-Land, an attraction at which visitors sat in moving seats that took them past intricate models of a future world, as shown in large, detailed dioramas. Futurama II featured spectacular highways, of course, but it also included other futuristic scenarios such as stations and even undersea communities.[40]

Writer Gay Talese noted that visitors experienced Futurama II in several different ways, depending on their ages and backgrounds. Children, he said, saw it as "a marvelously incomprehensive joy ride," whereas teenagers experienced it as "a plausible picture of their future." For older visitors, especially those in their 60s and 70s, however, this new Futurama was "a world they will never see—trips to the moon, hotels beneath the seas, planet-hopping in lunar rovers."[41] According to Talese, many older people were sorry they would probably miss these things, but at least one person reported confidence that the world Futurama II presented would eventually arrive. Fairgoer Margaret Stine, then 66 years old, said, "If there's one thing our generation has learned, it is never to doubt the future."[42]

Futurama II was a very successful exhibit that wowed visitors. Indeed, when a reporter asked a group of Roman Catholic nuns from the neighboring state of Connecticut which part of the Fair was their favorite, they picked Futurama II. Remarkably, they made this choice even though another exhibit, which was mounted by the Vatican, included the Pietà, a world-famous sculpture by the Renaissance artist Michelangelo that had never before traveled to the Americas.[43]

Many other companies also created exhibits in which futuristic themes were at least part of the attraction. Under a giant domed building, General Electric presented Progressland. Produced with "Walt Disney's magic touch," the Carousel of Progress employed "electronic figures to enact a warm, whimsical drama."[44] More overt futurism was evident in another section of the General Electric Pavilion. It purported to show "to the general public for the very first time," an exhibit about "awe-inspiring atomic fusion—a man-made sun that may in the far-off future become man's greatest power source."

Meanwhile, the Travelers Insurance Company created a building that looked like a red flying saucer that had landed in New York City. In another exhibit, Electric Power and Light created the "Brightest Show on Earth" in a "12-billion candle power Tower of Light" building that looked as though it was from a science-fiction movie.[45]

The IBM building was yet another futuristic showpiece. A towering ovoid structure which, if appearances were any indication, could have served as the design for a moon base, the pavilion housed exhibits that focused on computers.

Along with practical displays of computer power, IBM also presented an exciting attraction called the Information Machine. The exhibit featured "an astounding special-purpose theatre experience with multiple screens and projectors and which had a pneumatically-controlled grandstand that raised the audience 50 feet off the ground."[46] The immersive show emphasized how powerful computers would soon help humanity solve problems and make sense of things. It was one of the more accurate visions at the Fair.

These and other future-oriented exhibits were not the only things on display at the Fair. However, they were much emphasized and undoubtedly helped reinforce a vision of the future that, by 1964, was already well-established and even familiar. The futurism of the World's Fair had some previously unseen nuances. However, there was little about it that visitors would not have seen before. Much of the future it portrayed was familiar from *The Jetsons*, the 1962 Seattle World's Fair, and countless advertisements, television reports, newspaper and magazine articles, books, and other sources.

The 1964–1965 New York World's Fair was not particularly successful from a financial perspective. It never generated the revenues that its backers had imagined, and it disappointed its organizers in that respect. Still, it attracted millions of visitors, many of whom would remember it as a place where mid-century futurism was on display for the world to see. Undoubtedly, its impact on young visitors was significant enough to create, for many, a fantasy-like picture of what the world might be like in the coming years.

Some of the Fair's organizers originally had hoped to recreate the same sense of optimism that they remembered from the 1939 World's Fair a generation earlier. The exposition may have met those goals to some extent, but it did not turn out to be the entryway to the future that so many of its exhibits optimistically envisioned. In looking to already-aging ideas about the future for inspiration, the Fair created what appeared to be a valiant, last-ditch effort to salvage the sense of optimism and expectations for a bright future that had captured much of the American imagination for many years. True, some predictions eventually became a reality. In terms of gadgets, technologies, and scientific breakthroughs, predictions for those sorts of things were often more or less on the mark. As for the broader notion that the future would be wondrous and bright, however, those predictions were already starting to look precarious.

A half-century after the 1964 World's Fair closed, Janice Melnick, administrator of Flushing Meadows Corona Park, was asked what she thought the Fair had meant to visitors 50 years earlier. "I think for many people, the fair represents this last moment of true optimism," Melnick said. "We were looking into the future, and the future was going to be bright. That really struck a chord with a lot of people."[47]

Jon Margolis has noted that the 1964 World's Fair was a "determined celebration of middle-class life, technology, and the shiny future that awaited all Americans."[48] If so, that celebration was premature. By the middle of the 1960s, the world as it was—a world that was unraveling in many ways—was already making rosy predictions about the world of the future appear naïve and unrealistic. A person could still watch *The Jetsons* or visit the World's Fair in Flushing Meadows and forget about such things for a while. It would be increasingly difficult to continue doing so as time marched forward.

6

The Specter of Doubt

By the 1960s, Isaac Asimov was a well-known figure in America. To some, his fame rested on the success of his popular science-fiction novels and stories, which included the influential *Foundation* series and *I, Robot*. However, he was also an academic with impressive credentials, including a doctorate in chemistry from Columbia University and a faculty appointment at Boston University, which brought him recognition as a public figure beyond the ranks of science-fiction enthusiasts. As a result, the media often looked to Asimov as someone who could usefully comment on science, technology, and the future. Such was the case in 1964 when editors of the *New York Times* asked him to speculate about what a world's fair might be like 50 years hence. The result was a fascinating article, "Visit to the World's Fair of 2014,"[1] which the paper published in the summer of 1964.

Asimov made numerous predictions, speculations, and pronouncements in his essay. Some of these proved to be mostly accurate, while others missed the mark, and still others remain difficult to classify one way or the other. Many of his predictions concerned everyday living and technologies that he thought would find their way into ordinary households. He speculated about such things as "auto-meals" (which a kitchen appliance would prepare on its own), robots that might perform routine cleaning chores, devices running on radioisotope batteries, and large, flat television screens that could be mounted on the wall.

Looking beyond the home, Asimov also speculated about the sources of energy that would power the gadget- and technology-rich future world. He presumed that an "experimental fusion power plant" would be developed, even if that technology was not entirely ready for widespread use by 2014. He also wrote of "power stations in space," which would collect the sun's rays and redirect them to earth with "huge parabolic focusing

6. The Specter of Doubt

devices." More mundanely, though somewhat more accurately, Asimov foresaw massive "solar-power stations" that would be situated "in a number of desert and semi-desert areas—Arizona, the Negev, [and] Kazakhstan."[2] Communications in the 21st century would be revolutionized by 1964 standards, according to Asimov's predictions. Even contacting people who were then living on the moon would be easy.

Not surprisingly, perhaps, Asimov's predictions seemed to presume that the corporate world of 1964 America would persist and that it would have a similar influence over life in the future. He suggested that the General Motors pavilion in a world's fair of 2014 would still be a central exhibit, though he predicted that the company's focus would change. Highways, he thought, would have "passed their peak" by 2014, but there would still be a need for multiple transportation systems to meet growing demand. For this, he discussed a rise in frictionless driving in which vehicles—presumably the descendants of 1960s-style automobiles, buses, and trucks—would employ "jets of compressed air" that would "lift land vehicles off the highways, which, among other things, will minimize paving problems." The transportation of the future would also include self-driving vehicles controlled by "robot brains." The driver would "Set for particular destinations," after which the car would "then proceed there without interference by the slow reflexes of a human driver."[3]

Although he devoted relatively little attention to the subject of space travel, Asimov did make a few predictions about that, as well. Beyond presuming some human presence on the moon, he suggested that there would be progress on sending humans to Mars. But he was realistic about how difficult the challenges of traveling to Mars would be—so much so that he speculated that even by 2014, "only unmanned [sic] ships will have landed on Mars." Still, he guessed that there would be a keen interest in sending people there and wrote that a "manned expedition will be in the works."[4]

Asimov's predictions mostly centered on developments that were to come about because of continuing advances in technology and science. As a writer with a background in both chemistry and science fiction, these, perhaps, were the types of things that readers expected from him. Some of Asimov's most interesting speculations, however, involved more than science and technology; they involved underlying beliefs and presumptions about humankind and human behavior overall. In his remarks, one can see the influence of that era's keen interest in controlling nature, for example. He also seemed to possess a faith that almost all problems could be solved by applying science and human ingenuity.

Asimov expressed a particular viewpoint regarding the relationship between humankind and nature early in his essay, although he mentioned it only in passing. "One thought that occurs to me," he wrote, "is that men [sic] will continue to withdraw from nature in order to create an environment that will suit them better." At the time, this may have seemed like an ordinary sentiment that would hardly raise any questions. However, the idea that humans can "withdraw from nature" is a more complicated and loaded proposition than Asimov may have realized. The thought that people could invent "an environment that will suit them better" presumes a very high degree of confidence in humankind's ability to make wise choices. To some, humankind's past experiences might suggest that such confidence might not be warranted.

From this one sentence, it is impossible to know the full extent of Asimov's thoughts on these matters since, after saying this, he immediately moved on to another topic. Still, the social and political world in which Asimov wrote his essay also exuded this kind of confidence. It was a time in which Western societies still regarded the natural world as a nearly inexhaustible source of material for human use—as something that was there for humans to use as they wished. The American consumer society of the mid–20th century depended on such ideas. Humans, after all, had mastered the power of the atom, and they had taken their first steps into space. Finally, they were exerting control over nature, or that, at least, seemed to be what many people thought. That there might be severe negative consequences for how humans used and interacted with the environment was not a consideration to many people's way of looking at the world and nature at the time.

Elsewhere in his article, however, Asimov seemed less sure that people would be as successful in creating their destiny as this viewpoint might have suggested. The final section of his article is primarily devoted to issues that Asimov foresaw as potentially problematic. The first of these was the world's exploding population.

In 1964, the total world population was roughly 3.2 billion. Asimov predicted that by 2014, "there is every likelihood" that that figure would rise to about 6.5 billion. That would more than double the number of humans on earth in just 50 years. (In fact, Asimov underestimated this growth; the actual number in 2014 was more than 7 billion.) In the United States alone, Asimov predicted that the population would rise from around 191 million to roughly 350 million, with "Boston-to-Washington, the most crowded area of its size on earth."[5] (Asimov over-estimated this figure; the actual number was around 319 million.)

Such growth would result in many changes, Asimov said. One consequence that he envisioned involved humankind pushing into previously under-populated or unpopulated areas, such as deserts or even undersea. (This was similar to General Motors' *Futurama II* exhibit at the 1964

6. The Specter of Doubt 129

World's Fair.) Agriculture would need increased production to feed the world's burgeoning population, too, and Asimov suggested that "processed yeast and algae" would become an everyday foodstuff. More ominously, Asimov spoke of a growing chasm between the haves and the have nots. Technology would help combat this, but it would prove to be only "partial success," he said, adding, "A larger portion than today will be deprived ... [and] further behind when compared with advanced positions of the world."[6]

"Would there be solutions?" Here, Asimov was circumspect, and he suggested that there were "only two general ways of preventing this: (1) raise the death rate; (2) lower the birth rate."[7] A higher death rate would hardly be palatable, obviously, so realistically, population control would have to be the answer, he thought. That, of course, would require influencing human behavior at a deeply personal and fundamental level.

Oral contraceptives—an invention that is arguably one of the most impactful of the 20th century—were approved for use by the FDA several years earlier in 1960. However, matters regarding reproduction remained a controversial and contested subject, especially when questions involved the role of government. Still, Asimov speculated that by 2014, "there will, therefore, be a worldwide propaganda drive in favor of birth control by rational and humane methods and, by 2014, it will undoubtedly have taken serious effect."[8]

In the early 1960s, Asimov was not alone in predicting the future, of course. Many Americans were also looking ahead. When Asimov predicted tomorrow's world for the *New York Times*, he was joining a chorus of voices who were already doing much the same.

For example, a collection of magazine essays written by Arthur C. Clarke, another astrofuturist science-fiction writer, was published as a book two years before Asimov's piece for the *New York Times*. Clarke's *Profiles of the Future*, first released as a hardcover book, brought his vision of the coming world to a broad audience when subsequently released as a mass-market paperback. Like Asimov, Clarke focused heavily on technology and communications breakthroughs—notably including space exploration and fusion reactors. Despite admirable enthusiasm, in retrospect, he was overly optimistic about the timeline. Indeed, Clarke expressed supreme confidence that scientific and technological progress would quickly triumph over whatever hurdles and impediments were ahead. Such faith was, perhaps, consistent with the times. In any case, both Clarke and Asimov brought futurism's wide-eyed sense of awe into the new decade and before an ever-widening audience.

Meanwhile, from a very different perspective, an esteemed group of scholars, officials, and specialists looked at the issue. In the summer of 1964, the popular magazine *U.S. News and World Report* conducted a long and detailed set of interviews with these individuals. The interviews were published in an extensive piece titled "What the future holds for America."[9]

Asimov and Clarke mostly looked at the future through a lens that heavily emphasized the technological and the scientific. Other considerations received far less attention. By contrast, the group interviewed by *U.S. News* placed more weight on the social and political realms of life in America. Indeed, this group considered a future that addressed the difficulties facing the nation in the mid–1960s. Such problems were envisioned as numerous. They included overpopulation, poverty, race relations, women's rights, education, the economy, national defense, and more.

The possibility of explosive population growth was a significant concern. Dr. Joseph L. Fisher, a former presidential advisor and then president of the nonprofit Resources for the Future organization, foresaw the U.S. population growing to 330 million by the year 2000, with much of the growth located in sprawling urban areas. Fisher was asked if he thought there was "likely to be a need in this country to limit births." He responded that he did not see "any need for limiting births beyond what they are." More interestingly, he said that population growth would not be "the reason for which people in this country might wish to do family planning."[10] Instead, as was characteristic of that age, he presumed that Americans would successfully negotiate around any issue that arose due to the increasing population.

His view was part of his broader beliefs that humankind possessed the power to tame or otherwise control nature and the environment. As he explained:

> "I look upon it in a broad, philosophical way, that the whole adventure of man is to understand and assume increasing degrees of control or influence over his environment and over himself. It seems to me that, as techniques and institutions permit birth control it becomes another thing in the total environment over which men [sic] can have some influence if they wish. So this is the reason I would advocate families using birth-control if they wish to."[11]

Still, demographers expected the population to rise significantly. Therefore, it was not difficult to imagine that this would apply pressure to some aspects of American life and that this would require the government's attention. Poverty, for example, was an important issue in 1964.

President Johnson had declared a "war on poverty" in his State of the Union speech in January. The fight against poverty was also a centerpiece in his plans for building what he called a "Great Society"—an idea

6. The Specter of Doubt

he articulated in a speech delivered at the University of Michigan in May of that year. In Johnson's view, the Great Society would be achieved when America was a fairer and more equitable nation. He hoped to bring this about through an ambitious series of federal legislative initiatives.

According to statistics gathered by the Bureau of the Census, Johnson was right that poverty was a major problem. The overall poverty rate in the nation in 1964 was about 19 percent.[12] However, among African Americans, Latinos, and other people of color, the number was substantially higher. So, if the United States wanted to reduce the number of people living in poverty going forward, then creating more employment opportunities and options would be needed. That, at least, was the prevailing assumption.

In his *U.S. News* interview, Dr. Homer C. Wadsworth, executive director of the Kansas City Association of Trusts and Funds, foresaw a need for increased educational opportunities. He also called for bolstering job creation in the private sector, expanding public works, increasing support for the arts, and other measures.[13] In foreseeing a world in which America successfully reduced poverty, then, Wadsworth's remarks were generally supportive of Johnson's Great Society program.

Other interviews covered a broad range of topics. For example, law professor Daniel H. Pollitt said that "race relations" and "equal protection" were the critical issues that needed to be solved. Oceanographer Roger Revelle urged more adult education to address the needs of future society. Sociologist David Riesman spoke of increasing opportunities for women. Famed anthropologist Margaret Mead recommended a universal form of national service for "fitting back together a society that's become fragmented—and fragmented in a great many ways."[14]

The comments of these and other public figures in the *U.S. News* article presented a picture that was concerned with the practical, social, and political world. This perspective was somewhat atypical in the era of mid-century futurism when consumer and technological perspectives usually dominated the conversation. In many ways, however, the commentary expressed in the *U.S. News* piece provided a dose of reality to the very lofty visions of future life that Americans had been encountering for decades.

Nothing in the *U.S. News* article suggested that a better, more comfortable, and more technologically oriented world was out of reach. Those interviewed in the magazine were largely pragmatists, however, and they did not talk about such things in any detail. Instead, they looked at existing conditions and tried to imagine a path to the future based on a realistic assessment of the present. They did not throw cold water on the familiar techno-consumerist futurism of the previous years. However, they spoke with the realization that building a positive future would require much work and that there would be many real-world complications.

In talking about the future, Isaac Asimov, Arthur C. Clarke, and the *U.S. News* panel of experts took somewhat different approaches. As a result, their views differed in some respects. Even though Asimov's and Clarke's visions probably flew higher and were less constrained by the problems of the present day than was the case with the more practical ideas offered in the *U.S. News* item, there was still a hint of concern about how a positive future could come about. Johnson's planners purposefully identified various problems that needed resolutions. But even Asimov and Clarke also realized that some issues—especially inequalities and rising population—held the potential to affect life negatively.

Since there are always problems, admitting this was not a new development, *per se*. What did seem to be new were the cracks, however small, that appeared to be forming in the previously imposing edifice of American confidence. There was not yet a crisis of faith in America or its future, but troubling signs had already appeared on the cultural landscape.

Several years earlier, a loosely connected series of books written by journalist and social critic Vance Packard started to ask serious questions about American consumerism and many aspects of postwar American society. In what is probably the most well-known of these books, *The Hidden Persuaders* (1957), Packard aimed a spotlight on the inner workings of the advertising and influence industries. When he wrote about motivational research and about the sophisticated psychological techniques that shaped public tastes and attitudes, it was likely the first time that many readers had even heard of such things. But the implications of the book were clear—the worlds of consumerism and politics were less straightforward than they previously appeared. Instead, according to Packard, the public was the target of a complex web of manipulation that subtly influenced patterns of consumption and ways of thinking. Given that the postwar futurism was tightly bound to normative attitudes about consumerism and a distinctive American view of politics, this raised a specter of doubt. Was the dominant, optimistic view of the future mostly the result of unseen manipulation?

Packard wrote many popular books. He was not a social scientist, nor was he working with any pretense of being an academic researcher. Still, he had a gift for identifying topics that would interest the public, especially regarding the mysteries of American society. As a reviewer for the *New York Times* concluded, with *The Hidden Persuaders*, Packard had produced a "fascinating book" that was "frightening, entertaining, and thought-provoking."[15] It may have lacked social science rigor, as some readers thought, but it was popular. His writings promoted a way of looking at U.S. consumerist society that differed from the boosterism of businesses and government.

Two years later, another of Packard's books, *The Status Seekers* (1959), cast a similarly skeptical eye on a different aspect of American society. In critiquing prevailing social structures, he targeted what he called "hidden barriers," which he viewed as primarily related to class. The class structure, Packard thought, caused much of the unease and unhappiness that were discernible in some quarters of American society. From his perspective, then, class was implicated in limited social mobility. It threw up roadblocks to economic success, and—to phrase it differently—to achieving the American Dream. Such suggestions, though hardly revolutionary by later standards, again diverged significantly from the sorts of ideas that Americans usually encountered in writings about the U.S. homeland.

To be sure, such notions were not eagerly embraced by all. Some objected on ideological grounds. Others, including prominent sociologists, such as Lewis Coser and Seymour Martin Lipset,[16] were critical of Packard's methods and reasoning. Admittedly, Packard was not employing the careful analysis or rigorous standards that social scientists demanded in their work. Despite its shortcomings, however, *The Status Seekers* helped popularize the view that the structure of society held some people back. That overall perspective, expressed in various forms and venues, would come to resonate with many Americans in the coming decade.

In 1960, Packard issued a volume titled *The Waste Makers*. It hit at another core aspect of postwar American life: consumption. At the time, planned obsolescence was a cornerstone of American business. This way of assuring continuing consumption was based on the idea that people would buy new things if existing products broke or if they came to believe their existing products were no longer "new" or fashionable.

The first idea is straightforward and utilitarian: If products have limited lifespans and stopped functioning, they will soon need replacing. This presumably generates predictable demand and continuing business.

The second idea—the more intriguing of the two—is based on something very different, however. Why would consumers buy a new item if they already owned a working item that adequately served the same function? The answer to this question is social—not utilitarian in the usual sense. Because even if goods remained in working order, the idea is that consumers will still replace them if they believed these products are no longer fashionable or no longer suitable for modern life. Who, according to this line of reasoning, would want to be seen with last year's model or with some out-of-fashion product? This would send the wrong message to others and, in a highly competitive society, it would also challenge one's self-esteem. Instead, the way to secure one's identity as a successful person is to consume the latest products conspicuously. This rationale was a cornerstone in consumerism of that time, and it continues to be a powerful impulse in consumer-based societies.

In his book, Packard showed that consumption had become self-justifying and self-replicating—an endless cycle. In an economy that depended in no small measure on consumer spending, there was an argument for that point of view. To expose the underbelly of consumption, as Packard did, however, was another matter altogether. It was probably not one that everyone in the society was anxious to see exposed so openly.

In these and other writings, Vance Packard explored many aspects of American life that were familiar on the surface. However, in previous years, there seldom had been as much emphasis on the downside of the consumerist society as Packard offered in his books, at least in works aimed at the general public. As for the role that this kind of thinking played in visions for the future, it may not matter whether, or to what degree, Packard was right or wrong in his assessments. What was more significant, in terms of thinking about the future, was that Packard brought attention to undercurrents in American thought that had often been drowned out. After all, for several decades, consumerism and progress were deeply entwined in messaging about the future, and Americans seldom questioned their supreme confidence in America and its institutions. If, as a reading of Packard's works might suggest, that trust was either misplaced or vastly overstated, what would that say about conjectures about an envisioned future built on these same ideas?

Packard's books raised questions about some of the basic underlying tenets in American life. He may have seemed like a gadfly to some people who were not sympathetic to his general perspective. However, in some ways, his disapproval may have seemed mild compared to what was to come. Indeed, in the early 1960s, several other writers also presented disturbing analyses of American society. A pattern was starting to emerge that was not consistent with some of the essential underlying presumptions that had fueled mainstream American futurism of the mid–20th century.

Perhaps the most explosive allegations came in Rachel Carson's *Silent Spring* (1962). In this bestselling book, the marine biologist took on the powerful pesticide and chemical industry. She leveled grave charges about the consequences of use, promotion, over-use, and misuse of chemical pesticides and about the damaging health and environmental effects that resulted. Carson had written a book called *The Sea Around Us* in 1951, and its success had earned her a measure of fame and a solid reputation. What was clear in that volume was that she knew her material well and had a strong affinity for the natural world. What is more, at a time when scientists often published works for an audience of other scientists, Carson was an extremely gifted writer. She expressed scientific concepts in compelling prose that was accessible to ordinary readers.

Silent Spring begins with a short chapter titled "A Fable for Tomorrow." It was nothing like the typically rosy visions of the future that Americans knew. Instead, Carson told the story of a mythical "town in the heart of America" and of a "strange blight" and "mysterious maladies" bringing death and ruination. What was the cause of this tragedy? "The people had done it to themselves," she wrote.[17] As becomes evident later in the book, she is talking about "the sudden rise and prodigious growth"[18] of the pesticide industry. She was deeply critical of humankind's obsession with the "control of nature"—an obsession she characterized as arrogant.[19] Though aimed at one industry, her argument, in a general sense, applied to many. She declared publicly and forcefully that modern progress came with a cost, even if that cost was often hidden. The promised future of wonder and ease, in other words, would hardly be free.

Despite widespread perceptions to the contrary, Carson never called for an outright ban on all pesticides. But she did hope that people would think more deeply about the harmful effects posed by the increasingly large-scale use of these chemicals. She wanted to eliminate, or very carefully control, the most harmful of those chemical agents. To many people, especially since that time, such a call may seem relatively straightforward and nothing unusual. To the pesticide industry in 1962, however, it was taken as an all-out assault that was not only a threat to the industry but also to the continued success of the American way of life.

The industry's displeasure resulted in a vicious series of attacks on Carson's book, her abilities as a marine biologist, and even her personhood. Some of the critical comments directed at her were highly sexist. She was called a "hysterical woman," for example, with the implication that her concerns were ill-founded and should be dismissed.[20] In another effort to discredit her, one company published a mocking rebuttal of *Silent Spring* in the October 1962 edition of its corporate magazine. Titled "The Desolate Year," the article claimed that even a single year without pesticide use would prove to be devastating.[21]

Industry efforts were ineffective in quelling the uproar that Carson's warnings provoked. The CBS television network aired an hour-long news special on the topic of pesticides not long after the controversy about *Silent Spring* began. Although weakened from her battle against the breast cancer that would take her life in 1964, Carson appeared for an interview to reaffirm her position. "Can anyone believe it is possible to lay down such a barrage of poisons on the surface of the Earth without making it unfit for all life?" she asked.

To get the other side of the story, CBS interviewed Robert White-Stevens, a scientist representing the chemical industry, for a reaction. On television, he came across as smug and dismissive. He claimed that Carson's conclusions were "gross distortions of the actual facts, completely unsupported by scientific experimental evidence."[22] More than that, he said, "If man [sic] were to faithfully follow the teachings of Miss Carson, we would return to the Dark Ages, and the insects and diseases and vermin would once again inherit the Earth." Without explicitly using the word "future," White-Stevens' argument was pesticides were essential for the bright world of tomorrow that business and industry promised to deliver.

President Kennedy was aware of *Silent Spring* and the politically charged storm surrounding it. Observing the book's notoriety, he directed the Science Advisory Committee to examine the issues Carson had raised. The committee's findings were issued the following year in a document called *The Uses of Pesticides*. The report confirmed and validated Carson's conclusions. With momentum for change building, new federal laws addressed some of Carson's most pressing concerns the next year. By then, a nascent movement was emerging—the ecology movement.

In 1965, a book from consumer advocate Ralph Nader launched a devastating attack that aimed at the heart of mid-century American business—the automobile industry. Nader's book, *Unsafe at Any Speed: The Designed-In Dangers of the American Automobile*, claimed that this industry had manufactured and sold products of dubious safety to the unsuspecting public. More than that, he argued that some of the unsafe features in American automobiles were intentional choices. Shockingly, he contended that such features were business decisions that the company had made with little regard for the consumer.

This message brazenly challenged the public standing of the esteemed automobile industry. However, Nader, whose pedigree included degrees from Princeton and Harvard, had little use for American car culture or the evocative symbolism of the automobile. Indeed, he held a decidedly different view. "For more than half a century," he wrote, "the automobile has brought death, injury, and the most inestimable sorrow and deprivation to millions of people." Statistics gave credence to Nader's point of view. He cited "$8.3 billion in property damage, lost wages, and insurance overhead expenses."[23]

More disturbing than that, the number of highway fatalities from automotive accidents had been trending upward for some time. In 1965, the year of the book's publication, Federal Highway Administration records show that more than 47,000 people died from injuries sustained in such accidents in just that year.[24]

6. The Specter of Doubt

According to Nader, the situation would only get worse without some bold and direct action. He also claimed that powerful forces stood in the way of making the changes necessary for improved highway safety. Those forces were primarily institutional. "A great problem of contemporary life," he noted, "is how to control the power of economic interests which ignore the harmful effects of their applied science and technology."[25] The "traffic safety establishment,"[26] as he called it, represented the interests of the automobile manufacturers and other businesses and groups aligned with it. Primarily for that reason, he said, laws and regulations too often benefited this "establishment" rather than the driving public. The result was an unacceptably high cost to the public, in terms of both lives and dollars, all to the benefit of industry profits.

Nader was launching a direct attack on the mighty automobile industry—an industry that had spent years promoting itself as part of the future. One of Nader's most damning statements appears at the end of his text:

> There are men in the automobile industry who know the technical capability and appreciate the moral imperatives. But their timidity and conformity to the rigidities of the corporate bureaucracies have prevailed. When and if the automobile is designed to free millions of human beings from unnecessary mutilation, these men, like their counterparts in universities and government who knew of the suppression of safe automobile development yet remained silent year after year, will look back with shame on the time when common candor was considered courage.[27]

In concluding his book, Nader left readers to consider a perspective that was stunning within the context of that era. He suggested that the most powerful and influential industry in the United States knew how to make cars safer, but that industry had decided not to do so. If the wondrous consumer-oriented future required a deep faith in American institutions, then this was a potentially devastating realization.

The allegations made in *Unsafe at Any Speed* prompted enormous displeasure across the automobile industry overall and at General Motors, in particular. GM officials had good reason to be unhappy: Nader used the Corvair, one of the company's popular models, as the primary example of automobile safety lapses.

According to news accounts and court records, GM officials allegedly went to considerable lengths in trying to minimize the public relations damage from the book. In a subsequent lawsuit that Nader filed against GM in 1966, the author asserted that the automotive giant had violated his privacy rights by hiring a private investigation firm. He alleged that GM officials instructed the investigators to search for potentially compromising information about him. This action, Nader said, was part of "a campaign of intimidation against him in order to suppress ... [Nader's] criticism and prevent disclosure of information' about its [GM's] products."[28]

The charges cast General Motors in a negative light and drew even more adverse attention to the company. According to a document issued by the Court of Appeals of New York, Nader's lawsuit alleged that private investigators working for GM questioned his acquaintances regarding his "religious, social, ... racial and religious views" and about "his sexual proclivities and inclinations, and his personal habits." They also, according to claims in this document, "kept him under surveillance in public places for an unreasonable length of time," "made threatening, harassing and obnoxious telephone calls," and "tapped his telephone" as part of what the lawsuit called "a 'continuing' and harassing investigation." However, the most explosive charges were substantially more lurid than these allegations. The suit, as summarized by the Court of Appeals, claimed that the investigators "caused him to be accosted by girls [sic] for the purpose of entrapping him into illicit relationships."[29]

The case dragged on for a while. At one point, the private investigator apparently had enough, and he decided to provide evidence against his former client, General Motors. He then submitted a tape recording of a phone conversation that seemed to support some of Nader's charges. On the tape, an attorney for General Motors could be heard saying that the company wanted "to get something, somewhere, on this guy [presumably Nader] to get him out of their hair and to shut him up."[30]

Eventually, the suit was settled out of court, with General Motors admitting no wrongdoing. Nader received $425,000. Still, the case had compromised General Motors' reputation. As stated in an article published by the *New York Times*, Nader "got an apology for harassment" from the former president of General Motors even though he "denied that his company had intended any."[31] When interviewed by a reporter at the *New York Times* for this same article, the investigator involved "denied that he had accosted Mr. Nader with girls [sic] who were sex lures or made threatening or obnoxious telephone calls."

The exact details of what happened may never be fully known. However, it appears that in seeking to deflect criticism of its automobiles and business practices, General Motors may have inadvertently exacerbated the situation. Nader's allegations about the automobile industry helped kindle doubt where there appears to have been little beforehand. Regardless, *Unsafe at Any Speed* was a bestseller and earned Ralph Nader a prominent position on the public stage. The notoriety of his book and the charges it leveled would play a leading role in pushing Congressional action on auto safety, resulting in the National Traffic and Motor Vehicle Safety Act, which Lyndon Johnson signed into law in 1966.

6. The Specter of Doubt

Books by Vance Packard, Rachel Carson, Ralph Nader, and others provide some insight into the increasing doubt that was entering mainstream American life. Concurrently with their writings, moreover, an increasing number of magazine and newspaper articles, as well as television and radio news reports, also raised questions about the trustworthiness of American business and government.

Already, the Civil Rights Movement had begun to chisel away at the edifice of American confidence (at least among the white middle class), making it evident that the country and its institutions had failed a substantial proportion of its citizens through systematic racism. Within a few years, the rising women's movement, gay rights movement, and the large-scale opposition to the U.S. war in Vietnam, which began ramping up in 1964, would plunge American society into crisis. As public fissures developed and widened, the question remained as to what effect that would have on visions for future life.

Still, on balance, Americans remained optimistic. For the most part, they continued to possess faith in their society. In polling data from that time, for example, 76 percent of a random sample of Americans agreed that they could "trust the government in Washington to do a good job" either "just about always" or "most of the time."[32] This result was not very different from the results of a 1958 poll when the question was first asked. By 1970, things would be very different, with only 54 percent of respondents expressing similar confidence. A few years later, in 1974, during the Watergate crisis, the number dropped precipitously to only 36 percent. By 1980, only 25 percent of respondents agreed that they could trust the government "just about always" or "most of the time. It was nearly a complete reversal from the high approval rating of 1964."[33]

The story of Americans' disillusionment with their government—especially concerning the dramatic loss of faith in the 16 years after 1964—is one that has had ramifications well beyond that timeframe. Although the approval would improve slightly from time to time, at no time in the rest of the 20th century would the American public ever again reach 50 percent confidence, let alone surpass that figure, according to Pew Research. (The closest it would get would be in the middle of the Reagan years, at 44 percent in 1984.)[34]

The Pew Study also traced what it called the "national mood" over many years. As might be expected at a time when trust in government ran high, in 1964, more than 60 percent of respondents reported a positive mood about "the state of the nation." However, this number, too, plummeted over the following decade, dropping to a low of under 40 percent in 1974, before slightly recovering at various times throughout the rest of the century.[35]

Pew also examined "confidence in institutions" overall. When first gauged in 1967, confidence hovered near 50 percent. By the end of the 1970s, it dropped to under 40 percent.[36]

This dizzying array of statistics can be challenging to understand fully. As with all statistics, people might disagree about how closely they reflect reality and what they mean. However, these numbers suggest a portrait of the American mindset of the mid–1960s that is consistent with the events that transpired and with the social conditions that emerged at the time. It seems safe to conclude that the confidence that most Americans possessed just a few years earlier was starting to erode. Many things that the public previously took for granted increasingly seemed in doubt. Americans wondered if "progress" was always a good thing. They worried about its downsides. They began to question whether big business and the government truly had the public's interests at heart. More broadly, they began to doubt that American institutions could solve the nation's many problems. The bright and optimistic future required faith in those kinds of things. If they were in doubt, maybe the future as in doubt, too.

Second-guessing the future did not occur all at once or just because of one or two things, of course. Instead, it was a slower process—an unraveling. Yet, but the time NASA completed its moon mission in 1969, American confidence had already faded. Even that achievement was insufficient to jolt the American outlook back to where it had been or to restore the confidence that Americans continued to lose. It was a remarkable shift that affected how people envisioned the future.

The nation had not yet fully succumbed to the dour mood that was gathering steam, however. Some evidence of continuing optimism appeared in new science-fiction television shows. The networks aired several programs in the genre. Two of the most popular of such shows, *Lost in Space* and *Star Trek*, were strongly connected to mid-century futurist thinking, though in different ways.

CBS premiered *Lost in Space* in the autumn of 1965. The show adapts the basic story of *The Swiss Family Robinson*, a 19th-century novel by Johann David Wyss. In Wyss' book, the Robinson family becomes shipwrecked in the Caribbean while traveling to Australia. *Lost in Space* straightforwardly updates the exploits of the shipwrecked Robinson family by resetting their adventures in outer space. Although the rockets and futuristic technology dramatically differ from Wyss' story, the stories are otherwise similar. Indeed, the series was mainly a traditional adventure show with just a veneer of the future. It features familiar, if updated, stories.

Nonetheless, some elements in *Lost in Space* overtly connected the show to mid-century futurism. There were, for example, superficial similarities with *The Jetsons* animated comedy. The pastel-colored,

6. The Specter of Doubt 141

quasi-jumpsuit costumes that the Robinson family wore throughout the series would have been familiar in the Jetsons' world. The colorful apparel, which looked bright and modernist on color televisions of the era, undoubtedly also reminded viewers they were watching a story set in a future world.

The Robinsons' spaceship would have been at home in *The Jetsons*, as well, but its appearance was also reminiscent of other futuristic designs. The spacecraft on the show had the general look of a home that had been designed in 1960 by architect John Lautner, one of the early exponents of the Googie style. Lautner's building, known as the Chemosphere, had an octagonal structure and was perched on a thick concrete column overlooking Los Angeles. Although the Robinson spacecraft was round, rather than octagonal, the overall silhouettes of the two designs were quite similar. The fictional spaceship, like the costumes, read as futuristic at the time. However, it was futurism based on earlier futurism. There was little about it that was unique.

Lost in Space's familiar, almost retro type of futurism could also be found in the robot character, which was one of the series' main protagonists. The robot was designed by Robert Kinoshita, who had previously been one of the principal designers of Robby the Robot for the 1956 science-fiction movie *Forbidden Planet*. Robby was probably the most well-known robot of the American screen before the release of *Star Wars*. Not surprisingly, when Kinoshita designed a new robot for *Lost in Space*, he included several features from his earlier creation. Each robot, for example, had a plexiglass "head," a stout metallic torso, and bellows-style legs (which made it easier to maneuver on screen). The *Lost in Space* robot was imposing, but it was also cumbersome, bulky, and somewhat old-fashioned—a callback to the futuristic visions of an earlier era, which in some ways, it was. This series reinforced this link to the past when producers took *Forbidden Planet*'s Robby the Robot out of storage and used it alongside *Lost in Space*'s robot in one of the series' later episodes.

If American society was starting to lose confidence in the techno-consumerist futurism of mid-century, there was little evidence of this in *Lost in Space*. Separated from the rest of humanity, the Robinsons deal with the problems they encounter with the traditional male-centric heroism, assisted on occasion by futuristic gadgetry. Meanwhile, there is no evidence of the issues that real Americans faced in the mid–1960s. The series did not question the social roles of women, the dominant whiteness of its perspective, or the potential downsides of modern innovations.

The show's characters, for example, are mostly stereotypes of characters that appeared in countless movies and television shows. The series' main villain is a character named Dr. Smith, who was entertainingly portrayed by Jonathan Harris. Initially a saboteur, Smith soon evolves into a more comic than dangerous nemesis, whose incredible cowardice undermines his evil intentions. The main hero, meanwhile, turns out not to be the elder Robinson, who commands the mission, or the military attaché onboard. Instead, the series largely focuses on Will Robinson (played by Bill Mumy), the commander's young son.

Meanwhile, Will's mother and two sisters, nominally main characters in the series, seldom do anything that challenges the stereotypes that permeated television at the time. They occasionally perform acts of bravery and sometimes exhibit quick-witted abilities in a crisis. However, the female characters mostly represent a traditional view, which is interesting, considering that many Americans were starting to question this status quo around this time.

Overall, then, the storyline of *Lost in Space* mildly recalls the New Frontier ethos of just a few years earlier. However, the series' orientation seems to be as much a reflection of 1950s futurism as it was a product of the mid–1960s.

When producers of CBS television's *Lost in Space* needed a robot for the series, they consulted with Robert Kinoshita, who designed the robot for the classic 1956 science-fiction film *Forbidden Planet*. The *Forbidden Planet* robot, shown here in a mass-produced toy version that was manufactured some years later, was probably the most recognizable robot on the big or small screen until the debut of *Star Wars* in 1977 (iStock.com/daboost).

If *Lost in Space* has tenuous connections to the American Frontier Myth and the New Frontier ethos, such an association is far more evident in another series, *Star Trek*. That show premiered on the NBC network a year after *Lost and Space* began airing on CBS. William Shatner, in the role of Captain James T. Kirk, announces as much in the opening credits when he says, "Space, the final frontier." Indeed, the entire storyline of the series involves an exploratory mission, a supposedly peaceful voyage in the pursuit of "strange new worlds" and "new life and new civilizations."

When he initially pitched the series to the network, creator Gene

Roddenberry explained that the show would be like a science-fiction version of *Wagon Train*. The older show was a popular Western that aired first-run episodes from 1957 to 1962. In basing *Star Trek* on that show, Roddenberry established a connection between his series, which takes place in the 23rd century, and the mythology of the Old West and the American Frontier. Indeed, even a cursory consideration reveals that such connections, while sometimes muted and transformed, are not hard to find. The crew of the *Enterprise* may be on a peaceful mission, as the series takes pains to emphasize at many points, but it is also doing so aboard a heavily armed, state-of-the-art warship.

Still, *Star Trek* exhibits some aspects that run counter the presumptions of the Frontier myth. The crew of the *Enterprise*, for instance, are bound by a "Prime Directive," which mandates that they cannot interfere with the development of any of the civilizations they encounter. (At the time, audiences would have realized that this was the opposite of what the United States was doing as it prosecuted the war in Vietnam.) It is true that many of the civilizations the crew encounters are less developed than the technologically advanced Federation, which the crew serves. However, there are also episodes in which the crew of the *Enterprise* discovers that their state of development lags far behind some of those they encounter. (In an era before Colonialism was widely discredited, this also stood in stark contrast to central ideas in Westerns and the Frontier myth, more generally.)

As commander of the Starship *Enterprise*, Kirk leads a diverse crew, which was a remarkable feature for a network series of that era. The ship's officers include the half-human alien science officer, Spock, as well as men and women from a variety of racial and ethnic backgrounds. As scholar Emily S. Rosenberg has observed, "the interrelationships within groups of people on small crafts hurtling through space raised issues of gender, race, and class, allowing discussions relating to the contemporaneous civil rights and feminist movements."[37]

This diversity was a significant step towards broader representation in broadcast television, even though it was an early attempt and not entirely unproblematic, especially regarding lingering sexism. Still, the fact that the series even tried to present a diverse cast was a break from what was typical in television, the popular medium of the day. That break may not have been complete, and it may not have always been successful. In terms of diversity, however, *Star Trek* was forward-looking in a way that *Lost in Space*, which was a much more traditional show in such matters, was not.

One of *Star Trek*'s most famous scenes occurs in a 1968 episode titled "Plato's Stepchildren." In a groundbreaking television moment, it shows the white Captain Kirk kissing the African American communications officer, Uhura (played by Nichelle Nichols). It was a scene that would have been unimaginable on network television in an epoch before society's changing attitudes in the wake of the Civil Rights movement.

In some ways, *Star Trek* reflected traditional ideas and values. However, if often veered in another direction, especially in episodes that confront social issues. Indeed, a discernible strand of social consciousness appears throughout the series, which is what the show's creators wanted all along. Indeed, Roddenberry and the show's writers intentionally set out to challenge the status quo of the era and to comment, via allegory and science-fiction guises, some of the injustices they saw around them. As one writer concludes, *Star Trek*'s makers were "the original Social Justice Warriors.... For every destination that the *Enterprise* crew visited was, in essence, an exaggerated microcosm of different aspects of the American social condition: our fears, our aspirations, our most serious challenges at the time."[38]

The social commentary angle added a very current element to the series. In another way, however, *Star Trek* was perhaps somewhat less reflective of America's changing attitudes about the present and future. Indeed, *Star Trek* retained, and even glorified the long-held faith that rational problem-solving, scientific discovery and technological innovation could solve almost any problem, social or otherwise.

In one sense, the series is perhaps a last-gasp expression of the bright, optimistic type of futurism that the broader society no longer was sure it still believed. Technology and scientific discovery hold an elevated, unquestioned place in the show. The world of *Star Trek* is filled with futuristic gadgets that would have been at home in Arthur Radebaugh's *Closer Than We Think* comic strip a few years earlier. In the social realm, the society is meritocratic, and economic disparity is long-gone, to the extent there is no apparent need for money. The future, as *Star Trek* presents it, is progress as envisioned in the middle of the 20th century, writ large. Scientific problem-solving and technological innovation made it all possible.

Star Trek was a highly optimistic, even idealistic television series that aired during one of the nation's most divisive and troubled periods. However, despite its later popularity, it was not a hit at the time. The series struggled to reach the broad audience that the network desired, and NBC executives seriously considered canceling it on more than one occasion. They only renewed the series for a third and final season after a letter-writing campaign led by its most ardent fans.

By the time *Star Trek*'s third season went into production, the network slashed the budget and moved it to an unfavorable time slot on Friday nights. The situation did not look promising. Several months later,

6. The Specter of Doubt

NBC unceremoniously canceled the series. The last original episode aired on June 3, 1969. After that, it limped along with summer reruns until disappearing from NBC's schedule entirely in the fall.

Gene Roddenberry's series was never intended to be a realistic prediction of any specific future. Depictions of the future throughout popular culture seldom have that purpose. However, this is not to say that it was not trying to communicate something important about what the future could be. On that front, *Star Trek* made a bold statement, if not exactly a prediction. The series was an impassioned argument that humankind had within its grasp the tools to build a tomorrow that would be glorious and awe-inspiring. It could be something that people could embrace and anticipate with faith and confidence. Indeed, the "five-year mission" of the *Enterprise* represented just such a journey.

Within a few years, the series re-emerged as a successful syndicated show, with the original 79 episodes gaining new life in reruns. Later, numerous screen sequels and reboots further established *Star Trek* as an enduring pop-culture phenomenon. From a vantage point in 1969, however, all of that was yet to come. In any case, NBC's cancellation of *Star Trek*

In some respects a last-gasp expression of mid-century futurism, the original *Star Trek* television series projected a strong sense of optimism during years when American society was becoming increasingly pessimistic. The show featured many futuristic gadgets, as well as the distinctively designed *Enterprise*, the crew's huge spaceship, a model of which is depicted in this photograph (iStock.com/BrendanHunter).

came at a time when America was reaching a breaking point. Intergenerational conflict, the war in Southeast Asia, rising political discord, and other crises had shattered much of America's confidence.

Despite many downbeat conditions in the real world during the early summer of 1969, there was one event to which Americans could look with anticipation. Indeed, after nearly a decade of intense effort, NASA was preparing to launch three carefully trained astronauts for the boldest trip ever attempted.

7

Fading Tomorrows

In the middle of *Star Trek*'s original run on NBC television, Stanley Kubrick's imposing science-fiction film, *2001: A Space Odyssey*, brought a mesmerizing depiction of spaceflight to theaters. Unlike *Star Trek*, this was no cheaply made production with bargain-basement special effects. Instead, *2001*—based on Arthur C. Clarke's 1951 story, *The Sentinel*—effectively conveyed the sense of awe and wonder that Americans had long associated with space travel. Kubrick's film was unlike *Star Trek* in other ways, too. Its depiction of humankind's future in space had little of the aspirational optimism that was foundational to Gene Roddenberry's television show. Instead, *2001* was a sober and even foreboding affair. If Roddenberry envisioned a mostly promising tomorrow, Kubrick looked ahead with considerably more uncertainty and trepidation.

In the years since its release, *2001* has acquired a lofty reputation. Upon its premiere, however, many people had mixed feelings about it. Few, however, contested its brilliant visual design. Indeed, critics generally agreed that *2001* was a masterful representation of space travel in the not-too-distant future. The director spent many months and a small fortune in creating special effects that would render a journey to the moon and then to Jupiter in a convincing fashion. "There can be little doubt," wrote *Variety* critic Robert B. Frederick, "that the special effects in *2001* are the equal of any the screen has come up with."[1] To be sure, the film realistically depicted a "fantastic array of spaceships" and highly realistic "planetary shots," as Frederick noted. Kubrick showed audiences the vastness of space in a way that evoked feelings of awe and wonder.

While the film's imagery earned much praise, its story—its "plot, so-called," as Frederick described it—was less well-received and confused many people. Briefly stated, the narrative involves the discovery of an ancient monolith that was buried on the moon long before humans were capable of space travel. When experts conclude that the mysterious object originated in the vicinity of Jupiter, the government sends astronauts on a secret mission to investigate the monolith's origins. During the long and lonely journey, the spaceship's computer, HAL, malfunctions and then attempts to kill the crew.

As the one surviving crew member eventually makes his way to Jupiter, he is "subjected to a wild celestial ride through a series of galaxies that create a psychedelic effect."[2] From this point on, *2001* mostly leaves straightforward storytelling behind. The film ends with a series of surrealistic shots depicting the astronaut near the end of his life before finally switching to a shot of an embryo orbiting the earth, at which point the proceedings come to an end.

Visually, Kubrick's film was compelling. However, *2001*'s final segment was very idiosyncratic and hard to follow. Some viewers found it unsatisfying. The open-ended and cryptic nature of the story puzzled and even frustrated some viewers. Still, it was a film by Stanley Kubrick, whose previous films (including *Dr. Strangelove*) were highly regarded. It attracted much attention despite having a storyline that many viewers found to be inscrutable.

The film exudes a generally serious tone, but it possesses some wry elements that speak to the techno-consumerist futurism that had been prominent in previous years. These elements occur early in the story when an investigator travels to the moon for a conference about the mysterious object. In the year 2001, as depicted in the film, space travel to the moon appears to be more or less a routine matter. As the camera lingers on shots capturing the minutiae of the spaceship's voyage, viewers see that space travel in 2001 is very corporate.

As Stephanie Schwam discusses in her informative book about the film, Kubrick's associates made an organized effort to round up corporate input and sponsorship for *2001* during production.[3] In a lengthy space flight sequence that focuses on a spaceship called the *Orion*, the corporate logo of Pan Am airlines is plainly, even blatantly visible. Pan Am (officially Pan American Airways) was one of the most famous corporate brands in the world at the time. The inclusion of this and other corporate brands in the film reinforced an association between large businesses and the future. (Although the considerable on-screen presence of Pan Am in *2001* surely seemed to be a statement that the company would play a role in the future, that outcome was not to be. The company went out of business in the early 1990s.)

Other corporate connections appear in the film, too. A traveler headed to the moon stays at a Hilton Hotel onboard a space station. A sign for a space-station branch of the Howard Johnson's restaurant business (a chain that was once nearly ubiquitous across the United States) also appears in the background. The American Bell Telephone Company's logo is also visible on a computer screen.

IBM, which was very active in the computer business by this time, was also part of the film. In perhaps the most prophetic scene in the movie, an astronaut reads the news using an IBM Newsreader while having breakfast. (This fictional newsreader device looks very much like the tablet computers, such as Apple's iPad device, that became popular consumer products several decades later.) The IBM logo is visible in many other scenes, as well.

One of the main "characters" in *2001* is the deranged computer, HAL. Given that IBM, which was then the most recognized computer manufacturer in the world, helped with the film, Kubrick was aware that if HAL were associated with the company in the minds of audiences, the company might be regarded in a negative light. Recently published correspondence suggests that Kubrick asked one of his assistants about the matter. Kubrick is quoted as saying, "Does I.B.M. know that one of the main themes of this story is a psychotic computer?... I don't want to get anyone in trouble."[4] Ultimately, the IBM logo not used in a way that identified HAL with the company, though some viewers still have made the association. In any case, with HAL going awry in the film's storyline and murdering several members of the crew, the future that Kubrick depicted was clearly not one in which computers could be trusted.

2001: A Space Odyssey gave audiences an auteur's version of space adventure. In some respects, however, it was the latest in a long line of science-fiction movies showing the grandeur of space and the imagined dangers of encountering extraterrestrial life forms. Kubrick adds many layers and nuances, as well as some elements from the horror film genre, that elevate his film above earlier science-fiction movies of this sort. However, the film's narrative—true to its origins in Clarke's original story from the early 1950s—is mostly in that same tradition. Its depiction of routine space travel, in particular, reflects the same sorts of messages that had been ideas promoted in popular culture for many years.

Kubrick's primary, though somewhat indirect influence on thinking about the future was probably as much in the film's astonishing visual depiction of space and space travel as in anything to do with its plot. In that respect, too, it was somewhat a throwback since it was similar to imagery that was already familiar to the public. Seasoned space-artist Robert McCall provided paintings for the posters that promoted the movie. Indeed, Kubrick's cinematic depictions of space seemingly owe much to a visual vocabulary that McCall and other artists had been perfecting for many years.

Meanwhile, NASA was making enormous strides in real-world space travel. Fifteen months after *2001*'s theatrical release, the public had an opportunity to witness the culmination of the decade-long quest to send an American astronaut to the moon. On July 20, 1969, NASA's Apollo 11's lunar module, carrying NASA astronauts Neil Armstrong and Edwin "Buzz" Aldrin, safely landed on the lunar surface. The realization of John F. Kennedy's dream was at hand.

Not long after setting down in the moon's Sea of Tranquility, Armstrong positioned a television camera to beam images back to earth. A few moments later, he stepped onto the powdery lunar surface, telling a worldwide audience, "That's one small step for man, one giant leap for mankind." It was a moment that very few of the people who heard or saw it as it was broadcast live back on earth would ever forget.

Twenty minutes later, Aldrin joined him on the surface, and the world watched the two astronauts with intense interest. Armstrong and Aldrin had a busy schedule. Some of the activities that NASA planned were symbolically significant. Most prominently, the astronauts planted an American flag on the moon's surface. Other tasks were scientific and technological. The astronauts gathered rock samples, deployed experimental equipment, and photographed the surface. Meanwhile, Michael Collins, the third member of the Apollo 11 crew, orbited overhead in the command module, awaiting their return.

The astronauts' moonwalk was exciting, but it was also brief. Little more than two hours expired before Armstrong and Aldrin climbed back aboard the Eagle. After resting for several hours, they prepared for their return journey. Then, only 21 hours and 36 minutes after landing, the Eagle lifted off, en route to a rendezvous with Collins in the command module that was circling overhead.

On July 24, three days after heading back to earth, the Apollo 11 command module carrying the three astronauts splashed down in the Pacific Ocean. Less than a decade had passed since John F. Kennedy had challenged the nation to send Americans to the moon and return them safely to earth. Apollo 11's success was a remarkable achievement that seemed impossible just a few decades earlier. The futuristic dreams of yesterday had become a reality.

From a vantage point many years later, it is easy to forget how dangerous and uncertain the flight to the moon was. In most respects, the Apollo 11 mission was a spectacular success, but it was not without glitches. Although NASA had carefully prepared, preliminary testing could go only so far for a mission of such complexity. Disastrous unforeseen consequences remained possible. (That fact would become apparent a year later when an oxygen tank on Apollo 13 failed. The resulting crisis endangered the lives of the crew and forced NASA to cut the mission short.) Upon the

7. Fading Tomorrows

successful conclusion of the Apollo 11 mission, however, Americans celebrated. For a generation, human travel to the moon and beyond had been a hallmark of futuristic dreams. Those dreams were now a reality.

The Apollo 11 mission was a historic achievement, and its influence and effects were genuinely significant. Three astronauts journeyed to the moon and back safely, and nothing would take away from their bravery and skill. Nor could anything take away from the contributions made by thousands of hard-working people involved in that ten-year quest. A dozen years after Sputnik, American anxieties about space superiority finally could be put to rest. The United States had won the race to the moon.

However, it was a difficult time for America, and NASA's moon landing success would not change that. There were too many other concerns for Americans to become preoccupied with drawn-out jubilation. Indeed, many circumstances diverted Americans' attention away from the success

Less than a decade after John F. Kennedy challenged the nation to send a crewed mission to the Moon, American astronauts Neil Armstrong and Edwin "Buzz" Aldrin were walking on the lunar surface. Only twelve years after the Soviets stunned the world with their tiny Sputnik satellite, the successful Apollo 11 mission was evidence of NASA's astonishingly rapid progress in space science and technology. This photograph, which was taken by Armstrong, the mission commander, shows Aldrin on the Moon's surface on July 20, 1969 (NASA).

of the moon landing. For one thing, the race to the moon was over, but the Cold War was not. Tensions continued.

Furthermore, NASA's achievement came in the middle of the second-deadliest year for U.S. troops in Vietnam.[5] The war by then was deeply controversial, and the conflict appeared to be endless to many people. Large-scale protests were increasingly common across the country, further dampening America's quickly eroding confidence.

Added to this, America's increasing ambivalence about consumerism and its deepening distrust of U.S. institutions, generally, were two concerning developments. Then there were the shattering assassinations of civil rights icon Martin Luther King, Jr., and presidential candidate Robert F. Kennedy in rapid succession. These traumatic murders set the nation on edge just months before the moon landing. Thus, although the moon landing may have been the realization of a dream, that realization came in the context of rising skepticism and discouragement.

Most of the perceived threats of the Cold War had come from the outside. Now, however, discontent and anxieties often originated from within the nation's borders. Americans were losing faith in their own country's ability to solve its many pressing problems. Enthusiasm for the future was starting to fade, despite NASA's success. Ironically, NASA's spectacular achievement represented not only a beginning but also the end of an era—a game already won, yesterday's challenge completed. For much of the public, it did not necessarily say much about the future.

Given this context, it was perhaps less surprising than might have been expected when public enthusiasm for future moon missions began to wane. In Congress, which had always been aware of the enormous financial costs, support also faded. With so many earth-bound problems, many people felt that the nation's attention and resources should focus on issues closer to home.

After Apollo 11, NASA would send four more missions to the moon—one in December of 1969, two in 1971, and two in 1972. (The near-disaster of Apollo 13 in 1970 was the reason for the gap between 1969 and 1971.) After that, the subject of sending more humans to the moon came up occasionally, but little would come of it. NASA redirected its attention to its Challenger program and others that, to the general public, seemed less ambitious and less exciting that the quest to reach the moon had been. Arguably, no serious plans for Americans returning to the moon emerged until the 21st century. If space travels beyond a relatively conservative close-earth orbit were to be a big part of the future, as much mid-century futurism had envisioned, then the future was stalled.

More accurately, an optimistic future seemed less plausible. In the place of a once-utopian vision, new perspectives began to take hold. As

7. Fading Tomorrows

Americans considered the success of NASA's mission to the moon, ideas about space were evolving in popular culture. Meanwhile, a new wave of professionally minded futurists already had arrived on the scene.

In general, this wide-ranging group of futurists sought to bring the study of the future into the realm of systematic and scientific analysis. In a way, they aimed to "domesticate the future and bring it under control through a general theory of prediction," as one scholar has observed.[6]

These futurists brought a culture of academic-style problem-solving to bear in creating their visions of tomorrow's world. Ironically, they rose to prominence just as Americans were seemingly losing faith that their problems could be solved. Still, the new futurists' voices were influential in shaping conceptions in the late 1960s and early 1970s.

This goal-oriented, often institutionally oriented approach to futurism had been underway for many years. The RAND Corporation was one such organization where it thrived. Substantially before becoming well known to the general public, the organization developed expertise in scenario planning and defense forecasting beginning shortly after World War II. As part of the Douglas Aircraft Company, the RAND Corporation (the name derives from the phrase, "Research and Development") provided interdisciplinary research services and guidance that defense officials took seriously.

In 1946, for example, it produced a technical report called *Preliminary Design of an Experimental World-Circling Spaceship*. Its sponsor was Major General Curtis Lemay, who was then heading the U.S. Army Air Force.[7] In considerable detail, the report outlined "an engineering analysis of the possibilities of designing a man-made satellite" and "concluded that modern technology has advanced to a point where it now appears feasible to undertake the design of a satellite vehicle."[8]

Two years later, RAND was hired to "manage and integrate" the Air Force's satellite program.[9] In the process of doing this type of work, RAND researchers sometimes developed futuristic concepts, as was the case with weather satellites.[10] Significantly, RAND reports were classified and only available to defense officials at the time. Consequently, most of RAND's work remained hidden from public view.

RAND separated from Douglas to become an independent think tank in 1948, but it continued to perform essential and frequently classified work for the military. It was instrumental in producing research and analysis that led to the creation of the United States' ballistic missile program in 1955. That led to the eventual development of Thor, Atlas, and Titan rockets and to new technology that would be essential to later NASA programs.[11]

One of RAND's significant contributions to the study of the future was the Delphi Method, which dates from the 1950s. It was designed to be used in dangerous situations amid the ongoing threat of thermonuclear war, but it also had broader potential. As later described in RAND documentation, "The method entails a group of experts who anonymously reply to questionnaires and subsequently receive feedback in the form of a statistical representation of the group response.... The goal is to ... arrive at something closer to expert consensus."[12] The Delphi Method thus aimed to reduce uncertainty and crystallize expert opinion for practical use. The methodology proved to be very appealing to government and business leaders in the years to come.

By the early 1960s, RAND was becoming well-known to the general public, especially as newspapers and other media stories increasingly cited RAND as a source of expert opinion. The organizations' work on Cold War strategies and on managing the dangers of potential nuclear war earned it recognition in those dangerous years. By then, however, RAND had already played an influential part in shaping the Space Age, even if much of its early work was unknown to the general public. Its scientific and analytical approach to frightening nuclear issues contrasted with the often-hyperbolic approach that was often evident in the domestic U.S. political scene.

Around this time, another type of forecasting also took hold as the practice of strategic planning became a new point of emphasis among businesses, government agencies, and many other types of organizations. As the influential organization theorist Henry Mintzberg has noted, strategic planning "arrived on the scene in the mid-1960s." It was an heir, of sorts, to the scientific management principles developed by Frederick Taylor around the beginning of the 20th century.[13] The purpose of strategic planning was to make organizations more competitive by systematizing goal-setting and organizing operations to achieve identifiable outcomes. While narrower in scope than the broader concept of futurism, its orientation fit congruently within the path that thinking about the future was taking. Strategic planning offered a new element of purposeful, intentional analysis. Although it was still speculative, it was more tethered to the here-and-now than some of the fanciful, if highly imaginative visions of the future that U.S. culture had often produced before. Along with the rising dependence on think tanks such as RAND, then, the new enthusiasm for strategic planning helped set the stage for the new wave of futurists who started to gain recognition in the mid-1960s.

Like the strategic planners, the professional futurists mostly saw the world to come not as an empty canvas, but rather as a set of problems to be solved. Some amount of problem-solving was always part of futuristic

7. Fading Tomorrows

visions, of course. The new class of futurists, however, tended to mostly (though not entirely) see the problem-solving aspect of futurism differently from the techno-consumerist futurists. The latter group was largely responsible for creating the dominant picture of the future as it had existed in the preceding decades. The techno-consumerist futurists were interested in creating a world and improving a way of life—that is, through consumerism—that was well established and overwhelmingly accepted by the American public. Their visions of the coming world hardly ever questioned this as a starting point. Techno-consumerism futurism had only recently started to include an awareness that modern life had downsides. Few had awakened to that possibility before the years when Vance Packard, Rachel Carson, Ralph Nader, and others called their attention to growing problems. Of course, no one would have expected the champions of the techno-consumerism future to raise such doubts. Many of these people represented the corporate and institutional interests that had a stake in promoting that way of life.

By the mid–1960s, however, conditions were favorable for the emergence of a different approach. The general public seemed ready to accept a new way of thinking about the future. Perhaps they did not entirely reject the optimistic vision of tomorrow that American business and other institutions had been promoting for years. However, the public was starting to realize that the path to a positive future would not be as easy as they once thought. Environmental, social, and political problems had become too obvious and too numerous to avoid. Whatever the future might hold, it would undoubtedly require dealing with those issues, regardless of their source. To the futurists who took an increasingly prominent place in envisioning the world of tomorrow, those issues represented potential arenas in which to apply a modern, scientific approach.

It was surely not the case that the new futurists were fresh to the study of the future as a topic. They could be regarded as "new" only because they had not previously received widespread attention. In fact, some of them had been working on these issues for a very long time. But the new professional class of futurists had been working behind the scenes for governments and organizations. Therefore, the general public had very little awareness of them or their scientific approach. By the middle of the 1960s, however, their work drew notice. The public—or at least some segments of it—were now eager to hear what this "new," though not entirely new wave of futurists had to say.

A lengthy essay published in 1966 heralded the professional futurists' arrival to the national stage. It appeared in the widely respected *Time* magazine, a publication that remained an opinion leader in that decade. With the title, "The American passion for the future has taken a new turn," the article left no doubt that a new era of futurism had begun. "Leaving Utopians and science-fiction writers far behind," the essay read, "a growing number of professionals have made prophecy a serious and highly-organized enterprise."[14] The nation was awakening to the idea that the sobering realities of the 1960s might require a new approach to the world of tomorrow.

According to *Time*'s account, the new futurists foresaw many remarkable developments. By the year 2000, the article said, "Nearly all experts agree that bacterial and viral diseases will have been virtually wiped out."[15] The essay spoke of many other astonishing developments, too: the transformation of the oceans, complete with undersea farms; the ability to control the climate; advances in energy production so great that as few as 12 power stations could provide all of the nation's electricity; the development of computers that would replace many workers; the arrival of many medical marvels; and more.[16]

Some of these predictions were realistic. Others, including the suggestion that "everyone in the U.S., in effect, will be independently wealthy" by the year 2000,[17] were little more than pipe dreams. In general, when the predictions veered from science and technology to the social realm, the article's prognostications were sometimes dubious and revealed a mindset that seemed stuck in the 1960s. For example, similar to previous visions of the future that had long appeared in popular culture, the article said, "The kitchen, of course, will be automated." Like previous pictures of the future, the essay retained a sexist lens when discussing who would be working in that kitchen: "An A.D. 2000 housewife may well make out her menu for the week."[18]

Another prediction also revealed a point of view that was very consistent with then-current attitudes about the use of pharmacological substances to solve a myriad of problems:

> In general, drug control of personality will be widely accepted well before the year 2000. If a wife or husband seems to be unusually grouchy on a given evening, says RAND's Olaf Helmer, a spouse will be able to pop down to the corner drugstore, buy some anti-grouch pills, and slip them into the coffee.[19]

Overall, then, while reporting on a "new" era of futurism, *Time*'s account included much that was not actually new, especially concerning the nearly unquestioned faith in science and technology. To an extent, some of the professional futurists may have shared the general perspective expressed in the *Time* essay. In any case, the group of futurists consulted for the article were overwhelmingly white and male. They may have been highly educated, but other perspectives received almost no attention. As reported in *Time*, the new futurists seemed determined to develop a systematic way of envisioning tomorrow that would set their work apart from futurism of the past.

The new futurists employed varied and multidisciplinary theoretical methods in making their predictions. In some ways, they took their cue from works such as Frederick Polak's *The Image of the Future*, a book published in Europe.[20] Polak concludes that humans, by nature, are future-oriented. However, he also observes that it makes a difference whether people merely wait for the future to arrive, on the one hand, or if they try to shape it intentionally, on the other. Concluding that humans usually take a passive approach and that this causes undesirable outcomes, Polak argues for a more proactive role. He especially recommends paying attention to the images a society develops when they imagine the future and paying attention to the effects of psychology, emotion, and belief systems. His way of thinking about the future, then, was explicitly multi-dimensional. It provided important groundwork for later developments.

Meanwhile, other 1960s-era futurists were working out new philosophies and methodologies. Perhaps it was not surprising that as a relatively new discipline, the field had not yet fully coalesced. Into that context, the ongoing work of a few scholars, including Bertrand de Jouvenel, Ossip Flechtheim, and Daniel Bell, became instrumental in "disciplining an unruly field," as the historian of the future Jenny Andersson notes.[21]

Since the mid-1940s, German academic Ossip Flechtheim, who for a time also taught in the United States, had argued that colleges and universities should teach the future as a distinct subject. That was important, he suggested, if humankind wished to prevent a recurrence of the horrors that occurred in World War II. In 1945, Flechtheim published an academic article called "Teaching the Future" to make his case.[22] Several prominent intellectuals, including Lewis Mumford and Thomas Mann, were sympathetic to Flechtheim's ideas.[23]

Gradually, a growing number of researchers became interested in his general argument. Indeed, Flechtheim is sometimes credited with coining the term *futurology* around this time. Many people regard him as one of the several founding figures in the development of a structured, scientifically oriented approach to studying the future, writ large.[24]

After spending some time in the United States, Flechtheim was named director of the Institute for Future Studies at the Berlin School of Politics in 1954.[25] Over the following years, he produced works that greatly influenced the growing field of futures studies. Among his writings, his 1966 book *History and Futurology*[26] attracted much attention.

Meanwhile, French philosopher and social scientist Bertrand de Jouvenel published his formidable book, *L'Art de la conjecture*. It first appeared in the early 1960s in Europe and was soon translated into English as *The Art of Conjecture*. The book made a significant impact in the United States, creating a stir among American intellectuals who saw the future as a subject of inquiry.

In *The Art of Conjecture*, de Jouvenel provided a philosophical basis for futurology. He said that since the future had not yet arrived, it should be regarded not as a singular entity—not as *the* future, in other words—but rather as a set of possibilities. He argued for the study of futures, in the plural, instead of conceiving the topic as one specific future. It was an obvious distinction, perhaps, but it turned out to be significant for subsequent directions that studies of the future would take. It was also consistent with the scenario-planning approach that was a hallmark of RAND's work.

Meanwhile, in the United States, a new policy research center joined the increasing number of think tanks that aimed to understand important issues and make recommendations for their resolution. Established in 1961, the Hudson Institute soon became an east coast stronghold for futurism. It was a center for the scientific study of possible futures along the lines that the RAND Corporation had been undertaking on the west coast for some years.

One connection between the two organizations was Herman Kahn, who was one of the Institute's founders and had previously worked at RAND. Kahn already had conducted significant work on scenario planning in Cold War contexts, and specialists held him in high esteem. His presence at the Hudson Institute helped attract other academics who were also interested in the future. Among them was sociologist Daniel Bell, who was then teaching at Columbia University.

Bell was already a well-known figure. His prominence had been well established upon publication of his 1961 book, *The End of Ideology*. In that work, he argued that the old ways of thinking were outmoded and that the future would require something very different. He had also served on a presidential commission on technology, which brought him additional attention among policymakers. Thus, Bell systematically considered the future from his position as a highly trained academic. It was perhaps not surprising, then, that in 1965, the American Academy of Arts and Sciences (AAAS) appointed him to chair a new project, the Commission on the Future.

As Richard B. Halley and Harold G. Vatter note, with the AAAS's new project, "awareness of the futurist ferment was heightened within the American intellectual community."[27] Undoubtedly, with one of the country's most prestigious academic organizations venturing into the field, the study of the future suddenly gained a new aura of respectability, especially among many scholars and other national opinion leaders. The establishment of the Commission on the Future was an indication that a new type of academic futurism was taking hold in the United States. (In some ways, however, even the AAAS's project was mired in the past. Its overwhelmingly white male membership hardly reflected the growing awareness of the diversity that was emerging in the society at large.)

On a different but related front, Herman Kahn was covering similar ground through his work at the Hudson Institute. In 1967, Kahn and Anthony J. Wiener produced a new book for which Daniel Bell provided the introduction. In their *The Year 2000: A Framework for Speculation on the Next Thirty-Three Years*,[28] the authors argue that it is essential to scrutinize current situations to reduce surprise outcomes and other negative consequences. While acknowledging that unpredictable developments were not entirely avoidable, they still thought some useful results were achievable. Even among the academic community, not all readers were convinced of its conclusions, but the book was widely circulated and influential at the time.

The Year 2000 championed an analytic approach that reflected the new breed of academic futurist's way of conceiving the topic. It did mostly retain a technology-heavy framework. However, it also considered cultural and political factors somewhat more than was usual at the time.[29]

The burgeoning field of futures studies in the mid–1960s was, of course, much more complex and nuanced than shown in this very brief sketch. However, it seems clear that with the new, explicitly systematized and organized approach, futures studies gained prominence and prestige. The professional futurists' visions of what was to come seemed authoritative to many people. Many seemed to have an open mind about what this emerging group of experts had to say.

A new organization somewhat bridged the gap between the old-style futurism, which was grounded in an unbridled faith in technology and consumerism, and the new-style futurism of the professionals. That organization was the World Future Society. It was founded by a *National Geographic* science writer named Edward Cornish.

Like many people of his time, Cornish shared concerns about the potential dangers that could emerge from the Cold War and other trends in world affairs. From his work as a writer, he was also well versed in rapid developments in technology and science. Realizing these concerns would have a bearing on the coming world, he began writing a newsletter dedicated to futurology in 1965.[30] Cornish had little funding, but he sent copies of the newsletter to friends and other similarly-minded people, including R. Buckminster Fuller. Cornish's newsletter quickly built a readership. Soon, the modest publication became a full-fledged magazine,

The Futurist. It would become widely consulted among futurists and even attract some general readership.

With the success of his publication, Cornish founded the World Futurist Society (WFS) in 1966. Its purpose was to bring together people with similar interests in tomorrow's world. In addition to Fuller, who was intrigued by Cornish's idea from the start, prominent academic futurists, such as Herman Kahn, were also among those interested in the WFS's mission. Before long, the WFS also attracted many others. One was Marshall McLuhan, the communications theorist who wrote *The Gutenberg Galaxy* (1962), *Understanding Media* (1964), and *The Medium Is the Message* (1967).

Science-fiction writers Isaac Asimov and Arthur C. Clarke, and *Star Trek* creator Gene Roddenberry also became active. Academics, such as the revered anthropologist Margaret Mead, also were attracted to the organization. Over time, these and other prominent people in politics and other realms of society also became involved. With a combination of both new-style and traditional futurists on board, at least in terms of supporting the WSF's overall concept and mission, the Society gained much notice. For a time, it had little competition, especially as it was the only society covering this issue in depth until the creation of the World Futures Studies Federation (WFSF) in early 1973.

The WFS took its subject very seriously, but it also construed it widely. *The Futurist* published future-related articles on a variety of topics and tended to present information and ideas in a manner that ordinary people could understand.

Some of the magazine's early articles now sound far-fetched. One essay, for example, summarizes predictions from the Xerox Corporation. It concludes that life in the future "may become too easy" and that "people may need to take special pills to get a feeling of purpose and meaning into their lives."[31] Other articles, however, now seem to be on firmer ground.

At times, the magazine seemed to be aiming to heighten its credibility. For instance, the cover of the August 1969 issue featured "White House futurist" and future United States Senator Daniel P. Moynihan. Inside the magazine's covers, political scientist Richard Scammon, formerly the director of the U.S. Bureau of the Census, wrote the main article.

Overall, the World Future Society brought together futurists of many types and backgrounds while also providing a highly visible platform for those voices through its publications and conferences.

Elsewhere, a new CBS News television program, *The 21st Century*, was evidence that many people now regarded the future with a renewed sense of seriousness and purpose. Adding to the show's credibility, the legendary news anchor Walter Cronkite hosted the series, which debuted

7. Fading Tomorrows 161

in 1967. As described in a newspaper article of the time, *The 21st Century* aimed "to anticipate tomorrow's brave new world, a world that indeed will require extraordinary vision and courage."[32] The selection of Cronkite as the face of the series gave it a gravitas that was often lacking in presentations about the future. Widely regarded as "the most trusted man in America" and often fondly regarded as "Uncle Walter" by much of the public, Cronkite had delivered Americans major news stories for years.

In the new show, he traveled around the country to report on efforts to shape future life and to address conditions that might threaten the coming world if left unresolved. Some episodes of the weekly series were straightforwardly futurist. "The Weird World of Robots," for example, looked at current thinking in robotics, a field that had been in the public eye for some years.[33] Another typical episode, which examined the potential for automated highways and electric vehicles, included a segment in which Cronkite was shown driving the prototype of a car called the StaRRcar in the small suburban town of Westborough in central Massachusetts.[34] That episode also reported on new thinking about futuristic ideas that had been circulating for some time.

In other ways, however, *The 21st Century* spoke of tomorrow's world from a decidedly more contemporary angle. Those episodes squarely addressed issues that had come to widespread public attention only recently. One such matter was overpopulation. At the time, many people regarded escalating population growth as a grave threat to future happiness. *The 21st Century* devoted its May 19, 1969, episode, titled "The Food Revolution," to the topic, with a focus on "how to feed the ever-increasing population."[35] As presented by the series, such issues were far from abstract hypotheticals; they were disasters looming on the horizon that demanded a modern, scientific response. That the "most trusted man in America" was bringing these matters to public attention served to emphasize the seriousness of the issues. Overall, *The 21st Century* was consistent in tone and purpose with the many professional futurists whose prognostications were increasingly in the public eye.

Overpopulation was, in fact, the subject of a bestselling paperback book called *The Population Bomb*. Written by Paul Ehrlich, an entomologist at Stanford University, the 1968 book warned that a dire future was quickly approaching. There was nothing subtle or nuanced about Ehrlich's approach. Indeed, one edition of *The Population Bomb* features the title in bold letters along with the picture of a bomb with a lit fuse. The cover design includes a warning label that says: "While you are reading these words, four million people will have died from starvation. Most of them children."

Within the book's pages, many of Ehrlich's contentions were alarming. "At this late date," he wrote, "nothing can prevent a substantial increase in the world death rate."³⁶ He continued his dire warning, saying, "In the 1970s the world will undergo famines—hundreds of millions of people are going to starve to death."³⁷

As the example of Paul Ehrlich may suggest, the new futurists of the later 1960s often presented versions of the coming world that were cautionary, or sometimes outright fatalistic in tone. It often seemed that the future would almost certainly be problematic and that any hope of making things better would require bold, decisive action. In other words, a bright, optimistic future was no longer anything to be expected. Instead, for humanity to win the future, they would need to take careful, realistic, and possibly dramatic action.

Many people realized that the long-predicted techno-consumerist future was unfolding with many unforeseen consequences. Meanwhile, another segment of U.S. society was adopting a very different attitude. Indeed, a broad, multi-faceted movement known as the counterculture emerged by the later 1960s. Although there was a wide range of opinion within the movement, one common thread was its general rejection of many of society's norms and expectations.

The counterculture had little use for the trappings of middle-class life. They preferred to look different, they liked different music and styles, and they were open to using various drugs. More than that, though, these people, most of whom were young adults, were thinking very differently. Many of them rejected traditional American politics and considered other ideologies, some of which were much farther to the left than those offered by any of the major political parties. The movement attracted many people who had already been protesting the government and the American way of life, in general. However, as the counterculture blossomed, it became more than the sum of those parts.

In the mid–1960s, the middle-aged academic Timothy Leary, who advocated for the use of psychedelic drugs to achieve a higher level of consciousness, famously encouraged youth to "tune in, turn on, and drop out." To many who listened, Leary and others in the counterculture seemed to be saying that traditional, middle-class life in America was a dead end. The counterculture had little use for the techno-consumerist future. The movement did not want the quiet, carefree, suburban middle-class life that had been sold as the future to the American public for so many years. Instead, the counterculture envisioned a very different future. They imagined a world in which people would turn away from industrialization, consumerism, and conformity to middle-class values.

Most of the American public never fully shared the counterculture's outlook, but the movement's influence was profound and widespread enough to make a mark on the culture overall. Less than a month after NASA's triumphant landing on the moon, its force was evident at the Woodstock music festival. This milestone event attracted 400,000 people to a remote farm in upstate New York. Billed as "3 days of peace and music," Woodstock generated enormous media attention and was soon regarded as a significant event. In some ways, it seemed to demonstrate that mid-century futurism was dead, at least to this audience. Indeed, many young people now rejected the technologically inspired and consumer-driven picture of a wondrous world of tomorrow. The counterculture offered a simpler life, a life closer to the earth, and a way to live apart from the old institutions and old ways of thinking.

Interestingly, some members of the older generation became beloved figures within the counterculture movement. One such person was R. Buckminster Fuller, the designer-architect-futurist who was also associated with the World Futurist Society. Born in 1895, Fuller was old enough to be the grandfather of most people in the youthful counterculture movement. In some ways, he had the kind of traditional, privileged upbringing that would have made him anathema to young people who rejected polite society and its norms. However, Fuller had defied convention on many occasions, too. Twice expelled from Harvard—surely no small feat—his career was built upon the idea of doing things differently and coming up with new ways to think about the world and living in it.

That rebelliousness had resulted in several forays into futurism over the years. During the Great Depression, Fuller's bulbous, three-wheel automobile, the Dymaxion, gained some notice at the 1933–1934 Chicago's Century of Progress World's Fair. Unfortunately, the vehicle was involved in an accident that resulted in the death of the driver, which led to negative publicity. Fuller developed subsequent Dymaxion prototypes, but his designs did not do much to alter the course of the automotive world.

Fuller also worked on futuristic housing design. In the late 1920s and 1930s, he promoted what he called the Dymaxion House. He tinkered with the concept until he arrived at a circular design that would be constructed from aluminum. Its key feature was that its parts could be manufactured industrially and then shipped for assembly to any home site. As with the Dymaxion vehicle, he developed several iterations. However, the concept never gained traction. Like his automotive design, it seemed quirky, and it failed to resonate with the general public.

In the 1950s, Fuller's fortunes somewhat changed. After working for a brief time at Black Mountain College, he refocused much of his attention on geodesic dome designs. Using a clever arrangement of interlocking triangular aluminum struts that framed panels of fiberglass or some other lightweight material, these domes were highly scalable and easy to fabricate. They also had the advantage of being much lighter than traditional domes, making them feasible for uses where traditional domes would be too expensive or impractical.[38]

Unlike his previous work, which mostly continued to languish, Fuller's work with geodesic domes was much more successful. The Ford Motor Company included a Fuller geodesic design in one of its buildings in 1953, and he was later asked to design structures for use by the U.S. military.[39] Other applications for Fuller's geodesic dome followed. In the mid–1960s, he provided the design for the gigantic dome that housed the United States Pavilion at the Expo 67 (officially the 1967 International and Universal Exposition) in Montreal, Canada. By this time, Fuller was very widely known. He had even appeared on the cover of a 1964 issue of *Time* magazine, a sure sign that his days of marginalization were over.

Throughout the years, Fuller had been writing prodigiously. Somewhat utopian in outlook, he had always situated his bold concepts as contributions aimed to make life better. For that, Fuller believed that doing things differently and developing new ways of living would probably be necessary. He had already published much material before the 1960s, but in that decade, his writing started to attract a wide readership. He was not afraid of saying things boldly or provocatively, and now, many people were willing to listen to what he had to say.

Curiously, perhaps, Fuller was widely admired within the counterculture movement. This was mainly because of his famous *Operating Manual for Spaceship Earth*. This 1969 book, which partially was indebted to the nascent ecology movement, portrays the earth as a self-contained life-support system with limited resources. So, many of his ideas were at odds with the rampant consumerism that had led up to the 1960s. Indeed, his outlook sharply contrasted with the planned obsolescence and the "keeping up with the Joneses" that had fueled earlier futurist visions.

Fuller tirelessly promoted such concepts. Possessing imagination and enthusiasm, many people admired him. Of course, some were not enthusiastic about Fuller's rising status as a public intellectual.

An early version of his *Operating Manual* essay had appeared in a 1968 edited volume called *Environment and Change*. A reviewer for the *Bulletin of the Atomic Scientists* concluded that Fuller's contribution to that publication was the "longest, most pretentious, and emptiest essay" of the lot.[40] However, such criticism did not mute the influence of Fuller's *Operating Manual*. He continued to attract many followers, including many from the ranks of the professional futurists. Meanwhile, his message also appealed to counterculture people who were fed up with the status quo.

The year after Fuller's *Operating Manual for Spaceship Earth* was

7. Fading Tomorrows   165

published, a relatively new voice burst onto the publishing scene. In 1970, Alvin Toffler's book *Future Shock* created a sensation in the book world, and it quickly became a runaway bestseller. Building on recent thinking in futurology, Toffler presented a starkly different picture of the world-yet-to-be. Toffler's focused on "the 'soft' or human side of tomorrow" and "about what happens to people when they are overwhelmed by change."[41] His basic premise was that the pace of change was accelerating more rapidly than ever before and that humans were ill-equipped to deal with the implications of that fact. The "shock" element in the book's title, therefore, was similar to the anthropological concept of culture shock— disorientation caused by the unfamiliar.[42] As humankind raced into the future, Toffler concluded that this "future shock" would be debilitating unless people prepared for it. Otherwise, information overload might prove to present an insurmountable challenge. The book lays out his basic reasoning and the steps he proposed for dealing with the issue.

Toffler did make a few specific predictions, some of which came true and others of which missed the mark. However, making specific predictions was not his primary goal. Instead, he sought to change thinking and behaviors in a way that would facilitate adaptation to the unfolding future because the future, in his eyes, would not be entirely controllable. As one reviewer concluded, "The disturbing quality of Toffler's book resides in the skillful way in which he builds a case for the sudden death of permanence."[43]

Although overwhelming technological changes were a significant part of the book, Toffler also includes astute awareness of the major challenges that fast and large-scale social changes of the 1960s posed. Much of *Future Shock*'s significance arises from the inclusion of these multiple variables, which much futurism to that date had often ignored. In addition to evolving social norms and mores, he includes some discussion of race and some about women's issues. Toffler speaks broadly of the needs of democracy, too. He suggests that to improve the situation, people would need to think beyond the way of the "technocrat," who was "still thinking in top-down terms."[44] Instead, he urged the development of a system of feedback loops that would feed relevant information and reaction to those designing and implementing policies.

Despite the general optimism in most mid-century futurism, cautionary and sometimes fearful voices had warned of a potentially catastrophic future throughout the Cold War. Moreover, a multitude of developments in the 1960s served to reinforce the notion that the future might be much darker than was sometimes imagined. Toffler's views, which developed against this backdrop of rising uncertainty, recognized that technological and social change would almost certainly and unrelentingly continue to race forward. Accordingly, *Future Shock* includes chapters such as "Strategies for Survival," "Coping with Tomorrow," and "Taming Technology," all of which aimed to give readers an approach for dealing with what was to come. The book acquired a solid reputation—perhaps one that surpassed that of any futurist book written to that date. In many ways, it played a significant role in reorienting how American society would think about the world of tomorrow. One academic reviewer described it as "top priority general reading" about "an important concept, and a book of genuine relevance."[45] Over time, *Future Shock* and Toffler's subsequent books influenced many people. His reputation (as well as that of his wife and writing partner, Heidi Toffler) continued to grow.

Upon Toffler's death in 2016, former U.S. House speaker Newt Gingrich memorialized him. Toffler, he said, "had a remarkable impact on my life and the lives of millions, literally millions, of people—shaping how humans understand the world and the era that we live in."[46]

By the new decade, the bright, wondrous future, which techno-consumerist futurism had predicted from the 1930s into the 1960s, had itself become an artifact of the past. True, it would sometimes continue to surface from time to time. However, that specific way of envisioning the future increasingly seemed irrelevant.

The 1970s presented yet more challenges, few of which could be reconciled with the presumptions upon which mid-century futurism had been built. Americans were no longer sure about the path their society had taken in recent decades. Crucially, they also were no longer confident in the institutions that had molded their visions of tomorrow and that were supposedly going to deliver it. Instead, the 1970s would bring distrust, heightened by the "long national nightmare" (as President Gerald Ford would characterize it) of the Watergate scandal and resulting resignation of President Nixon. The nation would experience a bitter defeat in Vietnam. There would emerge a downbeat feeling, a malaise that lasted until the 1980s.

The allure of the world of tomorrow, as envisioned in the American imagination in the middle decades of the century, was thus greatly diminished. It had held sway in U.S. culture much too long to be regarded simply as a fad, but people now viewed it as yesterday's way of picturing the future. However, even as the mid-century vision of tomorrow faded, consumerism remained quite healthy, and faith in technology was still strong. Those impulses predated the techno-consumerist futurism, and they continued beyond it, and they would, indeed, be part of the actual future that unfolded in the following years.

To be sure, some of the mid-century futurists' predictions eventually came true. That certainly was the case in many significant techno-

7. Fading Tomorrows   167

logical developments, especially in terms of computers and electronic communications. Overall, however, the immediate future would turn out to be quite unlike the world that mid-century futurism had optimistically foreseen. Those visions, which for years had captured the American imagination, now often seemed naïve.

Still, the techno-consumerist futurism of the mid-century would continue to play a part in the coming years, although sometimes in unexpected ways.

Epilogue

It was 1973, and Americans had a future to meet. Maybe their expectations were not as lofty as they had been 15 years earlier, but the country had survived challenging times. Now, with the holidays fast approaching, the roadways beckoned. Americans had places to go and people to see.

Just as mid-century planners had anticipated two decades earlier, super-highways now crisscrossed the nation. Sleek, multilane roadways spectacularly channeled through cities and carved pathways across open fields and mountain passes. Americans, who had been on a car-buying spree for years, had places to go and the cars to take them there.

They did not, however, have gas.

Weeks earlier, in September, OAPEC, the Organization of Arab Petroleum Exporting Countries,[1] had instituted an oil embargo as a response to some of its members' displeasure with U.S. policy in the Middle East. With oil imports into the United States reduced to a trickle, gasoline was soon in short supply across the country, as it would be for some months. In many locales, drivers roamed the streets, hoping to find a gas station that was open and willing to sell them gasoline, albeit at inflated prices. Service stations often limited how many gallons a customer could buy and most cut back on their hours of operation. When they were open, long lines formed. If a station's supply of gas ran out—as was often the case—drivers were left frustrated and sometimes angry.[2]

Mid-century futurism had many components, but the automobile had long been one of its most prominent and potent emblems. Car culture had faded somewhat from the glory days of the 1950s. Although American cars still held symbolic value, the automobile unquestionably had lost a fair measure of its previous luster.

By the 1970s, a long series of developments eroded the mythic aura of the automobile in American culture. Ralph Nader's exposé in the 1960s had drawn attention to safety concerns and to a side of the industry that was perhaps darker than Americans had earlier imagined. Traffic, a problem that many futuristic proposals had aimed to solved for decades, was worse than ever. Moreover, there was growing recognition that the noxious fumes from gasoline-powered engines were not only unpleasant; they were contributing to health issues and harming the environment.

Now, with the 1973 oil crisis, yet another element in American car culture was laid bare. The nation's love affair with the automobile depended heavily on the availability of plentiful and relatively inexpensive oil. Those days seemed to be gone as the crisis drove home the point that those were not necessarily things that could be taken for granted going forward. The implications for the future were not insignificant. Considering that much of the techno-consumerist future—with its cars, and jets, and plastics—relied upon access to cheap and ample oil, the 1973 crisis further undermined the type of future that had been envisioned just a decade before.

By this time, Americans had much more on their minds than the price and availability of petroleum products, important as those factors were. The nation had already descended into the depths of the contentious, de-

An embargo that resulted from world political events plunged the United States into a severe oil crisis in 1973. The American public, which long had embraced car culture and had grown dependent on cheap petroleum, was suddenly confronted with gasoline shortages. This photograph, taken by David Falconer for the Environmental Protection Agency, shows motorists scrambling to purchase gasoline during the 1973 crisis in Portland, Oregon (National Archives).

stabilizing Watergate crisis—the political scandal that was the result of White House involvement (and a subsequent cover-up) in a break-in at the Democratic National Committee Headquarters in the Watergate complex in Washington, D.C.

Events leading up to the Watergate crisis shed some light on the strains that weighed down public confidence not only in the Nixon administration but also in the nation overall. Nixon had always regarded the antiwar movement with disdain, and his belief that public opposition to the war hampered his efforts to end the conflict on terms he found acceptable is well known. In mid-1971, however, that situation took a turn for the worse, heightening friction between the president and his supporters and the growing segment of the population that opposed Nixon's handling of the war.

Beginning on June 13, 1971, the *New York Times* began to publish leaked portions of a top-secret history of the war that had been compiled by the Department of Defense. In a series of front-page stories, the *Times* informed its readers about the so-called Pentagon Papers (officially called "Report of the Office of the Secretary of Defense Vietnam Task Force"). As published, the documents painted a damning picture of how the war had been reported to the American people by the government.

As far back to the 1950s, the documents revealed, U.S. administrations had not been entirely candid with the public. It appeared that on numerous occasions, the American people were either kept in the dark or worse, willfully misled about various details of the Vietnam conflict. Maybe if the war had already run its course, such revelations would have had little impact. That was not the case, however. Even with a reduced U.S. presence in the war by 1971, the conflict continued to drag on. Most Americans were sick of it by then, and many openly wondered if it might all have been a horrible mistake. With much of the public already soured on the war, revelations in the Pentagon Papers, which seemed to confirm the government had not been truthful to some degree, exacerbated the situation.

The administration took the matter to court, hoping to suppress the distribution of the documents, but the Supreme Court decided to permit publication to go forward. Soon after that, the administration prosecuted Daniel Ellsberg and an associate for revealing government secrets. Ellsberg, an ex-Marine and former RAND analyst, worked at the Pentagon in the 1960s, and he initially approved of America's war policy. Over time, however, he had second thoughts and reversed his opinion. By 1971, Ellsberg decided to take action. He secretly passed photocopied parts of the document to the *New York Times*, which began publishing the material shortly after that.

Epilogue

As Ellsberg's trial was underway, yet another secret was revealed: In September of 1971, two White House associates, G. Gordon Liddy and E. Howard Hunt, illegally broke into Ellsberg's office in a search for incriminating information. When it became known, the unlawful action doomed the government's case against Ellsberg and his associate, and the case was dismissed. Interestingly, however, a questionable pattern of behavior had been established.

The year after the break-in at Ellsberg's office, Liddy and Hunt were involved in yet another one, this time at the Democratic National Committee's offices at the Watergate complex. That fateful event precipitated a series of actions, accusations, and cover-ups that resulted in a full-blown Constitutional crisis.

The purpose of the Watergate break-in, which occurred in late May of 1972, was to wiretap phones at the DNC's main offices for political purposes. When police arrested five operatives in June, however, the intent and scope of the break-in remained obscure. Instead, it seemed to be a petty crime of little national interest.

By June, however, *Washington Post* reporters Bob Woodward and Carl Bernstein were looking more closely at what had transpired. After meeting with a secret informant (who years later was revealed to be an FBI official) and doing more research, Woodward and Bernstein discovered that a $25,000 check, since deposited in an account owned by one of the defendants, had been issued by the president's re-election campaign. With a connection to the White House established, the story began to gather steam.

At first, it did not significantly damage Nixon's reputation, however. Many people felt the president was probably not directly involved in any misdeeds that had been committed. Nixon handily won re-election in November.

For a time, things seemed to be going well for the president. Several weeks later, in January of 1973, Nixon announced that the United States signed an agreement with the communist government of North Vietnam, mostly ending U.S. participation in the demoralizing conflict in the region. In the coming weeks, many U.S. soldiers who had been held as prisoners of war by North Vietnam returned home.

Concurrently, in the early months of 1973, the Watergate situation began to unravel. It soon became a national obsession. As prosecutors looked beyond the small group of men initially arrested for the break-in, more and more people connected with the White House were swept up in the investigations. By May, a Select Committee of the Senate launched hearings on the growing scandal as revelations and allegations against the administration mounted.

By the time that OAPEC declared its oil embargo in the fall, Watergate was a full-fledged crisis that seemed poised to drive Nixon from office. After that time, Richard Nixon's situation would go from bad to worse. Finally, as it appeared that articles to impeach the president were on the verge of being passed in the House of Representatives, Nixon resigned on August 9, 1974.

A month later, the new president, Gerald R. Ford, granted Nixon a pardon for any crimes that the disgraced former president may have committed. In a speech Ford gave after taking the oath of office, he said what many Americans probably hoped was true. "My fellow Americans," he said, "our long national nightmare is over."

By then, many Americans felt uneasy, disappointed, and discouraged. Ironically, in many ways, America was probably safer than it was a generation earlier. The Cold War continued, but the public perceived it as less dangerous than before. Meanwhile, Americans worried about new kinds of enemies. Increasingly, many people thought that those enemies were within America itself. The worry was not like that of the 1950s when fear of communism caused Americans to fear enemy agents or sympathizers. Now, the fear was that the enemy might be even closer than that.

Throughout the later 1960s, the American public's trust in government generally fell precipitously. Many factors were in play, including the bitter divisiveness of the ongoing war in Vietnam. In 1964, it will be recalled, survey data indicated that 77 percent of Americans felt they could "trust the government in Washington always or most of the time," according to the Pew Research Center.[3] As late as October 1972, just weeks before that year's presidential election, more than half of Americans, 53 percent, reported similar confidence. However, when polled again after the oil crisis, the unfolding months of the Watergate scandal, and Richard Nixon's resignation, American trust had mostly evaporated. Only a paltry 36 percent of Americans still trusted the government.[4] An overwhelming majority of Americans surveyed did not.

In popular culture, Hollywood soon picked up the theme of fading American confidence. Numerous films across several genres centered on various manifestations of distrust and on the feeling that somehow the nation was heading in the wrong direction

In director Don Siegel's *Dirty Harry* (1971), a no-nonsense police officer confronts a world in which crime runs rampant, and the legal system is ineffective in combatting it. Within this scenario, the film introduces San Francisco police detective Harry Callahan (played by Clint Eastwood). A no-nonsense, reactionary antihero, Callahan is disgusted by the situation and decides to make up his own rules as a result.

Callahan is a cold and detached character, and he seems just as likely

Epilogue 173

to shoot suspects as to interrogate them. He is calm but also smug and hyper-violent. Seeing his superiors and the courts as weak and ineffective, Callahan ignores them and takes matters into his own hands. As a vigilante acting within the system, he spends the film meting out his idea of justice via the use of his massive .44 Magnum handgun, which in some ways is a co-star of the movie.

The idea of the world gone to ruin and overrun by crime stands in stark contrast to the world typically envisioned in mid-century futurism. Crime and social ills are not isolated problems to be solved with traditional methods, according to the storylines in such films. Instead, these ills are shown not as problems within the system, but rather as the main, if undesired, elements that define the system, which is shown as very broken, and perhaps too far-gone to be repaired. Indeed, in *Dirty Harry*—as in its sequels and other 1970s vigilante films, such as *Death Wish* (1974)—almost everything about society has gone wrong. These movies all contain at least implied indictments of liberalism, and, by implication, of the American system overall—the same system that created and promoted visions of an idealized techno-consumerist future over many years.

The protagonists in the 1970s vigilante movies tend to rely on one response to the societal ills that they see around them: violence. These films appeal, supposedly, to the frustrations of their audiences. Whether this is true or not is a matter of debate. However, the fact the era's vigilante movies were popular and financially successful is suggestive, at least, that many people by this time thought that modern life in America was going in the wrong direction. In any case, it is difficult to imagine how the world depicted in such films could exist concurrently with the bright world of mid-century futurism that had held considerable cultural power just a decade earlier.

Some films took the theme of America unraveling to even greater depths. Some of the most obvious of these placed conspiracies at the centers of their stories. Popular movies with conspiracy-oriented themes were nothing new. For decades, and especially in the tense years of the early Cold War, Hollywood frequently turned to conspiracy theorizing to make thrillers and other popular films.

At the height of the Red Scare of the late 1940s and 1950s, Hollywood churned out many conspiracy films, usually with an espionage angle. Movies such as *I Was a Communist Spy for the F.B.I.* (1951), *My Son John* (1952), *Big Jim McLain* (1952), and others were a familiar part of the era's movie scene. Even a decade later, the conspiracy theme emerged in well-known films such as *The Manchurian Candidate* (1962). One element in almost all of such movies was critical: The conspiracies involved foreign nations—external forces that are attacking America. Indeed, very few films depict a conspiracy coming from within an American institution. (The most notable exception is *Seven Days in May* [1964], which is a story about a conspiracy within the Pentagon that is led by a delusional general.)

By the mid-1970s, however, conspiracy movies were portraying a very different situation. Now, conspiracy-oriented films tended to tell stories in which the danger emanated from within the United States. So, the enemy is almost always people within the American system—often government officials or business executives—and, by implication, the system itself. In a way, the changing portrayal of conspiracies in movies reflected the gnawing feeling that Walt Kelly depicted in his famous syndicated comic strip, *Pogo*, when one character said, "We have met the enemy, and he is us."[5]

The breakdown of confidence and moral purpose evident in 1970s movies focusing on conspiracy theories emerged in many movies. Two prominent examples, however, stand out in the development of this thematic trend.

In 1973, *Executive Action* presented alarming conspiracy theories regarding the assassination of John F. Kennedy. One of the scriptwriters was Dalton Trumbo, who was blacklisted years earlier as one of the "Hollywood Ten." Another was Mark Lane, the author of a book, *Rush to Judgment* (1966), which dismissed the conclusion that Kennedy's assassination was the result of a lone gunman. Although it was hardly a major motion picture, *Executive Action* attracted some attention due to its controversial storyline. In addition, the cast had considerable star power. The presence of Burt Lancaster, Robert Ryan, and Will Geer assured that the press paid attention to it.

The film presents a hypothetical version of the assassination, with mysterious people and complicated motives. It suggests that the Warren Report was wrong or a cover-up and that the truth is far darker and more conspiratorial than the public had been led to believe. As critic Roger Ebert wrote at the time, the film seems to suggest that "November 22, 1963 [the date of Kennedy's death] was the day things started to go wrong for America."[6]

Another prominent example of a new era of conspiracism in U.S. popular culture appears in the 1975 thriller *Three Days of the Condor*. The film, which is directed by Sydney Pollack, stars box-office favorite Robert Redford as CIA analyst Joe Turner. When the story begins, Turner spends most of his days at a nondescript office combing through reading materials in a meticulous search for clues of clandestine enemy activity. One day, however, he returns from lunch to find that all the other CIA employees at the office have been ruthlessly murdered. Turner panics and calls a secure number in Washington to report the crime to CIA officials. From there, things get even more dangerous and confusing.

Eventually, it becomes clear that the assassinations were carried out under orders that came from within the CIA itself. The plot has many twists and turns and, in some ways, is a standard thriller. What is remarkable about this film, however, is its portrayal of the CIA, or factions within it, as the primary enemy. A generation earlier, such a cynical storyline would have been shocking. By 1975, however, it was accepted as a relatively uncontroversial plot element. With all that had transpired in American culture and politics over the previous decade and a half, the idea seemed no more outlandish than some of the events that had really happened. It provided another piece of evidence of dampening American expectations.

Many other films with conspiracy themes appeared at the time. These included Alan J. Pakula's acclaimed docudrama about the Watergate scandal, *All the President's Men* (1976). That film further exposed a downbeat, suspicious attitude that had become common by that time.

Mid-century futurism always blended faith in technology and scientific discovery, on the one hand, and the power of consumerism, on the other. The former implied that almost every issue could be addressed by using the methods of science and then applying technological solutions to them. The latter, meanwhile, was supposed to lift American lifestyles to ever greater heights. But now there was doubt. The darkening national mood did not seem to be a problem that technology or consumer spending could solve.

After years of revelations that cast doubt on business corporations and other institutions, this kind of faith was in short supply. It dawned on many that modern life had a significant downside. The steep decline of confidence in government dealt a blow to mid-century futurism. Said differently, technology no longer seemed to have all the answers. Worse than that, it sometimes seemed to be adding to society's problems. The same could be said for consumerism, which no longer seemed to provide a reliable pathway to the glorious world of tomorrow. Some sort of future was still on the horizon, of course, but many Americans were not confident that it would be good.

A look at other movies from the era illustrates this point. Stanley Kubrick's follow-up to *2001* tells the story of an especially bleak future. In *A Clockwork Orange* (1971), the world of tomorrow is nightmarish, indeed. The film depicts aimless youths, untethered to any social norms. They organize their lives around shocking acts of violence and recklessness. *A Clockwork Orange* is a lawless, crime-ridden world that is many,

many times darker and more hopeless than the bleak present-day world of *Dirty Harry*, which was released the same year.

Many other era science-fiction movies were also very bleak. *Omega Man* (1970) tells a near-future story in which a lone scientist is the last remaining human who has not been killed or rendered into a zombie-like mutant as the result of biological warfare. *Silent Running* (1972) pictures future-earth as ecologically ruined and barely able to sustain life, which leads humankind to abandon the planet amid desperation and conflict. The future-world depicted in *Soylent Green* (1973) is ravaged and overpopulated. The world is running so low on food and sustainable resources that the authoritarian government oversees the distribution of food products secretly and grotesquely made from deceased humans.

Some of these films depict a dysfunctional society that is easily amused and distracted by unusual and terrifying activities and contests. In *Westworld* (1973), visitors can immerse themselves in what amounts to a highly realistic theme park, one part of which is a replica of a town in the Old West. The guests engage in role-playing and interact with incredibly lifelike robots. Things take a frightening turn when the robots malfunction and begin targeting the human guests. This film's sequel, *Futureworld* (1976), involves conspiratorial corporate malfeasance, murder, human cloning, and robots.

Death Race 2000 from 1975 portrays a futuristic society that is addicted to televised spectacles. The most popular event in that world is a cross-country automobile race in which the drivers earn bonus points for each pedestrian and innocent bystander that they manage to run over and presumably kill along the route.

Even the lighthearted comedy *Sleeper* (1973), in which director Woody Allen tells the story of a man who awakens after two centuries in hibernation, hardly presents a world of optimism and confidence. The film includes many tropes from the heyday of mid-century futurism. These include farms with vegetables as big as automobiles, futuristic cars running on automated roadways, mood-altering technologies, and more. On another level, the society in this future-world has become dull, intolerant, and authoritarian. Indeed, Allen's film is awash in references to mid-century futurism, but he portrays these as mostly empty, pointless, and even comically ridiculous. They do not appear to evoke any sense of utopian wonder. Instead, it is as though their appearance reinforces the notion that many past depictions of the future were hopelessly naïve and impossible to take seriously. In *Sleeper*, mid-century futurism is shown as something laughable.

In general, many movies of the era depict the future as an outright dystopia. As commonly portrayed, the world of tomorrow is one in which technology is used to support authoritarian societies, and consumerism is a source of waste, toxic excess, and empty living. The very forces that were supposed to deliver a rosy future, in other words, now appear as sources of an envisioned downfall. Many films show a future to be feared—a world gone horribly wrong. It did not take long for the cinema's depictions of dystopian futures to become so prevalent movies that they began to resemble a trope. In any case, the sunny, optimistic world of mid-century futurism increasingly faded from view.

Memories of the bright, techno-consumerist future did not entirely disappear, but Americans' attitudes about it changed. To some, mid-century futurism now seemed naïve or even blatantly misguided. To others, however, it looked more like a lost opportunity—something that society could have achieved but did not. Surprisingly, some people developed powerful feelings of nostalgia for this once-imagined future that never materialized. Although the label was not widely used until much later, retrofuturism was emerging, especially within popular culture. Although the term *retrofuturism* has multiple meanings, Elizabeth Guffey and Kate C. Lemay usefully note that it "represents a loss of faith."[7] As they note, "If futurism is a term that describes our anticipation of what is to come," then "retrofuturism is the remembering of that anticipation."[8]

By the middle of the 1970s, a wave of nostalgia swept over America, as evident in the popularity of the television series such as *Happy Days*, which presented a sanitized television version of 1950s America. Interestingly, people also began to feel nostalgia for the future—or more accurately for the visions of the future presented in earlier years.

In time, a widespread affection for the never-materialized lost future—the retrofuture—would become commonplace in the cultural landscape. Although this lost future never existed outside the imagination, it still represented something authentic and meaningful, as Guffey and Lemay suggest. Retrofuturism, it seems, resembles the same sort of feelings that many adults have for the presumed lost innocence and lost opportunities of their youth—a longing for what might have been.

NASA, for example, sometimes referred to the enthusiasm of the early Space Age. The agency had once been at the forefront of a new era and a symbolic beacon of the future. Even though it no longer commanded the attention that it once did, in various programs, it continued to promote the optimism and wonder of space into this new era. Working for NASA, artists such as Rick Guidice and Don Davis produced inspired space art, including concept illustrations of an imagined space colony, that harkened back to the kinds of imagery that Robert McCall created some years earlier.

America sought to put on a brave and optimistic face in 1976, the

178 Epilogue

Although much of the exuberance that accompanied mid-century futurism just a decade earlier had largely faded, NASA continued to promote expansive dreams for space exploration into the 1970s. In the 1970s, the agency's Ames Research Center commissioned imaginative illustrations for possible space colonies, including this one by the accomplished artist Rick Guidice (NASA Ames Research Center).

year the nation celebrated its bicentennial. That effort was not altogether successful. In the presidential election that autumn, Gerald Ford, who had inherited the presidency just two years earlier, was booted from office. Jimmy Carter—the ex-governor of Georgia, a former Navy officer, a peanut farmer, and a Washington outsider—narrowly won the popular vote and was elected in his place. Carter faced many problems, unexpected issues, and crises. He had some successes, but he presided over the country during a time of general malaise.

On the popular culture front, one bright spot appeared in 1977 with the release of George Lucas's relatively low budget *Star Wars*. Few people, including the studio executives who initially approved the production, had expected the movie to amount to much. If it seemed to be a throwback to motion pictures from a much earlier day, that was because in some respects, it was. Lucas initially set out to make a new version of *Flash Gordon*, the futuristic comic-strip and movie-serial character who delighted newspaper readers and matinee movie audiences a generation earlier. The

Epilogue 179

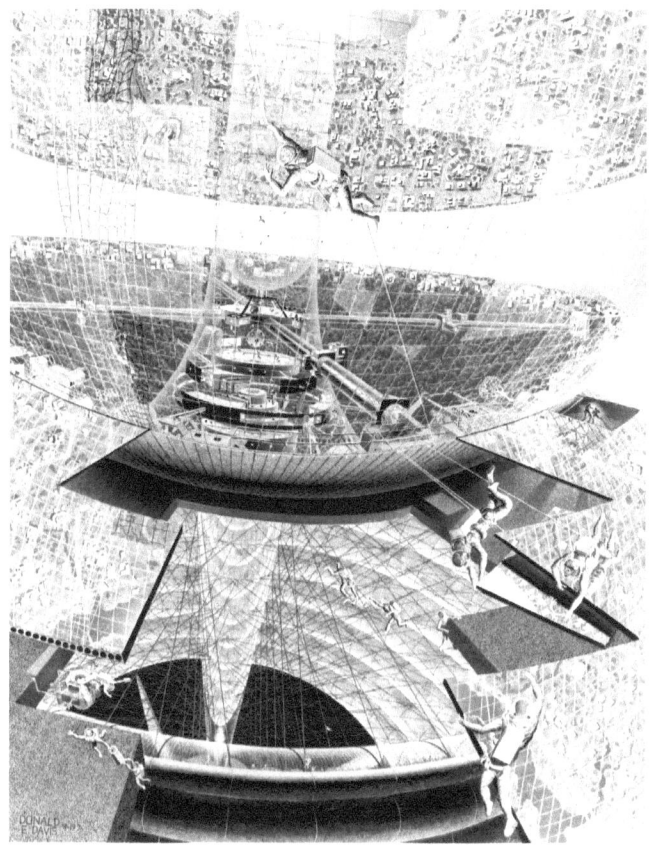

American artist Don Davis was also commissioned to create illustrations of futurist space colonies for NASA's Ames Research Center in the 1970s. His work evokes the sense of wonder and astonishment that was the hallmark of space art produced in the heyday of mid-century futurism some years earlier (NASA Ames Research Center).

cost of obtaining rights to the Flash Gordon character proved to be too high, but Lucas eventually retooled his concept.[9] With a new scenario and original set of characters, the reworked idea became *Star Wars*.

Ostensibly, *Star Wars* could hardly be about an American future or even the future of any earth-dwellers. As the film opens, a scrolling introduction tells viewers that the story they will see is from "a long time ago in a galaxy far, far away." The film is nothing of the sort, of course. It has a distinctly American point of view, and its entire universe is modeled after the real world of the 20th century. In many ways, moreover, *Star Wars* is a throwback to the early years of mid-century futurism. The film presents levitating transports (which appear to be little more than versions of flying cars), shiny robots, exotic spaceships, and many remarkable gadgets. Indeed, *Star Wars* embodies retrofuturism in many respects. It presents an ample supply of futuristic technology and gadgetry of the types that appeared in popular culture many years earlier. More importantly, for its original 1970s audience, it tapped in the nostalgia for an era in which life seemed simple, and technology evoked a sense of wonder. It was a throwback, then, to the time when mid-century futurism emerged and thrived.

Unexpectedly, *Star Wars* grew into a cultural phenomenon that generated much enthusiasm and substantial financial returns. In its wake, Hollywood looked to cash in on renewed nostalgia for retro-science fiction. Within just a few years, new movies based on old franchises appeared in theaters. These included *Superman* (1978), *Star Trek: The Motion Picture* (1979), and *Buck Rogers in the 25th Century* (1979). While the success of *Star Wars* was not necessarily the sole motivation for any of these productions, each benefited from the fondness of old-style futurism that they evoked even, as was the case with *Star Wars: The Motion Picture*, when the original course material was not very old.

These films look backward to evoke a sense of the future. Such movies were not indicative of the direction in which science-fiction films were headed overall. Indeed, many of the new science-fiction films aligned with a dark, cynical, and apocalyptic mood. *Capricorn One* (1978), for example, is a science-fiction and conspiracy-theory movie in which the government fakes a space mission to Mars. It is at once both outlandish and also one of the most cynical films of its type. *Alien* (1979) updates the monsters-in-space movie tradition with a horror angle. It also prominently features a corporate conspiracy subplot and is consistent with an "enemy within" theme. Many more films from the genre adopted a similarly gloomy perspective, which stood in stark contrast to the generally more optimistic *Star Wars* films and movies of that type.

The downbeat attitude about the direction of society continued in movies from other genres, as well. In the suspense film *Coma* (1978), otherwise healthy patients have routine surgery but mysteriously end up unconscious afterward. With next of kin believing there is no hope, the comatose patients are shipped off to a medical facility where villains secretly harvest their organs for the black market. The Australian action film *Mad Max* (1979), meanwhile, deals with a violent, post-apocalyptic wasteland. In its world, society has completely collapsed. In another example, the action film *Escape from New York* (1981) depicts a near-future world in which the United States has wholly decayed—so much so that the entire island of Manhattan is cordoned off and used as a lawless prison.

By the time the science-fiction film *Blade Runner* was released in

1982, American audiences were well-accustomed to movies in which society is very damaged and prospects for things to get better appear dim. The film features many elements from mid-century futurism: robots (in the form of incredibly lifelike androids), flying cars, cities that extend far into the sky, and high-end technology of many kinds. But these elements are now part of a perpetually dreary, authoritarian world just a hair's breadth away from the type of society portrayed in George Orwell's *1984*.

This turn to ruinous and apocalyptic visions of the near and distant future gained momentum. Incarnations of a dark future became as commonplace in some genres of American movies as visions of a bright tomorrow had been in consumer culture a generation earlier. That does not mean, of course, that Americans literally thought life in the real world was doomed to become like the dismal futures they often saw on screen. But audiences frequently encountered the dark-future theme. It was repeated over and over. Given the number of such movies released, it seems reasonable to conclude that at some level, this vision made an impression with many Americans.

By the time of the 1980 presidential election, Americans were ready for a change. High-profile adverse events in the previous months continued to weigh heavily on the national mood. The partial meltdown of a reactor at the Three Mile Island nuclear power station was one unnerving reminder that technology could go wrong. Meanwhile, in the political world, the Iran hostage crisis, which Jimmy Carter's administration was unable to resolve, appeared to add further evidence that America's power to shape world events was limited. Such developments, combined with other factors and a generally downbeat outlook, contributed to Ronald Reagan's election as the nation's 40th president. With his avuncular manner and plain speech, Reagan campaigned on bringing a new attitude to the American people. He aimed to sweep away the negativism, as he saw it, of the decade, and to replace it with a new spirit of optimism.

In many ways, the early years of Reagan's presidency did seem to provide the nation with a reset. The administration surely had its critics, but few would likely have argued that change of some sort had not come. Indeed, four years later, as Reagan campaigned for re-election in 1984, his campaign would characterize his first term as "Morning in America," as a new beginning in a new era.

Remnants of mid-century techno-consumerist futurism continued into this new decade and beyond, but as a cultural force, that idea increasingly was associated with the past. Some of its aesthetic elements, especially from the 1950s and 1960s, would occasionally resurface as style features for home décor and business design. "Mid-century modern," a term used to refer to the forward-looking and sleek architecture and furniture from those decades, would gain renewed popularity more than 50 years after this aesthetic originally appeared, for example. Mid-century rockets, business and product names with Atomic Age associations, and other elements from the futurism of the era frequently resurfaced in ironic or nostalgic manifestations.

Film, television, comic books, graphic novels, popular music, and many other popular culture forms often referenced this futurism, though almost always with a self-awareness that it referred more to past visions than future ones. Of course, some aspects of mid-century futurism—tail fins on cars would be a prominent example—began to look hopelessly dated, and, to many people, quaint examples of how unusual, and maybe even bizarre, past ideas about the future now seemed to be.

Considering the multitude of predictions during the years when mid-century futurism was fashionable, it is not surprising that many prognostications eventually turned out to be accurate, at least to some degree. The era of modern computing had already arrived, and its ultimately transformative effects on society were starting to become visible. There were also great strides in mobile communications and other electronic technologies, which seemed to come at an ever-quickening pace.

However, it is also true that some aspects of mid-century futurism now look dubious and even misguided. Indeed, the trouble-free life of leisure, a world of towering cities in the clouds, flying cars, humanoid robots, routine rocket trips, and other marvels that were hallmarks of mid-century futurism, have yet to materialize. And it is by no means a given that it would be an entirely positive development if they did.

It turned out that predicting technological innovations and consumer preferences was much easier than predicting changes in the social environment. Mid-century futurism generally neglected to take the existing social order sufficiently into account during its heyday. As often seen, predictions about the world to come often presumed that the social world of tomorrow would mostly look like the social world of today. It was largely a phenomenon intended for and appealing to white, middle-class consumers. It was, after all, the spending habits of these people that mattered most to the corporate interests that promulgated mid-century futurism. The failure to fully recognize that the social world would not stand still and that women, people of color, and other marginalized groups would not indefinitely sit on the sidelines was a significant shortcoming. Indeed, this failure is probably one reason for mid-century futurism's decline.

Despite a widespread retreat into nostalgia and retrofuturism, there is no denying that for a time, mid-century futurism was a real and powerful phenomenon. It emerged, in part, from the convergence of science,

Epilogue 183

technology, and consumerism, but it was never solely about those things. There was always something more—a creative and more aspirational spirit, a renewed sense of awe and wonder as people looked to a world of new possibilities.

That said, there is also no denying that mid-century futurism was a highly imperfect vision with significant limitations, including elements of sexism, racism, and triumphalist ideology that imagined tomorrow's world as America's world. These elements, often implicit and frequently so taken for granted that they remained unacknowledged, contributed to its undoing.

Ronald Reagan took the oath of office for his second term in January of 1985. That summer, director Robert Zemeckis' charming teenage comedy film, *Back to the Future*, became a huge hit with American audiences. Nominally a science-fiction movie, it depicts a white, middle-class suburban teenager who travels back in time to the height of the Atomic Age. He arrives there via a modified automobile—the iconic DeLorean, a short-lived darling of the automotive world that featured a sleek design and gleaming stainless-steel.

Back to the Future looked to the past with a sense of longing and with a bittersweet recognition of what might have been. In that respect, it

The iconic DeLorean automobile was a short-lived darling of automotive enthusiasts. A modified DeLorean was featured prominently in the popular movie comedy *Back to the Future*, a nostalgia-driven hit with American audiences in 1985 (iStock.com/Roberto Galan).

resembled the mindset of many Americans, not only in the 1980s but for years to come.

The following year saw a tragic coda to the futurism that had held sway in American society in previous decades. On January 28, 1986, NASA's space shuttle *Challenger*, with a crew of seven that included public school teacher Christa McAuliffe, took off on a highly anticipated mission. Moments later, however, it exploded mid-air. As a shocked television audience watched, the remnants of the shuttle fell into the Atlantic Ocean. The entire crew perished.

NASA had experienced tragedies before, but the horrifying failure of NASA's then-premier spacecraft was deeply wounding and seemed to call into question many aspects of America's space program.

America's dreams of the future did not die that day, of course. Life has misfortunes and setbacks, but people eventually move on. Indeed, people will always dream of the future in one way or another. But if it was not already apparent by that time, the exuberance of mid-century futurism, which had helped shape the hopes and aspirations of several generations, was long gone. America would need to build new dreams of tomorrow.

Chapter Notes

Preface

1. Tom Buckham, "World's First Rocket-Belt Flier Recalls Its Ups and Downs," *The Daily Gazette*, April 22, 1991.
2. *Ibid.*

Introduction

1. H.G. Wells, *The Discovery of the Future* (New York: B. W. Huebsch, 1913), 22.
2. *Ibid.*, 24.
3. *Ibid.*, 33.
4. *Ibid.*, 59.
5. "New Cult in Art Drapes the Nude, Bars Sentiment," *Evening World*, December 4, 1911.

Chapter 1

1. These events are recounted in "Youth Thinks Fair Is Great, But Misses 'Shoot-the-Shoots,'" *Brooklyn Eagle*, May 1, 1939.
2. "Assortment of Marvels," *New York Times*, April 20, 1939.
3. This figure is cited in Jessica Weglein, et. al, "Historical Note," *New York World's Fair 1939 and 1940 Incorporated Records 1935–1945* (New York: The New York Public Library Manuscripts and Archives Division, 2008), vii.
4. "Strides in Lighting laid to Fair's Magic," *New York Times*, May 20, 1939.
5. *Ibid.*
6. "R.C. Engelken Dies; Lighting Engineer," *New York Times*, January 20, 1944.
7. R. C. Engelken, "Lighting the New York World's Fair," *Journal of Electrical Engineering* 59 (May 1940): 179.
8. "Night Brings a Fairyland," *Brooklyn Eagle*, May 1, 1939.
9. Robert W. Rydell, *World's Fairs: The Century-of-Progress Expositions* (Chicago: University of Chicago Press, 1993), 116.
10. "Here is the Fair," *New York Times*, April 30, 1939.
11. Richard Wurts, et al., *The New York World's Fair, 1939-1940* (New York: Dover, 1977), 3.
12. *Ibid.*, 3.
13. *Ibid.*, 5.
14. *Your World of Tomorrow* (New York: Rogers-Kellogg-Stillson, 1939), 5.
15. *Ibid.*, 4.
16. *Ibid.*, 9.
17. *Ibid.*, 6.
18. *Ibid.*, 6.
19. "Town of Tomorrow: Demonstration Home No. 2, The House of Plywood, New York World's Fair 1939" (brochure, unspecified source, 1939), archived at the Art Institute of Chicago.
20. "Town of Tomorrow: Demonstration Home No. 5, The Small Home of Brick, New York World's Fair 1939" (brochure, unspecified source, 1939), archived at the Art Institute of Chicago.
21. *Ibid.*
22. "Town of Tomorrow: Demonstration Home No. 18, The Electric Home, New York World's Fair 1939" (brochure, unspecified source, 1939), archived at the Art Institute of Chicago.
23. "The World's Fair—Some Do's and Don'ts for Prospective Visitors," *Reading Eagle*, July 16, 1939.

24. "World's Fair Visitors Tour 1960 City of Broad Streets, Sunshine, Space and Air" (press release), General Motors Corporation (Detroit, MI), April 29, 1939, archived at the Art Institute of Chicago.

25. James Mauro, *Twilight at the World of Tomorrow* (New York: Ballantine, 2010), 171.

26. These details are recounted in *Ibid.*, 171–72.

27. "Spectacular Vista in General Motors World of the Future at Fair" (press release), General Motors Corporation (Detroit, MI), April 29, 1939, archived at the Art Institute of Chicago.

28. B. Alexandra Szerlip, *The Man Who Designed the Future: Norman Bel Geddes and the Invention of Twentieth-Century America* (Brooklyn: Melville House, 2017), 240.

29. "World's Fair Visitors Tour 1960 City of Broad Streets, Sunshine, Space and Air" (press release), General Motors Corporation (Detroit, MI), April 29, 1939, archived at the Art Institute of Chicago.

30. "Farm of the Future" (press release), General Motors Corporation (Detroit, MI) (undated, presumably circa April 1939), archived at the Art Institute of Chicago.

31. Robert W. Rydell and Laura Burd Schiavo, eds., *Designing Tomorrow: America's World's Fairs of the 1930s* (New Haven: Yale University Press, 2010), 9.

32. "The Exhibits: An Amazing Array," *New York Times*, April 30, 1939.

33. Andrew F. Wood, *New York 1939–1940 World's Fair* (Charleston, SC: Arcadia, 2004), 55.

34. Thomas Georges, *Digital Soul: Intelligent Machines and Human Values* (Boulder, CO: Westview Press, 2003), 47.

35. These details are discussed in Amanda Kooser, "Elektro: 1939 Smoking Robot Saved from Oblivion," *C/NET*, April 5, 2012, https://www.cnet.com/news/elektro-1939-somking-robot-saved-from-oblivion.

36. *Ibid.*

37. This is part of the copy for "The Middleton Family at the New York World's Fair," *Saturday Evening Post*, June 24, 1939, 100.

38. Mordaunt Hall, "A Technical Marvel," *New York Times*, March 7, 1927.

39. Noel Sharkey, "The Return of Elektro, the First Celebrity Robot," *New Scientist*, December 17, 2008, https://newscientist.com/article/mg20026873-000-the-return-of-elektro-the-first-celebrity-robot/.

40. Wood, *New York's 1939–1940 World's Fair*, 77.

41. David A. Mindell, *Between Human and Machine: Feedback, Control, and Computing Before Cybernetics* (Baltimore: Johns Hopkins University Press, 2004), 132.

42. This account appeared in "Seeing by Wire," *Albuquerque Morning Journal*, July 1, 1914.

43. A.M. Low, "Scientist Predicts Wonders of Age 500 Years Hence; Famous Engineer Now at Work on Tele-vision Enabling Long Distance Sight," *South Bend News-Times*, February 8, 1920.

44. These details are expressed in a news release issued by RCA on May 5, 1935, as reproduced in Stephen Herbert, *A History of Early Television*, vol. 3 (New York: Routledge, 2004), 13–15.

45. "Ceremony Is Carried by Television as Industry Makes Its Formal Bow," *New York Times*, May 1, 1939.

46. O.B. Hanson, "Here Comes Television!" *Think* 4, no. 12 (1939): 36.

47. Helen Astor, "Women and World Order," *Think* 4, No. 12 (1939): 10.

48. "Survey to Aid World [sic] Fair," *New York Times*, April 10, 1937.

49. Lizabeth Cohen, *A Consumers' Republic: The Politics of Mass Consumption in Postwar America* (New York: Random House, 2003), 33–41.

50. "21 Fair Advisers on Consumer Quit," *New York Times*, February 28, 1939.

51. Among the signatories of the mass-resignation letter were a number of prominent and well-connected women, including Ruth W. Ayres, the group's acting secretary; Emily Newman Blair, former chair of the Consumers Advisory Board; Ruth Brindze; a writer, Anna M. Cooley, of Columbia University; Alice Edwards of the American Home Economics Association; Florence Fallgatter of Iowa State College; Frances F. Gannon, Deputy Commissioner of Markets, City of New York; and more than a half dozen others. See "21 Fair Advisers on Consumer Quit," *New York Times*, February 28, 1939.

52. "Tempest Raised at Fair by

Undraped Forms Divine," *The Evening Star*, June 11, 1939.
53. *Ibid.*
54. La Guardia is quoted in *Ibid.*
55. "Sheriff Asks La Guardia's Help After 'Miss Nude' Show at Fair," *The Evening Star*, June 2, 1939.
56. Steven Gregory, *Black Corona: Race and the Politics of Place in an Urban Community* (Princeton: Princeton University Press, 2011), 45.
57. *Ibid.*, 45–46.
58. "Hitler Boasts of Nazi Arms; Assails Boycott," *Brooklyn Eagle*, May 1, 1939.

Chapter 2

1. Raymond Loewy, "What of the Post-War World?" *New York Times*, September 26, 1943.
2. Henry R. Luce, "The American Century," *Life*, February 17, 1941, 61.
3. *Ibid.*
4. *Ibid.*, 65.
5. *Ibid.*
6. *Ibid.*
7. "Takes Bright View of Realty Future: Noyes Predicts New York City Will Play Large Part in Post-War Activity," *New York Times*, January 31, 1943.
8. "Crowley Discusses Post-War Banking," *New York Times*, March 29, 1943.
9. The study, which was led by Bernard M. Baruch, was reported in "Baruch Maps Way to Preparedness for Shift to Peace," *New York Times*, February 19, 1944.
10. *Ibid.*
11. "Johnston See a Bright Future for Women in Jobs After the War," *New York Times*, April 1, 1944.
12. Lester B. Granger, "Victory Through Unity," *Opportunity: A Journal of Negro Life* 21 (January 1943): 147.
13. This appears in an advertisement for The Prudential Insurance Company of America that was published in *Life*, June 7, 1943, 18.
14. *Ibid.*
15. "Those Post-War Miracles," *The Nation*, September 18, 1943, 320–22.
16. Lizabeth Cohen, *A Consumers' Republic: The Politics of Mass Consumption in Postwar America* (New York: Vintage, 2004), 428, n. 25.
17. Harry S. Truman, "Speech before the Society of Plastics Industry at Hot Springs, Virginia," May 4, 1942 (press release), Harry S. Truman Library and Museum, https://www.trumanlibrary.gov/library/truman-papers/press-release-file-1937-1945/may-4-1942-society-plastics-industry-hot-springs.
18. Mary Madison, "In a Plastic World," *New York Times*, August 22, 1943.
19. *Ibid.*
20. *Ibid.*
21. Loewy, "What of the Post-War World?"
22. *Ibid.*
23. This account is drawn from U.S. Department of Energy, "Informing the Public, August 1945," *The Manhattan Project: An Interactive History* (n.d.), https://www.osti.gov/opennet/manhattan-project-history/Events/1945-present/public_reaction.htm.
24. *Ibid.*
25. Harry S. Truman, "Statement by the President of the United States" (press release announcing use of the atomic bomb), August 6, 1945, Harry S. Truman Library and Museum, https://www.trumanlibrary.gov/library/research-files/press-release-white-house.
26. *Ibid.*
27. The report, subsequently issued as a trade book, was initially printed by the government and distributed as Henry De Wolf Smyth and United States Army, *Atomic Bombs: A General Account of the Development of Methods of Using Atomic Energy for Military Purposes Under the Auspices of the United States Government, 1940–1945* (Washington, D.C.: War Department, 1945).
28. Henry Winfield Secor, "Disintegrate One Gram of Hydrogen—Lift 10 Woolworth Buildings 300 Feet," *The Evening World*, September 23, 1919.
29. "Tinkering with Angry Atoms May Blow Up the Earth," *Morning Tulsa Daily World*, May 21, 1922.
30. "Scientists Split Uranium, Create Record Discharge of Atomic Energy," *Life*, April 24, 1939, 52.
31. Laurence's working relationship with the War Department was explained in an editor's note that appeared in William L. Laurence, "Drama of the Atomic Bomb Found Climax in July 16 Test," *New York Times*, September 26, 1945.

32. Ibid.
33. Ibid.
34. Howard W. Blakeslee, "Atomic Bomb: None Can Tell Extent of Destructive Effects," *Schenectady Gazette*, August 9, 1945.
35. "Atomic Bomb Ban Urged by Dr. Urey: Scientist Calls for a World Government Able to Prevent Manufacture of Weapons," *New York Times*, October 22, 1945.
36. E.L. Woodward, "How Can We Prevent Atomic War," *New York Times*, January 13, 1946.
37. "Atomic Culture," Atomic Heritage Foundation, August 9, 2017, https://www.atomicheritage.org/history/atomic-culture.
38. Ibid.
39. See Gordon B. Arnold, *Projecting the End of the American Dream: Hollywood's Visions of U.S. Decline* (Santa Barbara, CA: Praeger, 2013).
40. W.L. Davidson, "We Can Harness the Atom," *Popular Science*, December 1945, 65
41. The popular line "What's good for General Motors is good for America" appears to be a misquoted version of a statement made in 1952 by Charles W. Wilson, then serving as the CEO of General Motors. Wilson's original comment was "What is good for our country is good for General Motors, and vice versa." See William Pelfrey, *Billy, Alfred, and General Motors* (New York: AMACOM, 2006), 277–278.
42. "Flying Automobile is Folding-Wing Biplane," *Popular Mechanics*, February 1922, 164.
43. "Flying Autos," *Flying Magazine*, September 1946, 22–23.

Chapter 3

1. "Charter of the United Nations," United Nations, October 24, 1945, https://un.org/en/charter/charter-united-nations/.
2. This topic is discussed in Gordon B. Arnold, *Conspiracy Theory in Film, Television, and Politics* (Westport, CT: Praeger, 2008), 19–29.
3. "History: 1950s," *Ad Age*, September 15, 2003, http://adage.com/article/adage-encyclopedia/history-1950s/98701/.

4. Jesse Hicks, "Atoms for Peace: The Mixed Legacy of Eisenhower's Nuclear Gambit," *Distillations*, July 19, 2014, https://sciencehistory.org/distillations/atoms-for-peace-the-mixed-egacy-of-eisnhower-nuclear-gambit.
5. Stewart Alsop, "Eisenhower Pushes Operation Candor," *Washington Post*, September 21, 1953.
6. Dwight D. Eisenhower, "Atoms for Peace," address to the General Assembly of the United Nations, New York, December 8, 1953.
7. Shawn J. Parry-Giles, "Dwight D. Eisenhower, 'Atoms for Peace,'" *Voices of Democracy 1* (2006), 122.
8. Racial discrimination and the growth of suburban housing are discussed at length in Richard Rothstein, *The Color of Law: A Forgotten History of How Our Government Segregated America* (New York: W.W. Norton, 2017).
9. Lizabth Cohen, *A Consumer's Republic: The Politics of Mass Consumption* (New York: Vintage, 2003), 266–267.
10. *Classic Car Book: The Definitive Visual History* (London: Dorling Kindersley, 2016), 32.
11. This ad appeared in several publications, including *Life*, January 7, 1957, 32.
12. A useful discussion of the chrome era appears in Michael Furman, *Automobiles of the Chrome Age, 1946–1960* (New York: Harry N. Abrams, 2004).
13. David Gartman, *Auto-Opium: A Social History of American Automotive Design* (New York: Routledge, 1994), 110.
14. "Aircraft Effect for '56 Dodge," *Detroit Tribune*, October 8, 1956.
15. "New Pontiacs on Display Here Friday," *Detroit Tribune*, November 7, 1956.
16. "GM Build First gas Turbine Car," *Tabor City Tribune*, February 28, 1954.
17. This ad appeared in *Fortune*, April 1954, 211.
18. This was published in *The American City*, March 1955, 26.
19. This ad appeared in *Industrial Design* 4 (1957): 8.
20. David Riesman, with Denney Reuel and Nathan Glazer, *The Lonely Crowd: A Study of the Changing American Character* (New Haven: Yale University Press, 1950).

21. Neal Gabler, *Walt Disney: The Triumph of the American Imagination* (New York: Random House, 2006), 483.
22. For these and other details, see Michael Barrier, *The Animated Man: A Life of Walt Disney* (Berkeley: University of California Press, 2007), 121.
23. Dennis Piszkiewicz, *Wernher Von Braun: The Man Who Sold the Moon* (Westport, CT: Praeger, 1998), 89.
24. Carl Jung, *Flying Saucers: A Modern Myth of Things Seen in the Skies* (London: Routledge & Keegan Paul, 1959).
25. Marina Benjamin, *Rocket Dreams* (New York: The Free Press, 2003), 39.
26. *Ibid.*
27. Tison Pugh and Susan Lynn Aronstein, *The Disney Middle Ages: A Fairy-Tale and Fantasy Past* (New York: Palgrave Macmillan, 2012), 151.

Chapter 4

1. Dwight David Eisenhower, *Dwight D. Eisenhower: Containing the Public Messages, Speeches, and Statements of the President* (Washington, D.C.: Government Printing Office, 1960), 865.
2. "Editorial," *Space Travel*, November 1958, 4.
3. For a comprehensive discussion of this topic, see De Witt Douglas Kilgore, *Astrofuturism: Science, Race, and Visions of Utopia in Space* (Philadelphia: University of Pennsylvania Press, 2003).
4. Emily S. Rosenberg, "Far Out: The Space Age in American Culture," in *Remembering the Space Age*, ed. Steven J. Dick (Washington, D.C.: National Aeronautics and Space Administration, 2008), 159.
5. De Witt Douglas Kilgore, *Astrofuturism: Science, Race, and Visions of Utopia in Space* (Philadelphia: University of Pennsylvania Press, 2003), 83.
6. *Ibid.*, 51.
7. John. W. Finney, "U.S. Missile Experts Shaken by Sputnik," *New York Times*, October 13, 1957.
8. Steve Garber and Roger Launius, "A Brief History of NASA," *NASA*, https://history.nasa.gov/factsheet.htm.
9. Amy Ryan and Gary Keeley, "Sputnik and U.S. Intelligence: The Warning Record," *Studies in Intelligence* 61, no. 3 (September 2017), https://www.cia.gov/library/center-for-the-study-of-intelligence/csi-publications/csi-studies/studies/vol-61-no-3/pdfs/sputnik-the-warning-record.pdf.
10. *Ibid.*
11. Gladwin Hill, "Officer Predicts Battles in Space," *New York Times*, February 20, 1957.
12. Walter Sullivan, "Soviet Expert Tells West of Test Rocket," *New York Times*, October 3, 1957.
13. William E. Burrows, *This New Ocean: The Story of the First Space Age* (New York: Modern Library, 1998), 139.
14. David Whitehouse, "First Dog in Space Died Within Hours," *BBC News, World Edition*, October 28, 2002, http://news.bbc.co.uk/2/hi/science/nature/2367681.stm.
15. Garber and Launius, "A Brief History of NASA."
16. *Ibid.*
17. James Kauffman, "NASA's PR Campaign on Behalf of Manned Space Flight, 1961–1963," *Public Relations Review* 17, no. 1 (Spring 1991): 57.
18. Edwin Diamond, *The Rise and Fall of the Space Age* (Garden City, NJ: Doubleday & Company, 1964), 83.
19. Megan Garber, "Astro Mad Men: NASA's 1960s Campaign to Win America's Heart," *The Atlantic*, July 31, 2013, https://www.theatlantic.com/technology/archive/2013/07/astro-mad-men-nasas-1960s-campaign-to-win-americas-heart/278233/.
20. John F. Kennedy, "Acceptance of Democratic Nomination for President" (speech to the Democratic National Convention, Los Angeles, CA, July 15, 1960), https://www.jfklibrary.org/learn/about-jfk/historic-speeches/acceptance-of-democratic-nomination-for-president.
21. John F. Kennedy, "Special Message to the Congress on Urgent National Needs" (speech to Congress, Washington, D.C., May 25, 1961), https://www.jfklibrary.org/archives/other-resources/john-f-kennedy-speeches/united-states-congress-special-message-19610525.
22. John F. Kennedy, "Address on the Nation's Space Effort" (speech at Rice University, September 12, 1962), https://jfklibrary.org/archives/other-resources/john-f-kennedy-speeches/rice-university-19620912.

23. "Man in the Moon's First Guest May be Woman, Panel Suggests," *New York Times*, September 4, 1957.
24. "Damp Prelude to Space: A Potential Lady Orbiter Excels in Lonesome Test," *Life*, October 24, 1960, 81.
25. Margaret A. Weitekamp, *Right Stuff, Wrong Sex: America's First Women in Space Program* (Baltimore: Johns Hopkins University Press, 2004), 117.
26. *Ibid.*, 151.
27. *Ibid.*, 146.
28. "She Orbits Over the Sex Barrier," *Life*, June 28, 1963, 28.
29. "The U.S. Team Is Still Warming Up the Bench," *Life*, June 28, 1963, 32–33.
30. Clare Booth Luce, "But Some People Simply Never Get the Message," *Life*, June 28, 1963, 31.
31. Sarah McLennan, "When the Computer Wore a Skirt: Langley's Human Computers, 1935–1970," *NASA*, https://crgis.ndc.nasa.gov/historic/Human_Computers.
32. *Ibid.*
33. Dwight's situation is thoughtfully discussed in Richard Paul and Steven Moss, *We Could Not Fail: The First African Americans in the Space Program* (Austin: University of Texas Press, 2015), 89–104.
34. *Ibid.*
35. Robert McCall, "Wild But Sane Ideas for Space Flight: *Life* Presents Some Imaginative New Concepts," *Life*, April 21, 1961, 48–52.
36. Caitlin McGurk, "Found in the Collection: Arthur Radebaugh's 'Closer Thank We Think,'" Billy Ireland Cartoon Museum (blog), December 27, 2012, https://library.osu.edu/blogs/cartoons/2012/12/27/found-in-the-collection-arthur-radebaughs-closer-than-we-think/.
37. Arthur Radebaugh as quoted in Matt Novak, "Before the Jetsons, Arthur Radebaugh Illustrated the Future," *Smithsonian*, April 2012, 30.
38. *Ibid.*

Chapter 5

1. Knute Berger, "Back to the Future: Why Seattle's World's Fair Mattered," *Seattle Magazine* (January 2012), http://www.seattlemag.com/article/back-future-why-seattles-worlds-fair-mattered.
2. This description is based on accounts appearing in "Century 21 World's Fair," Seattle Municipal Archives, Seattle, Washington, https://www.seattle.gov/cityarchives/exhibits-and-education/digital-document-libraries/century-21-worlds-fair, and Maysha Watson, "The History of the Seattle Center: A Timeline," *Seattle Magazine* (February 2012), https://www.seattlemag.com/article/history-seattle-center-timeline.
3. Muriel Lederer, "Seattle Looks Ahead to Century 21," *The Rotarian*, March 1961, 24–25.
4. Alan J. Stein, "Astronaut John Glenn Visits the Seattle World's Fair on May 10, 1962," HistoryLink.org, The Free Encyclopedia of Washington State History, February 18, 2002, https://historylink.org/File/3697.
5. *Seattle World's Fair 1962: Official Guidebook* (Seattle: Acme Publications, 1962), 8.
6. Lederer, "Seattle Looks Ahead to Century 21," 25.
7. *Ibid.*
8. These and other technical details are described in U.S. Department of Commerce, *United States Science Exhibit, Seattle World's Fair: Final Report* (Washington, D.C.: GPO, 1963), 18–19.
9. Bill Cotter, *Seattle's 1962 World's Fair* (Charleston, SC: Arcadia Publishing, 2015), 25.
10. "Seattle World's Fair, Washington State Coliseum, Seattle, WA, 1960–1962," Pacific Coast Architectural Database, http://pcad.lib.washington.edu/building/5972.
11. Stacy Warren, "To Work and Play and Live in the Year 2000: Creating the Future at the 1962 Seattle World's Fair," in *Meet Me at the Fair: A World's Fair Reader*, edited by Laura Hollengreen, Celia Pearce, Rebecca Rouse, and Bobby Schweizer (Pittsburgh: ETC Press, 2014), 476.
12. *Ibid.*, 479.
13. *Ibid.*
14. This general topic is treated at length in Gordon B. Arnold, *Projecting the End of the American Dream: Hollywood's Visions of U.S. Decline* (Santa Barbara, CA: Praeger, 2013).
15. Cotter, 29.

16. Joseph Barbera, quoted in Peter Joseph, *Good Times: An Oral History of America in the Nineteen Sixties* (New York: Charterhouse, 1973), 17
17. Ibid.
18. Matt Novak, "50 Years of the Jetsons: Why the Show Still Matters," *The Smithsonian*, September 19, 2012, https://www.smithsonianmag.com/history/50-years-of-the-jetsons-why-the-show-still-matters-43459669/.
19. Joseph Barbera, quoted in Scott Moore, "'Jetsons' Will Give Us a Look Ahead on New Year's Eve," *The Spokesman Review*, December 25, 1999.
20. Ibid.
21. Novak, "50 Years of the Jetsons."
22. Arnold B. Barach at al., *1975 and the Changes to Come* (New York: Harper & Row, 1962), 33, 37.
23. Ibid., 25.
24. Ibid., 46–47.
25. Ibid., 74–78.
26. Ibid., 84.
27. Ibid., 106.
28. Ibid., 136.
29. Ibid., 146.
30. Lawrence R. Samuel, *The End of Innocence: The 1964–1965 World's Fair* (Syracuse: Syracuse University Press, 2010), 3.
31. Robert Kopple quoted in Ibid., 3.
32. This account is drawn from Jon Margois, *The Last Innocent Year: 1964 and the Beginning of the Sixties* (New York: William Morrow, 1999), 198–200.
33. Samuel, *The End of Innocence*, 166.
34. Ibid., 167.
35. Ibid.
36. Stephen P. Alpert, "The Neutron Irradiated Dime, Atomic Energy Commission, New York World's Fair, 1964–1965," *TMAS Journal* 14, no. 1 (February 1974), 19.
37. This American Museum of Atomic Energy press release, presumably issued in 1954, is quoted in "Irradiated Dimes—1950s, 1960s," Oak Ridge Associated Universities, [1999], https://orau.org/ptp/collection/medalsmementoes/dimes.htm.
38. Joseph Tirella, *Tomorrow-Land: The 1964–1965 World's Fair and the Transformation of America* (Guilford, CT: Lyons Press, 2014), 206.
39. Donna R. Braden, "Ford Meets Disney at the Magic Skyway," *Fast Forward* (blog), www.thehenryford.org/explore/blog/ford-meets-disney-at-the-magic-highway.
40. Tirella, *Tomorrow-Land*, 206.
41. Gay Talese, "About the Fair: Elderly View the 'Futurama' as a World of Wonders They Will Never See," *New York Times*, May 1, 1964.
42. Ibid.
43. Gay Talese, "About the Fair: Member of Planned Parenthood Groaned as Sign Blinks Population Rise," *New York Times*, April 25, 1964.
44. "General Electric Progressland" (advertisement), *New York Sunday News, Special World's Fair Section*, April 12, 1964.
45. Ibid.
46. Dag Spicer, "IBM and the 1964 World's Fair," Computer History Museum, Mountain View, CA (April 16, 2014), https://www.computerhistory.org/atchm/ibm-and-1964-worlds-fair/.
47. Quoted in Beth J. Harpaz, "Revisiting the 1964 New York World's Fair, 50 Years On," *Daily Herald*, April 21, 2014.
48. Jon Margolis, *Last Innocent Year*, 199.

Chapter 6

1. Isaac Asimov, "Visit to the World's Fair of 2014," *New York Times*, August 16, 1964.
2. Ibid.
3. Ibid.
4. Ibid.
5. Ibid.
6. Ibid.
7. Ibid.
8. Ibid.
9. "What the Future Holds for America as the President's 'Idea Men' See It," *U.S. News and World Report*, June 22, 1964, 40–67.
10. Ibid., 42.
11. Ibid.
12. Ajay Chaudry, et al., *Poverty in the United States: 50-Year Trends and Safety Net Impacts* (Washington, D.C.: U.S. Department of Health and Human Services, 2016), 7.
13. "What the Future Holds for America as the President's 'Idea Men' See It," 50–51.

14. The comments of Roger Revelle, David Riesman, and Margaret Mead can be found, respectively, in *Ibid.*, 56, 52, 48.
15. A.C. Spectorsky, "The MR [sic] Boys Are Out to make You Buy and Buy," *New York Times*, April 28, 1957.
16. This matter is discussed in a book review from that era. See Robert Lekachman, "Popular Sociology: *The Status Seekers* by Vance Packard," Commentary, September 1, 1959, 270.
17. Rachel Carson, *Silent Spring* (Boston: Houghton Mifflin, 1962), 1–3.
18. *Ibid.*, 16.
19. *Ibid.*, 297.
20. Lisa Sideris and Kathleen Dean Moore, eds., *Rachel Carson: Legacy and Challenge* (Albany: State University of New York Press, 2008), 7.
21. "Desolate Year," *Monsanto Magazine*, October 1962, 4–9.
22. This quotation appears in Caitlin Johnson, "The Legacy of 'Silent Spring,'" *CBS Sunday Morning*, April 22, 2007, https://www.cbsnews.com/news/the-legacy-of-silent-spring/.
23. Ralph Nader, *Unsafe at Any Speed: The Designed-In Dangers of the American Automobile* (New York: Grossman Publishers, 1965), viii.
24. "Motor Vehicle Traffic Fatalities, 1900–2007," Federal Highway Administration, January 2009, https://www.fha.dot.gov/policyinformation/statistics/2007/pdf/fi2oo.pdf.
25. Nader, *Unsafe at Any Speed*, ix.
26. Nader devotes an entire chapter to this subject. See *Ibid.*, 232–295.
27. *Ibid.*, 346.
28. *Ralph Nader v. General Motors Corporation*, Court of Appeals of New York, 307 N.Y.S.2d 647, 25 N.Y.2d 560, 255 N.E.2d, January 8, 1970.
29. These quotations appear in *Ibid.*
30. These details are published in Franklin Jonas and Diana Klebanow, *People's Lawyers: Crusaders for Justice in American History* (Armonk, NY: M.E. Sharpe, 2002), 427.
31. Craig R. Whitney, "G.M. Settles Nader Suit on Privacy for $425,000," *New York Times*, August 14, 1970.
32. Pew Research Center for the People and the Press, *Deconstructing Distrust: How Americans View Government* (Washington, D.C.: Pew Research Center for People and the Press, 1998), 87.
33. *Ibid.*
34. Data for the question about the public's approval in government is reported for even-numbered alternate years only. See *Ibid.*
35. *Ibid.*, 25–26.
36. *Ibid.*, 25.
37. Emily S. Rosenberg, "Far Out: The Space Age in American Culture," in *Remembering the Space Age*, ed. Steven J. Dick (Washington, D.C.: National Aeronautics and Space Administration, 2008), 178.
38. Jason Perlow, "Star Trek: Discovery Continues the Mission of Futurism and Bold Social Commentary," *ZDNet*, September 21, 2017, https://zdnet.com/article/star-trek-a-mission-of-discovery-futurism-bold-social-commentary/.

Chapter 7

1. Robert B. Frederick, "Review: '2001: A space odyssey,'" *Variety*, April 2, 1968.
2. *Ibid.*
3. Stephanie Schwam, *The Making of 2001: A Space Odyssey* (New York: Modern Library, 2000), 44.
4. Aisha Harris, "Is HAL Really IBM?" *Slate*, January 7, 2013, https://slate.com/culture/2013/01/hal-9000-ibm-theory-kubrick-letters-shed-new-light-on-old-debate.html.
5. Official figures indicate that 11,780 American soldiers died in 1969, a number surpassed only the previous year, when the death toll was 16,899. These figures are listed in "Vietnam War U.S. Military Fatal Casualty Records," compiled by the National Archives, April 28, 2008, https://gov/research/military/vietnam-war/casualty-statistics.
6. Jennifer M. Gidley, *The Future: A Very Short Introduction* (New York: Oxford University Press, 2017), 45.
7. RAND Corporation, *50th Project Air Force, 1946–1996* (Santa Monica: RAND Corporation, 1996), 17.
8. Douglas Aircraft Company, *Preliminary Design of an Experimental World-Circling Spaceship* (Santa Monica, CA: Douglas Aircraft Company, 1946), i.

9. RAND Corporation, *Project Air Force*, 1946–1996, 18.
10. Ibid.
11. Ibid., 20.
12. "Delphi Method," RAND Corporation, [n.d.], https:// rand.org/topic/delphi-method.html.
13. Henry Mintzberg, "The Fall and Rise of Strategic Planning," *Harvard Business Review* (January-February, 1994): 107.
14. "The Futurists: Looking Toward A.D. 2000," *Time*, February 25, 1966, https:// content.time.com/time/subscriber/artcile/0,33009,835128-1,00.htm.
15. Ibid.
16. Ibid.
17. Ibid.
18. Ibid.
19. Ibid.
20. Frederick Polak, *The Image of the Future* (New York: Oceana, 1961).
21. Jenny Andersson, *The Future of the World: Futurology, Futurists, and the Struggle for the Post-Cold War Imagination* (New York: Oxford University Press, 2018), 9
22. Ossip Flechtheim, "Teaching the Future," *The Journal of Higher Education* 16, no. 9 (December 1945): 460–465.
23. Anderrson, 43–45.
24. Eberhard Fromm, "Vater der Futurologie. Ossip K. Flechtheim," *Berlinische Monatsschrift* 3, no. 8 (1999): 50–57.
25. Ibid.
26. Ossip Flechtheim, *History and Futurology* (Meisenheim am Glan: Hain, 1966).
27. Richard B. Halley and Harold G. Vatter, "Technology and the Future as History: A Critical Review of Futurism." *Technology and Culture* 19, no. 1 (January 1978): 53.
28. Herman Kahn and Anthony J. Wiener, *The Year 2000: A Framework for Speculation on the Next Thirty-Three Year* (New York: Macmillan, 1967).
29. This is noted, for example, in review of the book from that era. See Wilbert E. Moore, "Through a Glass Darkly," *Science* 160, no. 3828 (May 10, 1968): 647–648.
30. Tolon, Kaya, "The American Futures Studies Movement (1965–1975): Its Roots, Motivations, and Influences" (doctoral thesis, Iowa State University, 2011), 124.
31. "Life May Become Too Easy," *The Futurist* 3, no. 2 (April 1969), 3.
32. Jack Pitman, "Covering the News of Tomorrow," *Milwaukee Journal*, March 5, 1967.
33. "Television," *New York Magazine*, May 5, 1969, 14.
34. Scott Kirsner, "At 83, Cape Cod Entrepreneur Still Focused on the Future of Transportation," *Boston Globe*, July 22, 2009.
35. "Television," *New York Magazine* (May 5, 1969), 14.
36. This quotation is taken from a later edition: Paul Ehrlich, *The Population Bomb* (New York: Ballantine, 1970), 11.
37. Ibid.
38. Elizabeth Kolbert, "Dymaxion Man," *New Yorker* (June 9 & 16, 2008), www://newyorker.com/magazine/2008/09/dymaxion-man.
39. Ibid.
40. Arthur Roberts, "Vision of the Future," *Bulletin of the Atomic Scientists* 25, no. 5 (May 1969): 55.
41. Alvin Toffler, *Future Shock* (New York: Random House, 1970), 1.
42. Richard R. Lingeman, "Books of the Times: Future: Tense," *New York Times*, August 7, 1970.
43. Harold Shane, "We Must Learn to Face an Uncertain, Changing Future. But Can We?" *The Phi Delta Kappan* 52, no. 2 (October 1970): 126.
44. Toffler, *Future Shock*, 421.
45. Shane, "We Must Learn to Face an Uncertain, Changing Future," 126.
46. Newt Gingrich, "Remembering Alvin Toffler," *Politico*, December 31, 2016, https://www.politico.com/magazine/story/2016/12/alvin-toffler-obituary-future-shock-214561.

Epilogue

1. Although the names of the organizations are similar, OAPEC (Organization of Arab Petroleum Exporting Countries), which was established in 1968, is a separate entity from OPEC (Organization of Petroleum Exporting Countries), which was established earlier in 1960 and has membership from around the globe.
2. One account of the gas shortage situation in Boston, which is typical of the era,

can be found in Nils J. Bruzelius, "Long Lines Lead to Short Tempers," *Boston Globe*, December 30, 1973.

3. "Public Trust in Government: 1958–2019," Pew Research Center, April 19, 2019, https://www.people-press.org/2019/04/11/public-trust-in-government-1958-2019/.

4. *Ibid*.

5. Kelly was not the first to express this sentiment, but his use of this saying, first in a 1970 ecology poster that featured the Pogo character and subsequently in his syndicated comic strip, popularized its use. For more on the background, see James Eric Black, *Walt Kelly and Pogo: The Art of the Political Swamp* (Jefferson, NC: McFarland, 2015), 3.

6. Roger Ebert, "Executive Action," *Chicago Sun-Times*, November 20, 1973.

7. Elizabeth Guffey and Kate C. Lemay, "Retrofuturism and Steampunk," in *The Oxford Handbook of Science Fiction*, ed. Rob Latham (New York: Oxford University Press, 2014), 434.

8. *Ibid*.

9. Noel Brown, *The Hollywood Family Film: A History, from Shirley Temple to Harry Potter* (London: I.B. Tauris, 2012), 151.

Selected Bibliography

Alpert, Stephen P. "The Neutron Irradiated Dime, Atomic Energy Commission, New York World's Fair, 1964–1965." *TMAS Journal* 14, no. 1 (February 1974): 19.
Andersson, Jenny. *The Future of the World: Futurology, Futurists, and the Struggle for the Post-Cold War Imagination*. New York: Oxford University Press, 2018.
Arnold, Gordon B. *Conspiracy Theory in Film, Television, and Politics*. Westport, CT: Praeger, 2008.
———. *Projecting the End of the American Dream: Hollywood's Visions of U.S. Decline*. Santa Barbara, CA: Praeger, 2013.
Asimov, Isaac. "Visit to the World's Fair of 2014." *New York Times*, August 16, 1964.
Astor, Helen. "Women and World Order." *Think* 4, no. 12 (1939): 10, 53.
Barach, Arnold B., et al. *1975 and the Changes to Come*. New York: Harper & Row, 1962.
Barrier, Michael. *The Animated Man: A Life of Walt Disney*. Berkeley: University of California Press, 2007.
Benjamin, Marina. *Rocket Dreams*. New York: The Free Press, 2003.
Brosterman, Norman. *Out of Time: Designs for the Twentieth-Century Future*. New York: Harry N. Abrams, 2000.
Brown, Noel. *The Hollywood Family Film: A History, from Shirley Temple to Harry Potter*. London: I.B. Tauris, 2012.
Burrows, William E. *This New Ocean: The Story of the First Space Age*. New York: Modern Library, 1998.
Carson, Rachel. *Silent Spring*. Boston: Houghton Mifflin, 1962.
Chaudry, Ajay, et al. *Poverty in the United States: 50-Year Trends and Safety Net Impacts*. Washington, D.C.: Office of Human Services Policy, Office of the Assistant Secretary for Planning and Evaluation, U.S. Department of Health and Human Services, March 2016.
Cohen, Lizabeth. *A Consumer's Republic: The Politics of Mass Consumption*. New York: Vintage, 2003.
Corn, Joseph J., and Brian Horrigan. *Yesterday's Tomorrows: Past Visions of the American Future*. New York: Summit Books, 1984.
Cotter, Bill. *Seattle's 1962 World's Fair*. Charleston, SC: Arcadia Publishing, 2015.
"Damp Prelude to Space: A Potential Lady Orbiter Excels in Lonesome Test." *Life*, October 24, 1960.
"Desolate Year." *Monsanto Magazine*, October 1962.
Diamond, Edwin. *The Rise and Fall of the Space Age*. Garden City, NJ: Doubleday & Company, 1964.
Dick, Steven J., ed. *Remembering the Space Age*. Washington, D.C.: National Aeronautics and Space Administration, 2008.
Douglas Aircraft Company. "Preliminary Design of an Experimental World-Circling Spaceship." Santa Monica, CA: Douglas Aircraft Company, 1946.
Ehrlich, Paul. *The Population Bomb*. New York; Ballantine, 1970.

Selected Bibliography

Engelken, R. C. "Lighting the New York World's Fair." *Journal of Electrical Engineering* 59 (May 1940): 179–203.
Flechtheim, Ossip. *History and Futurology.* Meisenheim am Glan: Hain, 1966.
Franklin Jonas, and Diana Klebanow. *People's Lawyers: Crusaders for Justice in American History.* Armonk, NY: M.E. Sharpe, 2002.
Fuller, R. Buckminster. *Operating Manual for Spaceship Earth.* New York: Simon & Schuster, 1969.
Furman, Michael. *Automobiles of the Chrome Age, 1946–1960.* New York: Harry N. Abrams, 2004.
Gabler, Neal. *Walt Disney: The Triumph of the American Imagination.* New York: Random House, 2006.
Garber, Megan. "Astro Mad Men: NASA's 1960s Campaign to Win America's Heart." *The Atlantic,* July 31, 2013.
Garber, Steve, and Roger Launius. "A Brief History of NASA." Washington, D.C.: National Aeronautics and Space Administration, [n.d.]. https://history.nasa.gov/factsheet.htm.
Gartman, David. *Auto-Opium: A Social History of American Automotive Design.* New York Routledge, 1994.
Georges, Thomas. *Digital Soul: Intelligent Machines and Human Values.* Boulder, CO: Westview Press, 2003.
Gidley, Jennifer M. *The Future: A Very Short Introduction.* New York: Oxford University Press, 2017.
Gregory, Steven. *Black Corona: Race and the Politics of Place in an Urban Community.* Princeton: Princeton University Press, 2011.
Guffey, Elizabeth, and Kate C. Lemay. "Retrofuturism and Steampunk." In *The Oxford Handbook of Science Fiction,* edited by Rob Latham, 434–450. New York: Oxford University Press, 2014.
Hanson, O. B. "Here Comes Television!" *Think* 4, no. 12 (1939): 36, 66.
Herbert, Stephen. *A History of Early Television.* New York: Routledge, 2004.
Hicks, Jesse. "Atoms for Peace: The Mixed Legacy of Eisenhower's Nuclear Gambit." *Distillations,* July 19, 2014. https://sciencehistory.org/distillations/atoms-for-peace-the-mixed-egacy-of-eisnhower-nuclear-gambit.
Hughes, David Hughes. *The Complete Stanley Kubrick.* London: Virgin Publishing, 2001.
Jung, Carl. *Flying Saucers: A Modern Myth of Things Seen in the Skies.* London: Routledge & Keegan Paul, 1959.
Kahn, Herman, and Anthony J. Wiener. *The Year 2000: A Framework for Speculation on the Next Thirty-Three Year.* New York: Macmillan, 1967.
Kauffman, James. "NASA's PR Campaign on Behalf of Manned Space Flight, 1961–1963." *Public Relations Review* 17, no. 1 (Spring 1991): 57–68.
Kilgore, De Witt Douglas. *Astrofuturism: Science, Race, and Visions of Utopia in Space.* Philadelphia: University of Pennsylvania Press, 2003.
Kolbert, Elizabeth. "Dymaxion Man." *New Yorker,* June 9 & 16, 2008.
Lederer, Muriel. "Seattle Looks Ahead to Century 21." *The Rotarian,* March 1961.
Lekachman, Robert. "Popular Sociology: *The Status Seekers* by Vance Packard." *Commentary,* September 1, 1959.
Lingeman, Richard R. "Books of the Times: Future: Tense" [book review]. *New York Times,* August 7, 1970.
Luce, Clare Boothe. "But Some People Simply Never Get the Message." *Life,* June 28, 1963.
Margois, Jon. *The Last Innocent Year: 1964 and the Beginning of the Sixties.* New York: William Morrow, 1999.
Mauro, James. *Twilight at the World of Tomorrow.* New York: Ballantine, 2010.
McGurk, Caitlin. "Found in the Collection: Arthur Radebaugh's 'Closer Thank We Think.'" Billy Ireland Cartoon Museum (blog), December 27, 2012. https://library.osu.edu/blogs/cartoons/2012/12/27/found-in-the-collection-arthur-radebaughs-closer-than-we-think/.

McLennan, Sarah. "When the Computer Wore a Skirt: Langley's Human Computers, 1935–1970," Washington, D.C.: National Aeronautics and Space Administraton, [no date]. https://crgis.ndc.nasa.gov/historic/Human_Computers.
Mindell, David A. *Between Human and Machine: Feedback, Control, and Computing Before Cybernetics.* Baltimore: Johns Hopkins University Press, 2004.
Moore, Scott. "'Jetsons' Will Give Us a Look Ahead on New Year's Eve." *The Spokesman Review,* December 25, 1999.
Nader, Ralph. *Unsafe at Any Speed: The Designed-In Dangers of the American Automobile.* New York: Grossman Publishers, 1965.
Novak, Matt. "Before the Jetsons, Arthur Radebaugh Illustrated the Future." *Smithsonian,* April 2012.
Official Souvenir Program, Seattle World's Fair. Seattle: Acme Publications, 1962.
Packard, Vance. *The Hidden Persuaders.* New York: David McKay, 1957.
——. *The Status Seekers.* New York: David McKay, 1959.
——. *The Waste Makers.* New York: David McKay, 1960.
Parry-Giles, Shawn J. "Dwight D. Eisenhower: 'Atoms for Peace.'" *Voices of Democracy* 1 (2006): 118–129.
Paul, Richard, and Steven Moss. *We Could Not Fail: The First African Americans in the Space Program.* Austin: University of Texas Press, 2015.
Pew Research Center for the People and the Press. *Deconstructing Distrust: How Americans View Government.* Washington, D.C.: Pew Research Center for People and the Press, 1998.
Piszkiewicz, Dennis. *Wernher Von Braun: The Man Who Sold the Moon.* Westport, CT: Praeger, 1998.
Polak, Frederick. *The Image of the Future.* New York: Oceana, 1961.
Pugh, Tison, and Susan Lynn Aronstein. *The Disney Middle Ages: A Fairy-Tale and Fantasy Past.* New York: Palgrave Macmillan, 2012.
RAND Corporation. *50th Project Air Force, 1946–1996.* Santa Monica: RAND Corporation, 1996.
Riesman, David, Denney Reuel, and Nathan Glazer. *The Lonely Crowd: A Study of the Changing American Character.* New Haven: Yale University Press, 1950.
Rosenberg, Emily S. "Far Out: The Space Age in American Culture." In *Remembering the Space Age,* edited by Steven J. Dick, 157–184. Washington, D.C.: National Aeronautics and Space Administration, 2008.
Rothstein, Richard. *The Color of Law: A Forgotten History of How Our Government Segregated America.* New York: W.W. Norton, 2017.
Ryan, Amy, and Gary Keeley. "Sputnik and U.S. Intelligence: The Warning Record." *Studies in Intelligence* 61, no. 3 (September 2017): 1–16.
Rydell, Robert W. *World's Fairs: The Century-of-Progress Expositions.* Chicago: University of Chicago Press, 1993.
Rydell, Robert W., and Laura Burd Schiavo, eds. *Designing Tomorrow: America's World's Fairs of the 1930s.* New Haven: Yale University Press, 2010.
Samuel, Lawrence R. *The End of Innocence: The 1964–1965 World's Fair.* Syracuse: Syracuse University Press, 2007.
Schwam, Stephanie. *The Making of 2001: A Space Odyssey.* New York: Modern Library, 2000.
Sharkey, Noel. "The Return of Elektro, the First Celebrity Robot." *New Scientist,* December 17, 2008. https://newscientist.com/article/mg20026873-000-the-return—of-elektro-the-first-celebrity-robot/.
Sideris, Lisa, and Kathleen Dean Moore, eds. *Rachel Carson: Legacy and Challenge.* Albany: State University of New York Press, 2008.
Szerlip, B. Alexandra. *The Man Who Designed the Future: Norman Bel Geddes and the Invention of Twentieth-Century America.* Brooklyn: Melville House, 2017.
Tirella, Joseph. *Tomorrow-Land: The 1964–1965 World's Fair and the Transformation of America.* Guilford, CT: Lyons Press, 2014.
Toffler, Alvin. *Future Shock.* New York: Random House, 1970.

Selected Bibliography

Tolon, Kaya. "The American Futures Studies Movement, 1965–1975: Its Roots, Motivations, and Influences." Ph.D. diss., Iowa State University, 2011.
Watson, Maysha. "The History of the Seattle Center: A Timeline." *Seattle Magazine*, February 2012.
Weitekamp, Margaret A. *Right Stuff, Wrong Sex: America's First Women in Space Program*. Baltimore: Johns Hopkins University Press, 2004.
Wells, H.G. *The Discovery of the Future*. New York: B. W. Huebsch, 1913.
Wood, Andrew F. *New York 1939–1940 World's Fair*. Charleston, SC: Arcadia, 2004.
Wurts, Richard et al. *The New York World's Fair, 1939–1940*. New York: Dover, 1977.
Your World of Tomorrow. New York: Rogers-Kellogg-Stillson, 1939.

Index

ABC (American Broadcasting Network) 75, 112–113
Academy of Arts and Sciences Commission on the Future 158–159
Action Comics 52
advertising 4, 27, 43, 45, 54, 61–63, 67, 70–72, 75–76, 103, 125, 132
Aldrin, Edwin 150
Alien 180
All the President's Men 175
Allen, Woody 176
Amazing Stories 11
American Exceptionalism 4–5, 37, 54
American Rocket Society 86
American Telephone and Telegraph (AT&T) 26, 28–29
Anticipations of the Reaction of Mechanical and Scientific Progress 7
Apollo 11 150 -152
Armstrong, Neil 150–151
The Art of Conjecture 158
Asimov, Isaac 82, 126–130, 132, 160
Astor, Helen 31
Astounding Stories 11
astrofuturist writers 82–83, 116, 129
atom bomb 45–51, 63, 80
Atoman 52–53
Atomic Age 45–57, 58, 182, 183
Atomic Energy Commission 120–122
Atoms for Peace 64, 65

Back to the Future 183–184
Barach, Arnold 115–116
Barbera, Joseph 112
Baum, L. Frank 27
Becket, Welton 123
Bel Geddes, Norman 24–25, 31, 33, 123
Bell, Daniel 157, 158
Bell Rocket Belt 1–2; *see also* jet pack
Bernstein, Carl 171
Big Jim McLain 60, 173

Blade Runner 180–181
Boeing Corporation 108
Bonestell, Chesley 77, 102
Brave New World 12
Bubbleator 112
Buck Rogers 11, 17, 82, 180

Cagle, Myrtle 98
Capek, Karel 27
Capricorn One 180
car culture 55, 66–70, 104, 136, 168–169
Carpenter, Scott 89
Carson, Rachel 134–136, 139, 155
Carter, Jimmy 178, 179
CBS 75, 135–136, 140, 142, 160
Century of Progress International Exposition 14, 17
Century 21 Exposition 105–112, 118
Challenger 184
Chysler Corporation 25–26, 68, 122
Clarke, Arthur C. 78, 82, 116, 129–130, 132, 147–148, 160
A Clockwork Orange 175–176
Closer Than We Think 103–104, 144
Cobb, Geraldine "Jerrie" 97, 98
Collins, Michael 150
Coma 180
conformity 71, 104, 137, 162
The Conquest of Space 77
conspiracy theories 173–175
Cooper, Gordon 89
CORE (Congress on Racial Equality) 119
Cornish, Edward 159–160
Coser, Lewis 133
counterculture 162–163
Cronkite, Walter 160–161
Crowley, Leo T. 40
Crystal Palace Electric Exposition 14

Davis, Don 177, 179
Davy Crockett 94

199

200 Index

Death Race 2000 176
Death Wish 173
De Jouvenel, Bertrand 157
DeLorean automobile 183
Delphi Method 154
Democracity 20–21, 22, 25
Design for Dreaming 72–73
Destination Moon 78
Dietrich, Jan 98
Dietrich, Marion 98
Dirty Harry 172–173
Discovery of the Future 7–8
Disney, Walt 13, 73–75, 78, 81, 109, 123–124, 149–157
Disneyland (amusement park) 74–76, 78–80, 109
Disneyland (television series) 75, 77–80, 94
Douglas Aircraft Company 153
Dwight, Ed 100
Dymaxion 163

Earl, Harley 68
Ehrlich, Paul 161–162
Eisenhower, Dwight D. 64–65, 81, 83–87, 89
Electrical Experimenter 10
Elektro 27–28
Ellsberg, Daniel 170–171
The End of Ideology 158
Engelken Richard C. 18
Escape from New York 180
Executive Action 174
Exner, Virgil 68
The Exploration of Space 78
Explorer 1 88
Expo '67 164
Exposition Universelle 14

Farnsworth, Philo Taylor 29–30
Federal Aid Highway Act (1956) 67
Fisher, Joseph L. 130
Fisher, Katherine 32
Flash Gordon 11, 17, 82, 179
Flechtheim, Ossip 157
Flickinger, Donald 97
flying cars 2, 55, 80, 103, 113, 180
Flying Saucers: A Modern Myth of Things Seen in the Skies 77
Forbidden Planet 141, 142
Ford, Gerald R. 172, 178
Ford, Henry 67
Ford Motor Company 25–26, 55, 108, 122–123
Frank Reade Weekly Magazine 9
Friendship 7 91–92

From Earth to the Moon 7
Frontier myth 94–96, 142–143
Fuller, R. Buckminster 108, 159, 160, 163–164
Funk, Mary Wallace "Wally" 97
Futurama 24–25
Futurama II 123–124
Future Shock 165–166
The Futurist 160

Gagarin, Yuri 91
General Motors 24–25, 55, 68, 72–73, 108, 122–123, 137–138
geodesic dome 108, 163–164
Gingrich, Newt 166
Glenn, John 89, 91–92, 96, 98, 100, 107
Goddard, Robert H. 26
Golden Gate International Exposition (1939) 17
Good Housekeeping Institute 32
Googie architecture 114
Gorelick, Sarah 98
Grant, Harry Dart 8
Grissom, Virgil "Gus" 89, 91
Guidice, Rick 177, 178
Gutenberg Galaxy 160

Hanna, William 112
Happy Days 177
Harris, Jonathan 142
Hart, Jane B. 98
Heinlein, Robert 82
Hersey, John 49
The Hidden Persuaders 132–133
High Noon 94
Hiroshima (book) 49
Hiroshima (city) 45–47, 49–51
History and Futurology 157
Hixson, Jean 98
House Un-American Activities Committee 60
Hudson Institute 158, 159
Hunt, E. Howard 171
Hurrle, Rhea 98
Huxley, Aldous 12

I Was a Communist Spy for the F.B.I. 60, 173
IBM (International Business Machines Corp.) 109, 124, 149
The Image of the Future 157
International Bureau of Expositions 106–107, 118–119
International Geophysical Year 86
irradiator device 120–122
Italian Futurism 11

jet pack 1–2, 104, 113
The Jetsons 112–115, 118, 125, 140
Johnson, Katherine 100, 102
Johnson, Lyndon Baines 98, 100, 107, 119
Jones, Bassett 18
Jung, Carl 77

Kahn, Herman 158, 159
Kelly, Walt 174
Kennedy, John F. 1, 90–94, 100, 102, 117, 119, 136, 150–152, 174
Kimball, Ward 79
Kinoshita, Robert 141, 142
Kubrick, Stanley 103, 147–149, 175–176

La Guardia, Fiorello Henry 33
Laika 87–88
Lane, Mark 174
Lang, Fritz 12, 28
Laurence, William 46, 48–49
Lawrence, Robert 100–101
Leary, Timothy 162
Le Corbusier 13
Leverton, Irene 98
Ley, Willy 77
Liddy, G. Gordon 171
Lipset, Seymour Martin 133
Loewy, Raymond 25, 36, 45
The Lonely Crowd 71
Lost in Space 140–142, 143
Lovelace, William Randolph 97–98
Low, Archibald M. 29
Lucas, George 178–179
Luce, Clare Boothe 99
Luce, Henry 36–37

The Manchurian Candidate 173
Manhattan Project 45–47, 51
Mann, Thomas 157
McAuliffe, Christa 184
McCall, Robert 103, 149, 177
McCarthy, Joseph 60–61
McLuhan, Marshall 160
Mead, Margaret 131, 160
The Medium Is the Message 160
Menzies, William Cameron 20
Mercury 13 97–98
Metropolis 12, 28
Mintzberg, Henry 154
monorail 107, 109–110
Monsanto Chemical Company 64, 75, 76
Moon landing 150, 152, 163
Mumford, Lewis 157
Mumy, Bill 142
My Son John 60, 173

Nader, Ralph 136–138, 139, 155, 168
Nagasaki, Japan 45–49
NASA (National Aeronautics and Space Administration) 88–89, 91–93, 96–97, 100–101, 122, 140, 146, 149–153, 177–179, 184
National Advisory Committee for Aeronautics 88
National Aeronautics and Space Administration *see* NASA
NBC (National Broadcasting Company) 29–30, 75, 142, 144–145, 147
New Frontier speech 90–91, 92
New York World's Fair (1939) 15–35, 36–36, 94
New York World's Fair (1964) 117–125
Nichols, Nichelle 144
1984 (book) 3, 181
Nineteen Eighty-Four 3, 181
1975 and the Changes to Come 115
Nixon, Richard M. 90, 166, 170–173

OAPEC (Organization of Arab Petroleum Exporting Countries) 168, 172
oil embargo (1973) 168–169, 172
Omega Man 176
Operating Manual for Spaceship Earth 164
Operation Candor 64
Orwell, George 3, 181
overpopulation 128–129, 130, 161–162

Packard, Vance 132–134, 139, 155
Pakula, Alan J. 175
Pal, George 78
Pentagon Papers 170
Percy, the Mechanism Man 27
Perisphere 16, 18–19, 22, 25
planned obsolescence 71, 133–134, 164
plastics 43–44, 70, 76, 115, 169
Pogo 174
Polak, Frederick 157
Pollack, Sydney 174–175
Pollitt, Daniel H. 131
Popular Mechanics 10
Popular Science 10, 54–55
The Population Bomb 161–162
Powell, Adam Clayton 34
Preliminary Design of an Experimental World-Circling Spaceship 153
Profiles of the Future 129

race and race relations 24–25, 34, 37, 42–43, 62–63, 66–67, 71, 95,100–102, 104, 114, 117, 119, 130–131, 138–139, 141,143–144, 156, 159, 182–183

Index

Radebaugh, Arthur 103–104, 144
RAND Corporation 153–154, 158
RCA (Radio Corporation of America) 29
Reagan, Ronald 181, 183
Red Menace 60
retrofuturism 177, 182
Rey, Harold C. 51
Riesman, David 71, 131
robots 2, 27–28, 104, 112–113, 141–142, 161, 176, 180–182
Roddenberry, Gene 142–143, 145, 160
Roosevelt, Franklin, D. 29, 34
Rosie the Riveter 37
Rossum's Universal Robots (R.U.R) 27

Schirra, Wally 89, 93
Science and Invention 10
science fiction 7, 11, 53, 70, 82–83, 127, 180
SCORE satellite (Signal Communications by Orbiting Relay Equipment) 81
The Searchers 94
Seattle World's Fair (1962) *see* Century 21 Exposition
Shatner, William 142
Shepard, Alan 89, 91, 100
Silent Running 176
Silent Spring 134–136
Slayton, Deke 89
Sleeper 176
Sloan, Jerri 98
Smyth, Henry D. 47
Soylent Green 176
Space Needle 105, 106, 107, 113
Spacetarium 108
Sputnik 2 83–87, 87, 89
Star Trek 140, 142–145, 180
Star Wars 178–180
The Status Seekers 133
strategic planning 154
Stumbough, Gene Nora 98
Superman 52, 180

tail fins (automotive) 68–69, 182
Talese, Gay 123–124
Taylor, Moulton 56
television 29–30, 61–62, 71–72, 115
Tereshkova, Valentina 98–99
Things to Come 12, 20
Thiry, Paul 109
Three Days of the Condor 174–175
The Time Machine 7

Toffler, Alvin 165–166
Toffler, Heidi 166
Trimble, Bernice 98
Truman, Harry S. 43–46, 86
Trumbo, Dalton 174
trust in government 139–140, 172
Trylon 16, 18–19
The 21st Century 160–161
Twenty-Thousand Leagues Under the Sea 7
2001: A Space Odyssey 103, 147–149, 176

Understanding Media 160
United Nations 58–59, 64, 65
Unsafe at Any Speed: The Designed-In Dangers of the American Automobile 136–138

Verne, Jules 7
von Braun, Wernher 78–80, 81, 107

Wadsworth, Homer C. 131
Wagon Train 143
The War of the Worlds 7
The Waste Makers 133
Watergate scandal 170–172
Wells, H.G. 7–9, 12, 13, 47
Westinghouse Electric Company 26–28
Westworld 176
White-Stevens, Robert 136
Wizard of Oz 27–28
Woodstock music festival 163
Woodward, Bob 171
Woodward, E.L. 51
World Future Society 159–160
World Futures Studies Federation 160
The World Set Free 47
World War II 3, 36–40, 58, 99, 116, 157; atom bomb development 45–50; demobilization 41–32; German rockets 79–80, 82; plastics 43–44
World's Fair (Chicago, 1933) 14, 17
World's Fair Columbian Exposition 14
World's Fair (New York, 1939) 15–35, 36–36, 94
World's Fair (New York, 1964) 117–125
World's Fair (Seattle, 1962) 105–112, 118

Year 2000: A Framework for Speculation on the Next Thirty-Three Years 159

Zemeckis, Robert 183

www.ingramcontent.com/pod-product-compliance
Lightning Source LLC
Chambersburg PA
CBHW021354300426
44114CB00012B/1230